# *Beyond* BLACK BELT SUDOKU®

### FRANK LONGO

MARTIAL ARTS SUDOKU

SUPER TOUGH

PUZZLE WRIGHT PRESS

New York

# CONTENTS

Introduction

**3**

Puzzles

**5**

Answers

**155**

**PUZZLE**
WRIGHT
**PRESS**
New York

An Imprint of Sterling Publishing
387 Park Avenue South
New York, NY 10016

2   4   6   8   10   9   7   5   3   1

Published by Sterling Publishing Co., Inc.
387 Park Avenue South, New York, NY 10016
© 2011 by Frank Longo
Distributed in Canada by Sterling Publishing
C/o Canadian Manda Group, 165 Dufferin Street
Toronto, Ontario, Canada M6K 3H6
Distributed in the United Kingdom by GMC Distribution Services
Castle Place, 166 High Street, Lewes, East Sussex, England BN7 1XU
Distributed in Australia by Capricorn Link (Australia) Pty. Ltd.
P.O. Box 704, Windsor, NSW 2756, Australia

Sterling ISBN 978-1-4027-8070-7

For information about custom editions, special sales, premium and corporate purchases, please contact Sterling Special Sales Department at 800-805-5489 or specialsales@sterlingpublishing.com.

# INTRODUCTION

When you hear the term "X-wing," do you think of a Starfighter ship from *Star Wars*? Is a "jellyfish" only something to be avoided at the beach? Is a "Gordonian rectangle" less familiar to you than Pascal's triangle? If so, you probably haven't delved into the world of extreme sudoku, where these are some of the advanced solving techniques that are needed to get to the solution.

If you've never solved a sudoku puzzle before, here's how it works:

> **Fill in the boxes so that the nine rows, the nine columns, and the nine 3×3 sections all contain every digit from 1 to 9.**

Below is a sample puzzle on the left, and its solution on the right.

| | | | | | | | | |
|---|---|---|---|---|---|---|---|---|
| | | | | | | | | |
| | | 2 | | 1 | 8 | 4 | | |
| 9 | | 5 | | 7 | | 2 | | 6 |
| 1 | | 4 | 3 | 9 | 2 | | 7 | |
| | | | 7 | | 6 | | | |
| | 7 | | 1 | 4 | 8 | 9 | | 2 |
| 3 | | 2 | | 6 | | 8 | | 5 |
| 8 | 4 | 9 | | 3 | | | | |
| | | | | | | | | |

| | | | | | | | | |
|---|---|---|---|---|---|---|---|---|
| 4 | 2 | 1 | 6 | 8 | 3 | 5 | 9 | 7 |
| 7 | 3 | 6 | 5 | 2 | 9 | 1 | 8 | 4 |
| 9 | 8 | 5 | 4 | 7 | 1 | 2 | 3 | 6 |
| 1 | 5 | 4 | 3 | 9 | 2 | 6 | 7 | 8 |
| 2 | 9 | 8 | 7 | 5 | 6 | 4 | 1 | 3 |
| 6 | 7 | 3 | 1 | 4 | 8 | 9 | 5 | 2 |
| 3 | 1 | 2 | 9 | 6 | 7 | 8 | 4 | 5 |
| 8 | 4 | 9 | 2 | 3 | 5 | 7 | 6 | 1 |
| 5 | 6 | 7 | 8 | 1 | 4 | 3 | 2 | 9 |

If you are actually studying the two grids above because this is your first time trying sudoku, slowly close the cover of this book and back away without making any sudden movements. This is not a book for beginners. If you're just starting out, read *Mensa Guide to Solving Sudoku* by Peter Gordon and me. But if you're a seasoned pro and aren't intimidated by swordfish, XY-wings, XYZ-wings, alternating digits, finned X-wings, sashimi X-wings, Gordonian polygons, and other scary-sounding techniques, then your search for a book that will truly challenge you has finally ended.

I have found that the vast majority of sudoku puzzles that are labeled "hard," "expert," "challenger," and the like, in newspapers, magazines, and books, are not really all that difficult. And in a surprising number of cases, they are downright easy. They usually require only intermediate solving techniques. Some of them might require a combination of these techniques, but they are intermediate techniques nonetheless. Here, in *Beyond Black Belt Sudoku*, you will find puzzles truly worthy of the label "hard." (I should warn you that the puzzles in this book are even a notch harder than those in my previously toughest four-book series *Mensa Absolutely Nasty Sudoku*.)

The 300 all-new puzzles generally increase in difficulty, from "very hard" to "insane," as the book progresses. More advanced techniques are gradually added, and the numbers of instances of those techniques required for a single puzzle also increase.

Despite the difficulty of these puzzles, none of them require flat-out guessing to complete. All of the above-mentioned advanced techniques are simply methods that will logically get you to the next step in the solving process, whether you give them a fancy name or not. So if you're new to solving *really* hard sudoku puzzles, be patient, be willing to stretch your mind to see connections you wouldn't have thought to look for before, and be confident in knowing that there will always be something you can find that will get you to the next step. (That is, assuming you haven't made any errors!)

And just think, after you finish *this* book, you'll be able to impress those around you by tossing off any newspaper or magazine "super challenger" puzzle at lightning speed!

—Frank Longo

**1**

| 9 |   |   | 1 | 4 |   |   |   | 7 |
|---|---|---|---|---|---|---|---|---|
|   | 5 |   |   |   | 7 | 2 |   | 4 |
|   |   |   | 8 |   |   |   |   |   |
| 5 |   | 2 |   |   |   |   | 4 |   |
|   |   |   | 4 |   | 8 |   |   |   |
|   | 4 |   |   |   |   | 7 |   | 5 |
|   |   |   |   | 3 |   |   |   |   |
| 1 |   | 8 | 2 |   |   |   | 3 |   |
| 6 |   |   |   | 7 | 4 |   |   | 2 |

**2**

| in |   | 9 |   |   | 4 |   |   | 2 |
|---|---|---|---|---|---|---|---|---|
|   |   |   |   | 2 |   | 9 | 8 | 5 |
| 7 |   |   |   |   | 9 | 1 |   |   |
|   |   | 7 |   |   |   |   | 4 | 1 |
| 9 |   |   |   |   |   |   |   | 8 |
| 4 | 5 |   |   |   |   | 2 |   |   |
|   |   | 1 | 4 |   |   |   |   | 7 |
| 8 | 9 | 5 |   | 3 |   |   |   |   |
| 6 |   |   | 2 |   |   | 3 |   |   |

**3**

| | | 7 | | | | | | 3 |
|---|---|---|---|---|---|---|---|---|
| 8 | 3 | | | 2 | | | 9 | |
| | 2 | | | | 8 | | 5 | |
| | | 6 | | | 4 | | | |
| | | | 3 | 7 | 1 | | | |
| | | | 8 | | | 9 | | |
| | 9 | | 7 | | | | 1 | |
| | 4 | | | 5 | | | 3 | 8 |
| 1 | | | | | | 7 | | |

**4**

| 8 | | 7 | | 2 | | | | |
|---|---|---|---|---|---|---|---|---|
| | 6 | | | 9 | | | 8 | 1 |
| | | | | | | 3 | | |
| | | 8 | | | 2 | 5 | | |
| 4 | | | 9 | | 7 | | | 6 |
| | | 9 | 4 | | | 1 | | |
| | | 3 | | | | | | |
| 1 | 5 | | | 8 | | | 6 | |
| | | | | 1 | | 9 | | 8 |

**5**

| | | 7 | | 5 | | | | 3 |
|---|---|---|---|---|---|---|---|---|
| 3 | 9 | | | | | 7 | | |
| 6 | | | | | 7 | | | |
| 9 | | | 4 | | 2 | 5 | | |
| | 1 | | 8 | 7 | 9 | | 4 | |
| | | 3 | 5 | | 1 | | | 9 |
| | | | 2 | | | | | 7 |
| | | 1 | | | | | 3 | 4 |
| 8 | | | | 9 | | 2 | | |

**6**

| | 5 | 6 | | 4 | | | | |
|---|---|---|---|---|---|---|---|---|
| | | 1 | 5 | | | 8 | | |
| 8 | | | 7 | 3 | | | | |
| | 8 | | | | | 1 | 9 | |
| | | 3 | 9 | | 2 | 7 | | |
| | 1 | 9 | | | | | 6 | |
| | | | | 9 | 7 | | | 1 |
| | | 4 | | | 5 | 3 | | |
| | | | | 2 | | 6 | 8 | |

**7**

| | | 4 | | | 8 | | 2 | |
|---|---|---|---|---|---|---|---|---|
| | 2 | | | 5 | | | | |
| 3 | | 1 | 4 | | | 9 | | 7 |
| 9 | | | | | | | | 3 |
| | 1 | 8 | | | | 6 | 7 | |
| 7 | | | | | | | | 1 |
| 2 | | 5 | | | 1 | 3 | | 8 |
| | | | | 2 | | | 6 | |
| | 3 | | 8 | | | 7 | | |

**8**

| | | 3 | | | 2 | | | |
|---|---|---|---|---|---|---|---|---|
| 6 | | | 8 | | 1 | | 5 | |
| 1 | 2 | | 4 | | | | | |
| | | | | | | | 2 | 1 |
| | | 2 | 7 | | 4 | 5 | | |
| 7 | 9 | | | | | | | |
| | | | | | 8 | | 7 | 9 |
| | 1 | | 9 | | 5 | | | 3 |
| | | | 1 | | | 8 | | |

**9**

| | | 9 | | 1 | 6 | | | |
|---|---|---|---|---|---|---|---|---|
| 6 | 8 | 5 | | | | 7 | | |
| 1 | | | | | | | 3 | |
| | | | | 3 | | | | 5 |
| | | | 1 | 7 | 5 | | | |
| 3 | | | | 4 | | | | |
| | 2 | | | | | | | 8 |
| | | 8 | | | | 6 | 9 | 3 |
| | | | 4 | 6 | | 2 | | |

**10**

| | 2 | | 3 | 4 | | | | |
|---|---|---|---|---|---|---|---|---|
| 3 | | | 8 | | | | | |
| 5 | | | | | | 6 | | |
| | 5 | | 9 | | | 2 | | |
| | 9 | | 2 | | 6 | | 1 | |
| | | 7 | | | 4 | | 6 | |
| | | 9 | | | | | | 7 |
| | | | | | 9 | | | 6 |
| | | | | 3 | 1 | | 4 | |

| 3 | 7 |   | 1 | 4 |   |   |   |   |
|---|---|---|---|---|---|---|---|---|
|   |   |   |   |   |   |   |   | 3 |
| 9 | 2 |   | 3 |   | 6 |   |   |   |
| 5 |   |   |   | 7 |   | 9 | 8 |   |
|   |   |   |   | 2 |   |   |   |   |
|   | 3 | 8 |   | 6 |   |   |   | 4 |
|   |   |   | 9 |   | 4 |   | 1 | 8 |
| 8 |   |   |   |   |   |   |   |   |
|   |   |   |   | 3 | 8 |   | 5 | 9 |

| 9 |   |   |   | 5 |   |   | 8 |   |
|---|---|---|---|---|---|---|---|---|
|   | 4 | 8 |   |   |   | 9 |   |   |
|   |   |   | 3 |   |   | 2 |   | 4 |
|   |   |   | 7 |   |   |   | 6 | 5 |
|   |   | 6 |   |   |   | 1 |   |   |
| 4 | 9 |   |   |   | 3 |   |   |   |
| 2 |   | 9 |   |   | 6 |   |   |   |
|   |   | 4 |   |   |   | 6 | 7 |   |
|   | 5 |   |   | 1 |   |   |   | 3 |

**1 3**

| | | | | 8 | 4 | 6 | | |
|---|---|---|---|---|---|---|---|---|
| 9 | | | | 2 | | | 3 | |
| | | | 3 | | | 4 | | |
| | 6 | 8 | | | | 7 | | |
| 3 | | | | 1 | | | | 2 |
| | | 1 | | | | 5 | 9 | |
| | | 3 | | | 8 | | | |
| | 2 | | | 9 | | | | 8 |
| | | 5 | 4 | 6 | | | | |

**1 4**

| | 6 | | 4 | | | 3 | 5 | |
|---|---|---|---|---|---|---|---|---|
| 3 | | | 5 | | | | 6 | |
| 2 | | | | | | 8 | | 4 |
| | | 8 | | | 4 | | | |
| 4 | | | | | | | | 6 |
| | | | 8 | | | 1 | | |
| 1 | | 2 | | | | | | 5 |
| | 5 | | | | 7 | | | 2 |
| | 9 | 4 | | | 2 | | 3 | |

| | | 3 | 8 | | | | 4 | |
|---|---|---|---|---|---|---|---|---|
| | 8 | | | 2 | | | | |
| | | | | | 4 | | 2 | 5 |
| | 3 | | 1 | | | | 9 | 8 |
| | | | | 9 | | | | |
| 1 | 6 | | | | 7 | | 3 | |
| 9 | 5 | | 3 | | | | | |
| | | | | 1 | | | 5 | |
| | 7 | | | | 6 | 1 | | |

| | | | 9 | | 2 | | | |
|---|---|---|---|---|---|---|---|---|
| | 5 | | | | | 3 | 1 | 4 |
| | | 3 | | | | 8 | | |
| | 2 | | | 8 | | | | 3 |
| | | | 7 | | 9 | | | |
| 8 | | | | 4 | | | 5 | |
| | | 9 | | | | 2 | | |
| 1 | 8 | 5 | | | | | 6 | |
| | | | 6 | | 1 | | | |

| | | | 8 | | | | 1 | |
|---|---|---|---|---|---|---|---|---|
| | | 4 | | 3 | | | | |
| | 9 | | | | | | 6 | 7 |
| 2 | | 3 | | | 6 | | | 9 |
| | | | | 9 | | | | |
| 5 | | | 1 | | | 7 | | 8 |
| 6 | 4 | | | | | | 2 | |
| | | | | 6 | | 8 | | |
| | 8 | | | | 1 | | | |

| 1 | 8 | 4 | 5 | | | | | |
|---|---|---|---|---|---|---|---|---|
| | 7 | | | 3 | | 2 | | |
| | | | | | | 5 | 7 | |
| | | | 9 | | 1 | | | 7 |
| | | | | | | | | |
| 6 | | | 3 | | 5 | | | |
| | 4 | 3 | | | | | | |
| | | 5 | | 6 | | | 8 | |
| | | | | | 2 | 1 | 3 | 4 |

Puzzle 19

|   | 2 |   | 4 |   |   |   | 1 |   |
|---|---|---|---|---|---|---|---|---|
| 5 |   |   |   |   |   | 6 |   |   |
|   | 7 | 4 | 6 |   |   | 9 |   |   |
|   | 4 |   | 5 |   | 2 |   |   |   |
| 9 |   |   |   | 4 |   |   |   | 3 |
|   |   |   | 9 |   | 3 |   | 7 |   |
|   |   | 1 |   |   | 7 | 5 | 6 |   |
|   |   | 8 |   |   |   |   |   | 1 |
|   | 3 |   |   |   | 6 |   | 4 |   |

Puzzle 20

|   |   |   | 3 |   |   | 1 |   | 5 |
|---|---|---|---|---|---|---|---|---|
| 1 |   |   |   | 5 |   |   |   | 4 |
|   | 5 |   |   |   | 4 |   | 9 |   |
|   | 6 | 8 | 4 |   |   |   |   |   |
|   | 1 |   |   |   |   |   | 7 |   |
|   |   |   |   |   | 5 | 9 | 8 |   |
|   | 4 |   | 8 |   |   |   | 5 |   |
| 6 |   |   |   | 4 |   |   |   | 7 |
| 7 |   | 3 |   |   | 9 |   |   |   |

| | | 6 | 1 | | 9 | | 3 | |
|---|---|---|---|---|---|---|---|---|
| 9 | 7 | | 6 | 4 | | | | |
| 4 | | | | | | | | |
| | | 4 | | | | | | 1 |
| | 2 | | 3 | | 1 | | 8 | |
| 7 | | | | | | 5 | | |
| | | | | | | | | 6 |
| | | | | 1 | 8 | | 5 | 9 |
| | 9 | | 7 | | | 5 | 8 | |

| | | | 2 | 9 | | | | |
|---|---|---|---|---|---|---|---|---|
| | 1 | 3 | | | | | | 6 |
| | | 7 | | | 1 | | | |
| | | 6 | | 4 | | 2 | | 7 |
| | 2 | | | | | | 9 | |
| 1 | | 4 | | 7 | | 6 | | |
| | | | 8 | | | 9 | | |
| 6 | | | | | | 1 | 3 | |
| | | | | 5 | 3 | | | |

| | | | | | | | | 8 |
|---|---|---|---|---|---|---|---|---|
| | | | 6 | 7 | | | | |
| | 3 | | | | 5 | 9 | 7 | |
| | 8 | 4 | | 1 | 9 | 2 | | |
| | | 1 | | 5 | | 3 | | |
| | | 3 | 7 | 6 | | | 4 | 1 |
| | 7 | 2 | 4 | | | | 9 | |
| | | | | 9 | 6 | | | |
| 9 | | | | | | | | |

| | | | | 8 | | | 4 | 2 |
|---|---|---|---|---|---|---|---|---|
| 3 | | | | | | | 1 | |
| 4 | | | | 6 | 2 | 3 | | |
| 7 | | | 2 | 1 | | 9 | | |
| | 2 | | | | | | 8 | |
| | | 8 | | 7 | 4 | | | 1 |
| | | 9 | 3 | 4 | | | | 8 |
| | 3 | | | | | | | 6 |
| 5 | 4 | | | 2 | | | | |

| 3 | 1 |   |   |   |   |   |   | 7 |
|---|---|---|---|---|---|---|---|---|
|   |   |   | 9 |   |   |   | 6 |   |
|   | 7 |   | 1 |   |   |   |   | 8 |
|   |   | 3 | 7 |   | 9 | 6 |   |   |
|   |   |   |   |   |   |   |   |   |
|   |   | 8 | 4 |   | 3 | 5 |   |   |
| 1 |   |   |   |   | 2 |   | 9 |   |
|   | 4 |   |   | 8 |   |   |   |   |
| 9 |   |   |   |   |   |   | 2 | 4 |

|   |   |   |   |   |   |   | 2 | 5 |
|---|---|---|---|---|---|---|---|---|
|   | 2 | 3 |   |   | 7 |   | 8 |   |
|   | 4 |   |   |   | 1 | 6 |   |   |
|   | 1 |   |   | 8 | 2 |   |   |   |
| 5 |   |   |   |   |   |   |   | 7 |
|   |   |   | 9 | 5 |   |   | 3 |   |
|   |   | 4 | 2 |   |   |   | 1 |   |
|   | 7 |   | 4 |   |   | 9 | 5 |   |
| 1 | 3 |   |   |   |   |   |   |   |

| 8 |   | 3 |   | 1 |   |   | 2 |   |
|---|---|---|---|---|---|---|---|---|
|   |   |   |   |   |   |   | 9 |   |
|   |   |   |   | 8 |   | 4 | 3 |   |
|   |   | 4 |   |   | 3 |   |   |   |
|   |   | 1 | 7 |   | 4 | 6 |   |   |
|   |   |   | 9 |   |   | 2 |   |   |
|   | 4 | 5 |   | 3 |   |   |   |   |
|   | 2 |   |   |   |   |   |   |   |
|   | 6 |   |   | 4 |   | 1 |   | 5 |

| 4 |   |   |   |   | 8 |   |   | 7 |
|---|---|---|---|---|---|---|---|---|
|   | 8 |   |   |   |   |   |   |   |
| 3 |   |   | 1 | 9 | 5 |   |   |   |
|   | 2 | 5 |   | 1 |   | 8 |   |   |
|   |   |   |   |   |   |   |   |   |
|   |   | 1 |   | 3 |   | 5 | 6 |   |
|   |   |   | 8 | 4 | 9 |   |   | 2 |
|   |   |   |   |   |   |   | 5 |   |
| 2 |   |   | 7 |   |   |   |   | 3 |

**Puzzle 29**

| | | | 4 | | 7 | 8 | | |
|---|---|---|---|---|---|---|---|---|
| | | | | | | 4 | | 3 |
| 4 | | | | | 5 | | 2 | |
| 3 | | | | 8 | | 5 | 6 | |
| | 9 | | | | | | 8 | |
| | 8 | 5 | | 4 | | | | 9 |
| | 1 | | 3 | | | | | 8 |
| 2 | | 9 | | | | | | |
| | | 8 | 7 | | 1 | | | |

**Puzzle 30**

| | | | | 7 | | | | |
|---|---|---|---|---|---|---|---|---|
| | 6 | | | | | 9 | | 2 |
| 2 | | 4 | | | | | 8 | |
| 5 | 2 | 3 | 8 | | | | | 1 |
| | | | | 9 | | | | |
| 4 | | | | | 7 | 2 | 6 | 5 |
| | 7 | | | | | 5 | | 4 |
| 8 | | 5 | | | | | 3 | |
| | | | 3 | | | | | |

**3 / 1**

| | 4 | 7 | | | | 9 | | |
|---|---|---|---|---|---|---|---|---|
| | | | | 2 | | | | 5 |
| | | | 3 | | 4 | | | 2 |
| | 3 | | | | 6 | | | 9 |
| | 9 | | | 4 | | | 8 | |
| 7 | | | 9 | | | | 4 | |
| 5 | | | 7 | | 2 | | | |
| 4 | | | | 9 | | | | |
| | | 8 | | | | 5 | 1 | |

**3 / 2**

| | 1 | | 3 | | | | 8 | |
|---|---|---|---|---|---|---|---|---|
| | | 5 | | | | 9 | 3 | |
| | | | | | 2 | | | |
| 5 | | 7 | | 4 | | | | 3 |
| 8 | | | | 2 | | | | 4 |
| 9 | | | | 3 | | 7 | | 1 |
| | | | 5 | | | | | |
| | 5 | 6 | | | | 1 | | |
| | 2 | | | | 8 | | 4 | |

**Puzzle 3-3**

| | 2 | | 3 | | | | | |
|---|---|---|---|---|---|---|---|---|
| 3 | | 1 | | 5 | | | 6 | |
| | 4 | | | 6 | 2 | | 9 | |
| | | 2 | | | 3 | | | |
| 1 | | | 4 | | 8 | | | 7 |
| | | | 7 | | | 9 | | |
| | 3 | | 2 | 7 | | | 5 | |
| | 1 | | | 3 | | 6 | | 8 |
| | | | | | 6 | | 2 | |

**Puzzle 3-4**

| | | 3 | | 5 | | 9 | | |
|---|---|---|---|---|---|---|---|---|
| | | | | | | | 4 | 6 |
| | 1 | | 3 | | | | | |
| | 6 | | 5 | | | | 8 | 3 |
| | 4 | | | 6 | | | 9 | |
| 3 | 2 | | | | 8 | | 7 | |
| | | | | | 9 | | 1 | |
| 4 | 5 | | | | | | | |
| | | 1 | | 8 | | 7 | | |

**3/5**

| | 8 | | | 6 | | | | 2 |
|---|---|---|---|---|---|---|---|---|
| | | 3 | 4 | | 2 | | | |
| | | | 1 | | 3 | 5 | 8 | |
| 2 | 7 | | | | | | 5 | |
| | | | | 3 | | | | |
| | 4 | | | | | | 1 | 6 |
| | 6 | 7 | 3 | | 4 | | | |
| | | | 6 | | 9 | 8 | | |
| 1 | | | | 5 | | | 3 | |

**3/6**

| | 5 | | 4 | | 3 | | | |
|---|---|---|---|---|---|---|---|---|
| 3 | | | | | | 9 | | |
| 1 | | 8 | | | 7 | | 2 | |
| | 9 | | | 8 | | | | |
| 8 | | 1 | | | | 2 | | 3 |
| | | | | 4 | | | 1 | |
| | 1 | | 7 | | | 6 | | 8 |
| | | 7 | | | | | | 2 |
| | | | 5 | | 8 | | 9 | |

| 5 |   |   | 9 |   |   |   |   | 7 |
|---|---|---|---|---|---|---|---|---|
|   |   | 9 | 8 |   |   |   |   |   |
| 7 |   | 4 |   |   |   | 9 | 1 |   |
|   |   |   |   | 3 | 2 |   |   |   |
| 8 |   | 1 |   |   |   | 6 |   | 4 |
|   |   |   | 4 | 6 |   |   |   |   |
|   | 1 | 8 |   |   |   | 2 |   | 6 |
|   |   |   |   |   | 7 | 4 |   |   |
| 9 |   |   |   |   | 1 |   |   | 5 |

|   |   | 8 |   |   | 3 | 4 |   |   |
|---|---|---|---|---|---|---|---|---|
|   |   |   | 2 | 4 |   | 8 |   |   |
|   | 1 |   |   |   |   |   | 2 | 9 |
| 6 |   | 1 | 5 | 9 |   |   |   |   |
|   | 5 |   |   |   |   |   | 4 |   |
|   |   |   | 1 | 2 | 9 |   |   | 6 |
| 5 | 8 |   |   |   |   |   | 9 |   |
|   |   | 2 |   | 3 | 6 |   |   |   |
|   |   | 4 | 9 |   |   | 1 |   |   |

## 39

| | 7 | | | 9 | | 1 | 8 | |
|---|---|---|---|---|---|---|---|---|
| | | | | | | 6 | | 2 |
| | 1 | | 6 | 8 | | | 9 | |
| 9 | 3 | | | | | 8 | | |
| | | | | 1 | | | | |
| | | 2 | | | | | 6 | 9 |
| | 6 | | | 3 | 9 | | 7 | |
| 4 | | 5 | | | | | | |
| | 2 | 3 | | 6 | | | 1 | |

## 40

| | 4 | | 2 | 7 | | | | 5 |
|---|---|---|---|---|---|---|---|---|
| | | 1 | | | 3 | | | |
| 9 | | | | | 5 | | | |
| | | 9 | | 3 | 1 | 5 | | 7 |
| | 3 | | | | | | 1 | |
| 1 | | 5 | 7 | 9 | | 4 | | |
| | | | 3 | | | | | 4 |
| | | | 5 | | | 6 | | |
| 2 | | | | 4 | 8 | | 3 | |

**4 1**

| | | 3 | | 5 | | 2 | | |
|---|---|---|---|---|---|---|---|---|
| | | 8 | 9 | | | | 6 | |
| | | 5 | | | 8 | | | 7 |
| 8 | | | | 3 | | | 5 | |
| | | 4 | | | | 7 | | |
| | 2 | | | 1 | | | | 9 |
| 4 | | | 7 | | | 3 | | |
| | 7 | | | | 5 | 1 | | |
| | | 1 | | 4 | | 8 | | |

**4 2**

| | 4 | | | | | 9 | | |
|---|---|---|---|---|---|---|---|---|
| | 1 | | | 6 | 3 | 8 | | |
| 7 | | | 9 | | 5 | 1 | | |
| | | | | | | | | 4 |
| | 5 | | 6 | | 2 | | 3 | |
| 6 | | | | | | | | |
| | | 5 | 8 | | 4 | | | 7 |
| | | 8 | 1 | 7 | | | 2 | |
| | | 2 | | | | | 1 | |

| | | | 8 | | | | 6 | 2 |
|---|---|---|---|---|---|---|---|---|
| | | | | 6 | | 4 | | 3 |
| | | 7 | | 3 | 2 | | | |
| 7 | | | | | | 5 | 9 | |
| | | | 2 | | 9 | | | |
| | 4 | 3 | | | | | | 1 |
| | | | 7 | 8 | | 9 | | |
| 6 | | 5 | | 1 | | | | |
| 8 | 9 | | | | 5 | | | |

| | | | | | | | 6 | |
|---|---|---|---|---|---|---|---|---|
| 5 | | | 2 | | | 3 | | 7 |
| | | | | 3 | | 5 | | 4 |
| | 8 | | | 5 | | 7 | | |
| | 9 | 1 | | 7 | | 8 | 5 | |
| | | 7 | | 4 | | | 9 | |
| 2 | | 8 | | 6 | | | | |
| 9 | | 5 | | | 4 | | | 6 |
| | 1 | | | | | | | |

| | | 6 | | | 1 | | 2 | |
|---|---|---|---|---|---|---|---|---|
| 2 | | | | 4 | | 9 | | |
| 8 | | 1 | | | | 3 | | |
| | | | | | 9 | | | 3 |
| 9 | | | 6 | | 4 | | | 2 |
| 3 | | | 5 | | | | | |
| | | 8 | | | | 1 | | 9 |
| | | 3 | | 8 | | | | 7 |
| | 5 | | 2 | | | 8 | | |

| | 6 | 7 | | | | | | |
|---|---|---|---|---|---|---|---|---|
| | | | | 6 | 8 | | | 3 |
| | 9 | | | | 2 | 1 | | |
| | | | | | 9 | 6 | 7 | |
| | | 9 | | 2 | | 3 | | |
| | 2 | 1 | 6 | | | | | |
| | | 6 | 4 | | | | 3 | |
| 8 | | | 9 | 7 | | | | |
| | | | | | | 9 | 5 | |

| | 8 | | 4 | | 6 | 9 | | |
|---|---|---|---|---|---|---|---|---|
| | 4 | | | 8 | | | 2 | |
| | | 5 | | | 1 | | | |
| 7 | 9 | | | | | 4 | | |
| | | 4 | 6 | | 7 | 2 | | |
| | | 2 | | | | | 5 | 7 |
| | | | 2 | | | 3 | | |
| | 2 | | | 6 | | | 8 | |
| | | 6 | 8 | | 4 | | 1 | |

| 4 | | | 2 | | | | | |
|---|---|---|---|---|---|---|---|---|
| | 3 | | 9 | | | 1 | | |
| 7 | 2 | | 1 | | | | 5 | 4 |
| | | | 8 | 6 | | | 1 | 5 |
| | | | 5 | | 1 | | | |
| 6 | 1 | | | 4 | 3 | | | |
| 1 | 9 | | | | 8 | | 4 | 2 |
| | | 4 | | | 9 | | 6 | |
| | | | | 1 | | | | 8 |

| | | | | 6 | | | | |
|---|---|---|---|---|---|---|---|---|
| 5 | | | 2 | 1 | | | | 8 |
| | | 4 | | 5 | | | 1 | |
| | 6 | 2 | 1 | | | | | |
| 7 | | 1 | | 4 | | 3 | | 6 |
| | | | | | 2 | 1 | 9 | |
| | 2 | | | 3 | | 5 | | |
| 4 | | | | 2 | 8 | | | 9 |
| | | | 9 | | | | | |

| | | | | 1 | | | | |
|---|---|---|---|---|---|---|---|---|
| | 6 | | | 2 | | | 8 | 5 |
| | 5 | | 9 | | | 6 | | 1 |
| | 4 | | 3 | | | 8 | | |
| | | 6 | | | | 9 | | |
| | | 7 | | 8 | | | 3 | |
| 6 | | 5 | | | 2 | | 9 | |
| 2 | 8 | | | 3 | | | 6 | |
| | | | | 4 | | | | |

**5-1**

| | | | | | | | | |
|---|---|---|---|---|---|---|---|---|
| | | | | 9 | | | 6 | 3 |
| 8 | 7 | | | | | | 9 | |
| | | | | 3 | 4 | | | |
| | 1 | | | 9 | | | | 8 |
| 9 | | | 2 | 8 | 1 | | | 4 |
| 3 | | | 6 | | | 5 | | |
| | | 2 | 9 | | | | | |
| | 4 | | | | | | 7 | 6 |
| 7 | 3 | | | 4 | | | | |

**5-2**

| | | | | | | | | |
|---|---|---|---|---|---|---|---|---|
| | 1 | | | 9 | | | | 8 |
| | 6 | | 1 | | | | 4 | |
| 8 | | | | | | | 5 | 7 |
| 3 | 9 | | | | 6 | | | |
| | | | 2 | | 9 | | | |
| | | | 7 | | | | 1 | 2 |
| 9 | 8 | | | | | | | 4 |
| | 2 | | | | 3 | | 9 | |
| 5 | | | | 4 | | | 3 | |

| 8 |   |   |   |   | 5 |   | 4 |   |
|---|---|---|---|---|---|---|---|---|
| 6 |   |   | 7 |   |   |   |   |   |
|   |   |   | 3 |   |   | 8 |   |   |
|   | 7 |   |   |   |   | 1 |   |   |
|   | 1 |   | 5 | 6 | 4 |   | 3 |   |
|   |   | 5 |   |   |   |   | 9 |   |
|   |   | 1 |   | 8 |   |   |   |   |
|   |   |   |   |   | 3 |   |   | 5 |
|   | 4 |   | 9 |   |   |   |   | 3 |

|   |   |   |   |   |   |   |   |   |
|---|---|---|---|---|---|---|---|---|
|   | 7 |   | 4 |   |   | 6 | 3 | 8 |
| 6 |   |   |   | 8 | 2 |   |   | 5 |
| 7 |   |   |   | 6 |   | 4 |   | 2 |
|   |   | 6 |   |   |   | 9 |   |   |
| 2 |   | 4 |   | 1 |   |   |   | 3 |
| 4 |   |   | 2 | 7 |   |   |   | 6 |
| 3 | 6 | 9 |   |   | 8 |   | 1 |   |
|   |   |   |   |   |   |   |   |   |

| | | 2 | | | 5 | | 6 | |
|---|---|---|---|---|---|---|---|---|
| 1 | | 5 | | 6 | 7 | 8 | | 9 |
| | 7 | | | | | | | 5 |
| 4 | | | 5 | | | | | |
| | 9 | | | 7 | | | 8 | |
| | | | | | 9 | | | 3 |
| 8 | | | | | | | 7 | |
| 7 | | 9 | 2 | 8 | | 3 | | 6 |
| | 2 | | 7 | | | 4 | | |

| | | 9 | | | 4 | | 1 | |
|---|---|---|---|---|---|---|---|---|
| | | | | 9 | | | | 8 |
| | 1 | 6 | | 2 | 7 | | | |
| | | | | | | 3 | 7 | |
| | 4 | | | 6 | | | 5 | |
| | 7 | 2 | | | | | | |
| | | | 5 | 4 | | 2 | 9 | |
| 9 | | | | 1 | | | | |
| | 6 | | 3 | | | 5 | | |

**5/7**

| | 4 | | 2 | | | | | |
|---|---|---|---|---|---|---|---|---|
| | | | | 3 | | | | 5 |
| | 1 | 6 | | 4 | | | 8 | |
| 5 | | | 7 | | | 3 | | |
| 4 | | | | | | | | 8 |
| | | 9 | | | 1 | | | 2 |
| | 7 | | | 1 | | 4 | 2 | |
| 9 | | | 3 | | | | | |
| | | | | | 7 | | 5 | |

**5/8**

| | | 6 | | | 2 | | | |
|---|---|---|---|---|---|---|---|---|
| 4 | | | | | 1 | | 3 | 7 |
| | | | | | | 5 | | |
| 2 | | | | 7 | | 5 | | |
| 5 | | 1 | | 2 | | 6 | | 4 |
| | | 3 | | 5 | | | | 1 |
| | 8 | | | | | | | |
| 7 | 3 | | 4 | | | | | 8 |
| | | | 3 | | | 9 | | |

| | | | 7 | | 1 | 5 | | 3 |
|---|---|---|---|---|---|---|---|---|
| | | | | 9 | | 1 | 8 | |
| | | | | | 5 | | 9 | |
| | | 8 | | 7 | | | | 4 |
| 9 | | | | 6 | | | | 2 |
| 3 | | | | 4 | | 6 | | |
| | 9 | | 4 | | | | | |
| | 2 | 4 | | 1 | | | | |
| 7 | | 1 | 9 | | 2 | | | |

| | | 1 | 5 | 9 | | 6 | | |
|---|---|---|---|---|---|---|---|---|
| 5 | | 6 | | 1 | | | | |
| | 4 | | | | | | 1 | |
| | 9 | | | | | 2 | 7 | |
| 6 | | | | 2 | | | | 1 |
| | 8 | 3 | | | | | 5 | |
| | 6 | | | | | | 8 | |
| | | | | 5 | | 7 | | 2 |
| | | 2 | | 7 | 4 | 3 | | |

Puzzle 6/1:

| | 3 | | | 2 | | 5 | | |
|---|---|---|---|---|---|---|---|---|
| 5 | | 8 | | | 9 | | | 2 |
| 9 | | | 4 | | | | | |
| 2 | | | | | 1 | | | 7 |
| | | 1 | | 7 | | 3 | | |
| 3 | | | 9 | | | | | 4 |
| | | | | | 7 | | | 6 |
| 4 | | | 5 | | | 7 | | 3 |
| | | 7 | | 9 | | | 5 | |

Puzzle 6/2:

| 4 | | | | | 2 | | | 8 |
|---|---|---|---|---|---|---|---|---|
| | 8 | 2 | | | 9 | | 1 | |
| 3 | | | 1 | | | | | |
| 9 | | | 2 | | 6 | | 4 | |
| 7 | | | | | | | | 1 |
| | 6 | | 7 | | 3 | | | 2 |
| | | | | | 1 | | | 5 |
| | 1 | | 6 | | | 8 | 7 | |
| 5 | | | 9 | | | | | 6 |

## 6 3

| | | | 1 | | | | 6 | |
|---|---|---|---|---|---|---|---|---|
| | | 1 | | 6 | | | 5 | |
| | | | | | 9 | 1 | | |
| 2 | 6 | | 3 | | | 9 | | |
| 4 | | | | 8 | | | | 3 |
| | | 9 | | | 6 | | 4 | 2 |
| | | 6 | 8 | | | | | |
| | 1 | | | 2 | | 4 | | |
| | 4 | | | | 5 | | | |

## 6 4

| | | | | | 5 | 6 | 9 | |
|---|---|---|---|---|---|---|---|---|
| 1 | 6 | | 7 | | | | | |
| | | 4 | | | | | | |
| 6 | | | | | 4 | 3 | | 2 |
| | 1 | | 3 | | 8 | | 7 | |
| 4 | | 7 | 2 | | | | | 8 |
| | | | | | | 8 | | |
| | | | | | 9 | | 4 | 3 |
| | 2 | 5 | 8 | | | | | |

| 2 |   |   | 5 |   | 7 |   | 3 |   |
|---|---|---|---|---|---|---|---|---|
|   |   |   | 8 |   |   |   | 5 | 7 |
|   |   | 5 |   |   |   | 8 |   |   |
| 9 |   |   | 6 |   |   | 7 |   |   |
|   |   | 6 |   | 7 |   | 5 |   |   |
|   |   | 8 |   |   | 4 |   |   | 9 |
|   |   | 1 |   |   |   | 6 |   |   |
| 6 | 4 |   |   |   | 8 |   |   |   |
|   | 5 |   | 3 |   | 9 |   |   | 4 |

| 5 |   |   | 7 |   |   |   |   |   |
|---|---|---|---|---|---|---|---|---|
|   |   | 8 |   |   | 2 |   | 9 |   |
|   | 3 |   |   | 6 | 8 |   |   | 7 |
| 6 |   | 5 |   |   |   | 3 |   |   |
| 1 |   |   |   |   |   |   |   | 9 |
|   |   | 9 |   |   |   | 8 |   | 4 |
| 3 |   |   | 8 | 2 |   |   | 4 |   |
|   | 1 |   | 3 |   |   | 5 |   |   |
|   |   |   |   |   | 1 |   |   | 8 |

| 5 | 8 | 4 |   |   | 2 |   |   |   |
|---|---|---|---|---|---|---|---|---|
| 3 |   |   | 4 |   | 7 |   |   |   |
|   |   | 6 |   |   |   |   | 9 |   |
|   |   |   | 2 | 1 |   |   | 5 | 6 |
|   | 6 |   |   |   |   |   | 4 |   |
| 1 | 2 |   |   | 4 | 6 |   |   |   |
|   | 4 |   |   |   |   | 3 |   |   |
|   |   |   | 5 |   | 1 |   |   | 4 |
|   |   |   | 3 |   |   | 9 | 6 | 1 |

|   |   |   |   |   | 4 |   | 6 | 8 |
|---|---|---|---|---|---|---|---|---|
|   |   | 5 |   | 9 |   |   |   |   |
| 3 |   | 7 | 6 |   |   |   |   |   |
|   | 6 | 3 |   |   | 1 | 8 |   |   |
|   |   |   |   | 4 |   |   |   |   |
|   |   | 2 | 9 |   |   | 1 | 7 |   |
|   |   |   |   |   | 6 | 9 |   | 5 |
|   |   |   |   | 1 |   | 7 |   |   |
| 8 | 3 |   | 5 |   |   |   |   |   |

| | | | | 9 | | | | 2 |
|---|---|---|---|---|---|---|---|---|
| 7 | 1 | 9 | | | | | | |
| | | | 5 | | 7 | | | |
| 9 | 8 | | 1 | 2 | | | 3 | |
| | 3 | | | | | | 5 | |
| | 4 | | | 8 | 3 | | 2 | 1 |
| | | | 6 | | 4 | | | |
| | | | | | | 7 | 8 | 6 |
| 2 | | | | 3 | | | | |

| | 7 | | | 9 | | | | |
|---|---|---|---|---|---|---|---|---|
| | 5 | | 3 | | 6 | 7 | | |
| | 6 | | | | | 2 | 1 | |
| | | | 1 | | | 9 | | |
| 7 | | | 9 | | 4 | | | 6 |
| | | 3 | | | 8 | | | |
| | 4 | 9 | | | | | 7 | |
| | | 7 | 4 | | 3 | | 5 | |
| | | | | 5 | | | 4 | |

**7/1**

| | 5 | 3 | | | 2 | | | |
|---|---|---|---|---|---|---|---|---|
| 1 | 6 | | | | 7 | | 5 | |
| 4 | | | | | | | | 3 |
| | | | 7 | | | | 8 | |
| 2 | | | 4 | | 8 | | | 6 |
| | 8 | | | | 1 | | | |
| 6 | | | | | | | | 4 |
| | 7 | | 3 | | | | 6 | 1 |
| | | | 2 | | | 8 | 3 | |

**7/2**

| | 4 | | 3 | | | | 8 | |
|---|---|---|---|---|---|---|---|---|
| | | | 8 | | 6 | | | |
| | | 7 | | 9 | | | | 3 |
| | | 6 | | 1 | | | | 2 |
| | 2 | | 8 | | 3 | | 9 | |
| 7 | | | | 5 | | 8 | | |
| 4 | | | | 7 | | 1 | | |
| | | 2 | | 4 | | | | |
| | 5 | | | | 6 | | 4 | |

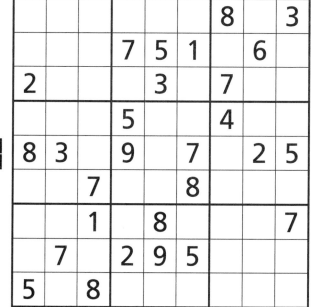

| 8 |   |   | 3 |   |   |   |   |   |
|---|---|---|---|---|---|---|---|---|
|   |   |   |   | 2 |   |   | 6 |   |
| 9 |   | 2 | 8 |   | 5 |   |   |   |
| 6 | 5 |   |   | 1 | 7 |   | 8 | 2 |
|   |   | 1 |   |   |   | 9 |   |   |
| 2 | 4 |   | 6 | 8 |   |   | 7 | 1 |
|   |   |   | 5 |   | 2 | 1 |   | 8 |
|   | 2 |   |   | 3 |   |   |   |   |
|   |   |   |   |   | 1 |   |   | 7 |

| 6 | 1 |   |   |   |   |   |   |   |
|---|---|---|---|---|---|---|---|---|
|   | 2 |   |   |   | 5 |   | 8 |   |
|   |   | 5 | 7 | 8 |   |   |   | 9 |
| 9 |   |   | 1 |   |   |   |   |   |
|   | 3 |   |   |   |   |   | 5 |   |
|   |   |   |   |   | 6 |   |   | 2 |
| 1 |   |   | 7 | 9 | 5 |   |   |   |
|   | 7 |   | 5 |   |   |   | 6 |   |
|   |   |   |   |   |   |   | 2 | 8 |

| | 1 | | | | | 6 | | |
|---|---|---|---|---|---|---|---|---|
| 8 | | 2 | 6 | | | 1 | | |
| 6 | | 7 | | 5 | | | | |
| | 7 | | | 9 | | | | |
| 2 | | 8 | 1 | | 5 | 4 | | 3 |
| | | | | 2 | | | 6 | |
| | | | | 8 | | 3 | | 1 |
| | | 4 | | | 3 | 5 | | 8 |
| | | 5 | | | | | 2 | |

| 5 | | 1 | | 2 | | | | |
|---|---|---|---|---|---|---|---|---|
| | | | 9 | 6 | | 3 | | |
| | 3 | | 4 | | | 2 | | |
| 2 | | 3 | | | | | 1 | |
| 6 | | 4 | | | | 8 | | 7 |
| | 7 | | | | | 6 | | 2 |
| | | 6 | | | 5 | | 2 | |
| | | 2 | | 4 | 9 | | | |
| | | | | 3 | | 7 | | 9 |

| 6 |   | 5 |   | 4 |   |   |   |   |
|---|---|---|---|---|---|---|---|---|
|   |   |   |   |   | 1 |   |   |   |
| 4 | 3 |   |   |   | 8 |   | 6 |   |
|   | 8 | 7 |   | 2 |   |   | 9 |   |
| 3 |   | 6 |   |   |   | 2 |   | 1 |
|   | 2 |   |   | 1 |   | 5 | 3 |   |
|   | 6 |   | 8 |   |   |   | 5 | 9 |
|   |   |   | 1 |   |   |   |   |   |
|   |   |   |   | 9 |   | 3 |   | 7 |

|   | 1 |   |   |   | 5 | 4 |   |   |
|---|---|---|---|---|---|---|---|---|
|   |   | 5 | 7 | 9 |   |   |   |   |
|   |   |   |   |   |   |   | 1 |   |
| 8 |   |   |   | 6 |   |   | 5 |   |
| 3 |   | 6 |   |   |   | 8 |   | 2 |
|   | 5 |   |   | 4 |   |   |   | 7 |
|   | 9 |   |   |   |   |   |   |   |
|   |   |   | 3 | 6 | 2 |   |   |   |
|   |   | 8 | 5 |   |   |   | 3 |   |

| 9 |   | 4 |   |   |   |   | 5 |   |
|---|---|---|---|---|---|---|---|---|
| 7 |   |   |   |   |   |   |   |   |
|   |   |   |   | 6 | 1 |   |   |   |
| 4 |   | 3 | 5 |   |   |   | 1 |   |
| 1 |   | 9 | 8 |   | 4 | 5 |   | 2 |
|   | 2 |   |   |   | 3 | 8 |   | 4 |
|   |   | 8 | 1 |   |   |   |   |   |
|   |   |   |   |   |   |   |   | 1 |
|   | 4 |   |   |   |   | 2 |   | 6 |

| 7 |   | 6 |   |   | 3 | 5 |   |   |
|---|---|---|---|---|---|---|---|---|
|   |   |   | 7 |   |   | 3 |   |   |
|   | 2 |   |   | 4 |   |   | 6 |   |
| 9 |   |   |   |   | 6 |   |   |   |
| 5 |   | 7 |   |   |   | 9 |   | 2 |
|   |   |   | 1 |   |   |   |   | 5 |
|   | 9 |   |   | 5 |   |   | 3 |   |
|   |   | 5 |   |   | 8 |   |   |   |
|   |   | 2 | 6 |   |   | 1 |   | 8 |

| | 8 | | | 9 | | 1 | | 7 |
|---|---|---|---|---|---|---|---|---|
| | | | 1 | | 4 | 8 | | |
| | 6 | | | | | | 9 | |
| | | | | 5 | | 2 | 6 | |
| 6 | | | 3 | | 1 | | | 9 |
| | 9 | 8 | | 2 | | | | |
| | 5 | | | | | | 2 | |
| | | 2 | 9 | | 8 | | | |
| 9 | | 1 | | 6 | | | 4 | |

| | 9 | | | | | | | 4 |
|---|---|---|---|---|---|---|---|---|
| | 8 | | | 1 | | 2 | 3 | |
| 4 | | | | 5 | | 9 | | |
| | | | 3 | | | | | |
| | 3 | | 5 | 6 | 2 | | 9 | |
| | | | | | 8 | | | |
| | | 1 | | 7 | | | | 8 |
| | 4 | 5 | | 3 | | | 1 | |
| 7 | | | | | | | 5 | |

| 4 |   | 3 |   |   |   | 8 |   |   |
|---|---|---|---|---|---|---|---|---|
|   | 2 | 9 |   |   |   |   | 7 |   |
| 5 |   |   | 2 |   | 1 |   |   |   |
|   | 7 |   | 5 | 8 |   |   |   | 3 |
| 2 |   |   |   |   |   |   |   | 7 |
| 3 |   |   |   | 2 | 9 |   | 1 |   |
|   |   |   | 4 |   | 6 |   |   | 2 |
|   | 9 |   |   |   |   | 1 | 5 |   |
|   |   | 2 |   |   |   | 7 |   | 6 |

|   | 2 | 1 |   |   |   |   |   | 5 |
|---|---|---|---|---|---|---|---|---|
|   |   |   | 3 |   |   |   |   | 1 |
|   |   | 9 |   | 8 |   |   | 2 | 4 |
|   |   | 5 | 8 | 3 |   |   |   |   |
|   | 4 |   |   | 1 |   |   | 5 |   |
|   |   |   | 7 | 4 | 1 |   |   |   |
| 6 | 7 |   |   | 2 |   | 5 |   |   |
| 9 |   |   |   |   | 3 |   |   |   |
| 8 |   |   |   |   |   | 6 | 3 |   |

| | | | | | | | | 5 |
|---|---|---|---|---|---|---|---|---|
| | | | | 8 | 3 | 7 | | |
| 4 | | 9 | 1 | | | | | |
| | | 8 | | 4 | 5 | | | |
| 9 | | | 8 | 7 | | | | 3 |
| | | 4 | 9 | | 2 | | | |
| | | | | 2 | 4 | | | 6 |
| | 5 | 7 | 3 | | | | | |
| 1 | | | | | | | | |

| | 7 | | | | 6 | | | 9 |
|---|---|---|---|---|---|---|---|---|
| | 1 | 9 | | | | 3 | 7 | |
| 5 | | | | | | | 4 | |
| 6 | | 7 | 4 | | 5 | | | |
| | | | | 8 | | | | |
| | | | 2 | | 7 | 9 | | 4 |
| | 6 | | | | | | | 7 |
| | 3 | 2 | | | | 4 | 9 | |
| 9 | | | 1 | | | | 3 | |

| | 5 | 6 | | 8 | | | 3 | |
|---|---|---|---|---|---|---|---|---|
| | 7 | | | 9 | 5 | 8 | | |
| | | | | | | | 4 | |
| 1 | | | | | | | 9 | |
| | | | 2 | 4 | 9 | | | |
| | 9 | | | | | | | 6 |
| | 3 | | | | | | | |
| | | 2 | 6 | 7 | | | 8 | |
| | 8 | | | 5 | | 9 | 1 | |

| | | | | | | 9 | 4 | 8 |
|---|---|---|---|---|---|---|---|---|
| | | 6 | | | | | 5 | |
| 7 | | | | 8 | 4 | 1 | | |
| | | | | 9 | | 5 | | |
| | | 1 | 7 | | 8 | 3 | | |
| | | 4 | | 2 | | | | |
| | | 7 | 9 | 6 | | | | 1 |
| | 6 | | | | | 8 | | |
| 9 | 1 | 2 | | | | | | |

Puzzle 9/1:

| 6 |   |   |   |   |   |   |   |   |
|---|---|---|---|---|---|---|---|---|
|   |   | 5 | 6 |   | 9 |   |   | 8 |
|   |   | 7 |   | 3 |   |   | 1 |   |
|   |   | 3 | 1 |   | 5 |   |   | 7 |
| 5 |   |   |   |   |   |   |   | 6 |
| 8 |   |   | 7 |   | 4 | 1 |   |   |
|   | 3 |   |   | 5 |   | 2 |   |   |
| 7 |   |   | 8 |   | 1 | 5 |   |   |
|   |   |   |   |   |   |   |   | 4 |

Puzzle 9/2:

| 5 |   |   | 4 |   | 5 |   |   | 1 |
|---|---|---|---|---|---|---|---|---|
|   |   | 8 |   | 7 |   |   | 2 | 6 |
| 4 |   |   |   |   |   | 3 |   |   |
| 5 |   |   | 6 |   | 7 |   | 9 |   |
|   |   | 2 |   | 8 |   | 6 |   |   |
|   | 8 |   | 5 |   | 4 |   |   | 7 |
|   |   | 3 |   |   |   |   |   | 8 |
| 8 | 9 |   |   | 1 |   | 5 |   |   |
| 2 |   |   | 7 |   | 8 |   |   |   |

**93**

| | 2 | | | 7 | 3 | | 5 | |
|---|---|---|---|---|---|---|---|---|
| | | | | | 8 | 6 | | |
| | | | 4 | | | 7 | | |
| 3 | | | | 8 | | | 6 | |
| | 7 | 6 | | | | 4 | 1 | |
| | 9 | | | 3 | | | | 5 |
| | | 2 | | | 7 | | | |
| | | 9 | 8 | | | | | |
| | | 3 | | 2 | 6 | | 9 | |

**94**

| | | 6 | | 1 | | | | |
|---|---|---|---|---|---|---|---|---|
| | | 1 | 4 | | 8 | | | 3 |
| | | | | | | | 9 | |
| | 2 | 4 | 6 | 9 | | | 7 | |
| | | 3 | | | | 9 | | |
| | 6 | | | 8 | 2 | 3 | 5 | |
| | 3 | | | | | | | |
| 9 | | | 2 | | 1 | 7 | | |
| | | | | 5 | | 4 | | |

| 1 | 5 |   | 6 |   |   |   |   | 8 |
|---|---|---|---|---|---|---|---|---|
|   |   | 8 |   |   |   | 9 |   |   |
|   |   |   | 4 |   | 5 | 1 |   |   |
|   | 2 |   |   |   | 8 |   |   |   |
| 6 |   |   |   |   |   |   |   | 1 |
|   |   |   | 3 |   |   |   | 2 |   |
|   |   | 6 | 9 |   | 7 |   |   |   |
|   |   | 5 |   |   |   | 8 |   |   |
| 3 |   |   |   |   | 6 |   | 4 | 2 |

|   | 8 |   |   |   | 6 |   |   |   |
|---|---|---|---|---|---|---|---|---|
|   | 1 |   |   | 5 |   |   |   | 9 |
|   |   |   | 3 | 9 |   | 4 |   | 7 |
|   |   |   |   |   |   | 1 | 4 |   |
|   |   | 2 |   |   |   | 3 |   |   |
|   | 4 | 6 |   |   |   |   |   |   |
| 7 |   | 1 |   | 3 | 8 |   |   |   |
| 2 |   |   |   | 6 |   |   | 5 |   |
|   |   |   | 9 |   |   |   | 7 |   |

| 7 | 8 |   |   |   |   | 9 |   |   |
|---|---|---|---|---|---|---|---|---|
|   |   |   |   | 5 | 9 |   |   | 1 |
|   |   | 6 |   |   | 1 |   |   |   |
|   |   |   |   |   |   |   | 8 | 5 |
|   | 4 |   | 3 | 2 | 8 |   | 1 |   |
| 1 | 2 |   |   |   |   |   |   |   |
|   |   |   | 2 |   |   | 4 |   |   |
| 2 |   |   | 5 | 9 |   |   |   |   |
|   |   | 4 |   |   |   |   | 2 | 3 |

|   | 6 |   |   |   | 5 |   |   | 1 |
|---|---|---|---|---|---|---|---|---|
| 1 |   | 8 |   |   | 2 |   | 6 |   |
|   |   |   |   | 8 |   | 4 |   |   |
| 5 |   | 9 |   |   |   |   |   |   |
|   |   | 3 | 4 |   | 8 | 2 |   |   |
|   |   |   |   |   |   | 8 |   | 3 |
|   |   | 2 |   | 1 |   |   |   |   |
|   | 7 |   | 2 |   |   | 1 |   | 9 |
| 3 |   |   | 8 |   |   |   | 7 |   |

| 8 | 5 |   | 7 |   | 2 |   | 4 |   |
|---|---|---|---|---|---|---|---|---|
|   |   |   |   | 3 |   | 2 | 8 |   |
|   |   |   | 8 |   |   |   | 7 |   |
|   | 2 |   |   |   |   | 8 | 6 | 7 |
| 5 |   |   |   |   |   |   |   | 3 |
| 4 | 8 | 3 |   |   |   |   | 9 |   |
|   | 4 |   |   |   | 3 |   |   |   |
|   | 7 | 2 |   | 5 |   |   |   |   |
|   | 9 |   | 2 |   | 6 |   | 5 | 4 |

|   |   | 3 | 9 |   |   |   |   | 1 |
|---|---|---|---|---|---|---|---|---|
|   | 6 |   |   | 1 | 3 |   |   |   |
| 5 |   | 9 |   |   | 4 |   |   |   |
|   | 9 | 5 |   |   |   | 6 |   |   |
|   |   |   | 2 |   | 1 |   |   |   |
|   |   | 7 |   |   |   | 5 | 4 |   |
|   |   |   | 4 |   |   | 1 |   | 6 |
|   |   |   | 1 | 2 |   |   | 3 |   |
| 6 |   |   |   |   | 5 | 7 |   |   |

|   |   |   |   |   |   |   |   |   |
|---|---|---|---|---|---|---|---|---|
| 4 | 1 |   |   |   |   | 9 |   |   |
| 9 |   |   | 8 |   |   |   |   |   |
|   |   | 7 | 2 |   |   |   | 3 |   |
|   |   |   | 7 |   |   |   | 2 | 5 |
|   |   | 9 |   |   |   | 8 |   |   |
| 7 | 3 |   |   |   | 8 |   |   |   |
|   | 4 |   |   |   | 6 | 7 |   |   |
|   |   |   |   |   | 1 |   |   | 9 |
|   |   | 6 |   |   |   |   | 5 | 3 |

|   |   |   |   |   |   |   |   |   |
|---|---|---|---|---|---|---|---|---|
| 8 | 9 |   |   |   |   | 1 |   |   |
|   | 2 | 4 |   |   | 1 |   |   |   |
|   |   |   | 8 |   |   | 3 | 9 | 4 |
| 5 |   |   | 3 |   |   |   |   |   |
|   | 8 |   | 1 |   | 9 |   | 4 |   |
|   |   |   |   |   | 6 |   |   | 1 |
| 3 | 4 | 7 |   |   | 8 |   |   |   |
|   |   |   | 7 |   |   | 4 | 5 |   |
|   |   | 6 |   |   |   |   | 3 | 7 |

| 6 |   |   |   |   | 7 | 2 |   |   |
|---|---|---|---|---|---|---|---|---|
| 9 |   |   |   |   |   | 6 |   | 5 |
|   | 7 |   |   | 8 |   |   |   |   |
| 5 | 6 |   | 2 |   |   |   |   |   |
|   |   |   |   | 7 |   |   |   |   |
|   |   |   |   | 4 |   |   | 5 | 9 |
|   |   |   |   | 5 |   |   | 4 |   |
| 1 |   | 8 |   |   |   |   |   | 3 |
|   |   | 4 | 7 |   |   |   |   | 6 |

|   |   |   | 8 | 7 | 5 |   |   |   |
|---|---|---|---|---|---|---|---|---|
|   |   | 4 | 1 |   |   |   |   | 7 |
|   | 2 |   |   | 3 |   | 6 |   |   |
|   |   |   |   |   |   |   |   | 6 |
|   | 6 | 9 | 5 |   | 1 | 8 | 4 |   |
| 7 |   |   |   |   |   |   |   |   |
|   | 3 |   | 9 |   |   |   | 7 |   |
| 4 |   |   |   |   | 6 | 1 |   |   |
|   |   | 5 | 7 | 1 |   |   |   |   |

**105**

| | | | 9 | | 2 | 4 | | |
|---|---|---|---|---|---|---|---|---|
| | | 9 | | | | | | |
| | 7 | | | | | | 6 | 5 |
| | 9 | 2 | | 1 | | | 8 | |
| 8 | | | | | | | | 4 |
| | 6 | | | 8 | | 7 | 9 | |
| 6 | 5 | | | | | | 1 | |
| | | | | | | 3 | | |
| | | 8 | 6 | | 3 | | | |

**106**

| 2 | | 4 | | | 9 | | | |
|---|---|---|---|---|---|---|---|---|
| | | | | 8 | | | 2 | |
| 5 | 8 | | 3 | | | 6 | | |
| 9 | | | | | 3 | | 4 | |
| | | 8 | | | | 7 | | |
| | 3 | | 2 | | | | | 8 |
| | | 7 | | | 2 | | 9 | 6 |
| | 6 | | | 1 | | | | |
| | | | 6 | | | 8 | | 2 |

| | 7 | | 8 | | | 4 | | |
|---|---|---|---|---|---|---|---|---|
| | | | | | 4 | 3 | 2 | |
| 9 | | | | | 3 | | 7 | |
| 8 | 9 | | | | | | | 2 |
| | | | 1 | 9 | 2 | | | |
| 2 | | | | | | | 5 | 7 |
| | 6 | | 9 | | | | | 5 |
| | 8 | 5 | 4 | | | | | |
| | | 9 | | | 1 | | 6 | |

| | | | | 5 | | 4 | | |
|---|---|---|---|---|---|---|---|---|
| | 8 | | 2 | | | 3 | | 5 |
| 6 | | | 8 | | | | 9 | |
| 3 | | | | 2 | | | | |
| | 7 | | 5 | | 8 | | 4 | |
| | | | | 4 | | | | 1 |
| | 5 | | | | 2 | | | 9 |
| 4 | | 3 | | | 9 | | 5 | |
| | | 1 | | 3 | | | | |

**109**

| | | 1 | 6 | | | | | |
|---|---|---|---|---|---|---|---|---|
| 8 | 4 | | | | 9 | | 5 | |
| 7 | | | 4 | | 8 | | 1 | |
| | 7 | | | 1 | | | 2 | 4 |
| | | | | | | | | |
| 5 | 1 | | | 9 | | | 6 | |
| | 5 | | 9 | | 1 | | | 3 |
| | 9 | | 3 | | | | 4 | 6 |
| | | | | | 6 | 2 | | |

**110**

| | | | | | | 7 | | |
|---|---|---|---|---|---|---|---|---|
| 7 | | | 1 | | 3 | | 6 | 4 |
| | | 3 | | | 7 | 2 | | 1 |
| | | | | 1 | | | 2 | 8 |
| 8 | | | 5 | | 2 | | | 3 |
| 1 | 2 | | | 9 | | | | |
| 3 | | 1 | 6 | | | 8 | | |
| 6 | 4 | | 8 | | 1 | | | 7 |
| | | 5 | | | | | | |

Puzzle 1:

| | | 6 | | 4 | | | | |
|---|---|---|---|---|---|---|---|---|
| 4 | | | | | 7 | | | 1 |
| | | 7 | 9 | | 2 | | 5 | |
| | 9 | 8 | | | 6 | | | |
| | | 1 | | | | 5 | | |
| | | | 1 | | | 4 | 7 | |
| | 8 | | 5 | | 4 | 1 | | |
| 3 | | | 7 | | | | | 9 |
| | | | | 3 | | 8 | | |

Puzzle 2:

| | | | | | 9 | 4 | | |
|---|---|---|---|---|---|---|---|---|
| | 5 | | | 6 | | 3 | 7 | |
| 8 | | 2 | | | 1 | | | |
| 3 | | | 2 | | | | | |
| | | 5 | | 1 | | 2 | | |
| | | | | | 3 | | | 9 |
| | | | 9 | | | 7 | | 8 |
| | 7 | 6 | | 8 | | | 5 | |
| | | 1 | 3 | | | | | |

**113**

| | | 9 | 7 | | | 3 | 2 | 6 |
|---|---|---|---|---|---|---|---|---|
| | 8 | | | | | | | |
| 7 | | | 2 | | | | | 4 |
| | | 6 | | | | | 3 | |
| | | 2 | 9 | | 6 | 4 | | |
| | 7 | | | | | 9 | | |
| 4 | | | | | 8 | | | 2 |
| | | | | | | | 7 | |
| 6 | 3 | 7 | | | 5 | 8 | | |

**114**

| | | | 9 | | | | 1 | |
|---|---|---|---|---|---|---|---|---|
| 2 | | | | | | 3 | | 7 |
| | | | 5 | 1 | | 9 | | |
| | | 7 | | | 4 | | | 3 |
| 5 | | 6 | | | | 7 | | 2 |
| 9 | | | 7 | | | 6 | | |
| | | 2 | | 8 | 1 | | | |
| 6 | | 3 | | | | | | 8 |
| | 5 | | | | 7 | | | |

| | 3 | | 6 | | | 7 | | |
|---|---|---|---|---|---|---|---|---|
| | | | | | | 9 | | |
| 7 | | 4 | | | | | 5 | 3 |
| 9 | 5 | | 2 | | 6 | | | |
| | | | | 5 | | | | |
| | | | 8 | | 1 | | 2 | 7 |
| 5 | 8 | | | | | 1 | | 4 |
| | | 1 | | | | | | |
| | | 7 | | | 3 | | 9 | |

| 5 | | 3 | | | | | 6 | 1 |
|---|---|---|---|---|---|---|---|---|
| | | | | | 1 | | | 2 |
| | | | | | | | 7 | |
| 4 | 6 | | | 8 | 3 | 2 | | |
| | | 2 | 9 | | 6 | 5 | | |
| | | 1 | 4 | 5 | | | 3 | 8 |
| | 3 | | | | | | | |
| 7 | | | 8 | | | | | |
| 8 | 5 | | | | | 7 | | 4 |

| | | | | | 5 | | | |
|---|---|---|---|---|---|---|---|---|
| 8 | | 7 | | 6 | | 4 | | |
| 5 | 1 | | | | | | 2 | |
| | | | | 9 | 4 | | | 8 |
| | 3 | | 6 | | 8 | | 4 | |
| 7 | | | 5 | 2 | | | | |
| | 4 | | | | | | 7 | 1 |
| | | 8 | | 5 | | 6 | | 9 |
| | | | 9 | | | | | |

| | 6 | 2 | 7 | | | | | |
|---|---|---|---|---|---|---|---|---|
| | | 1 | | 8 | | 5 | | |
| 3 | | | 6 | | 4 | | | |
| 5 | | | 1 | | | 8 | 4 | |
| | | | | 5 | | | | |
| | 8 | 3 | | | 9 | | | 5 |
| | | | 4 | | 6 | | | 7 |
| | | 5 | | 2 | | 1 | | |
| | | | | | 1 | 2 | 6 | |

| | | | 4 | 5 | | | | |
|---|---|---|---|---|---|---|---|---|
| | | 3 | | | 6 | 5 | | |
| | | | | 7 | | | 1 | |
| | 5 | 4 | | | | | | 8 |
| 1 | | | 7 | | 3 | | | 6 |
| 8 | | | | | | 3 | 2 | |
| | 9 | | | 2 | | | | |
| | | 5 | 6 | | | 2 | | |
| | | | | 4 | 9 | | | |

| | 8 | | | | 2 | | | 1 |
|---|---|---|---|---|---|---|---|---|
| | | | 1 | | | | 6 | |
| | | 1 | | | 3 | | 2 | 5 |
| | | 6 | | | | | 7 | |
| 4 | | | | 7 | | | | 6 |
| | 5 | | | | | 8 | | |
| 8 | 4 | | 9 | | | 2 | | |
| | 9 | | | | 4 | | | |
| 7 | | | 3 | | | | 8 | |

| | 9 | 3 | 1 | 2 | | | | 6 |
|---|---|---|---|---|---|---|---|---|
| | | | | 4 | | 5 | | |
| | | | | 3 | 1 | | | |
| 7 | | 4 | | | | | 2 | |
| | | | 5 | | | | | |
| | 2 | | | | | 6 | | 8 |
| | | 7 | 8 | | | | | |
| | | 6 | | 7 | | | | |
| 4 | | | | 3 | 2 | 8 | 5 | |

| 7 | | 2 | | | 5 | | 3 | |
|---|---|---|---|---|---|---|---|---|
| | 4 | 9 | | | 8 | | | |
| | | | | | | | 2 | |
| 1 | | | | | 2 | 3 | | |
| 3 | | | 1 | 7 | 6 | | | 4 |
| | | 7 | 8 | | | | | 6 |
| | 2 | | | | | | | |
| | | | 3 | | | 7 | 6 | |
| | 7 | | 4 | | | 9 | | 2 |

Puzzle 1-2-3:

| | | | | | | | 7 | |
|---|---|---|---|---|---|---|---|---|
| 3 | | | 6 | | | 2 | | 4 |
| | | 1 | | | | 6 | 9 | |
| | 2 | | 8 | 1 | | | | |
| 4 | | | 2 | | 9 | | | 8 |
| | | | | 4 | 6 | | 5 | |
| | 8 | 5 | | | | 9 | | |
| 2 | | 6 | | | 3 | | | 5 |
| | 3 | | | | | | | |

Puzzle 1-2-4:

| | 6 | | 5 | | 9 | 7 | | |
|---|---|---|---|---|---|---|---|---|
| 9 | | | | 8 | | | | |
| | | 3 | 2 | | | 6 | | |
| 5 | | 4 | | 6 | | | | 8 |
| | | | | | | | | |
| 2 | | | | 4 | | 5 | | 3 |
| | | 7 | | | 8 | 9 | | |
| | | | | 1 | | | | 6 |
| | | 8 | 3 | | 6 | | 2 | |

| | | 4 | | | 6 | | 5 | |
|---|---|---|---|---|---|---|---|---|
| | | 3 | | | | | 2 | |
| 7 | | | 2 | | 5 | 3 | 4 | |
| 3 | | | 7 | | | | | |
| | 4 | | 3 | 5 | 1 | | 9 | |
| | | | | | 2 | | | 3 |
| | 7 | 5 | 6 | | 3 | | | 2 |
| | 2 | | | | | 8 | | |
| | 3 | | 8 | | | 6 | | |

| | | 8 | 5 | | | 6 | 3 | |
|---|---|---|---|---|---|---|---|---|
| 7 | 2 | 6 | | | 4 | | | |
| | | | 2 | | | | | |
| 8 | | 7 | | | | | 2 | |
| | 9 | | | 2 | | | 8 | |
| | 5 | | | | | 7 | | 1 |
| | | | | | 9 | | | |
| | | | 3 | | | 1 | 4 | 8 |
| | 1 | 4 | | | 5 | 2 | | |

| | | 2 | | | 8 | | 5 | |
|---|---|---|---|---|---|---|---|---|
| 6 | | 3 | | | | | | 7 |
| | 8 | | 1 | | 4 | | | |
| | 7 | 1 | 3 | | | | 9 | |
| | | | | | | | | |
| | 6 | | | | 9 | 7 | 2 | |
| | | | 7 | | 1 | | 8 | |
| 7 | | | | | | 6 | | 5 |
| | 9 | | 5 | | | 2 | | |

| | 2 | | | 6 | | | | 3 |
|---|---|---|---|---|---|---|---|---|
| 9 | | | | 4 | | 1 | | |
| 3 | | 1 | | | 2 | | | |
| | | | | | 5 | | 9 | |
| 5 | | 3 | | | | 2 | | 8 |
| | 1 | | 4 | | | | | |
| | | | 7 | | | 4 | | 6 |
| | | 6 | | 8 | | | | 2 |
| 4 | | | | 1 | | | 5 | |

Puzzle 129:

| 2 | 5 |   |   |   | 8 | 3 |   | 4 |
|   | 6 |   |   | 5 |   |   |   |   |
|   |   |   | 3 |   |   |   |   |   |
| 7 |   |   | 2 |   |   | 5 | 4 |   |
| 9 |   |   |   | 4 |   |   |   | 2 |
|   | 2 | 6 |   |   | 9 |   |   | 7 |
|   |   |   |   |   | 6 |   |   |   |
|   |   |   |   | 8 |   |   | 7 |   |
| 8 |   | 9 | 1 |   |   |   | 6 | 5 |

Puzzle 130:

|   | 2 |   |   |   |   | 6 |   |   |
|   |   | 1 |   |   | 7 |   | 4 |   |
|   | 7 |   |   | 9 |   |   |   |   |
|   | 5 |   | 9 | 8 |   | 7 |   |   |
|   |   | 2 | 6 |   | 1 | 8 |   |   |
|   |   | 4 |   | 7 | 5 |   | 1 |   |
|   |   |   |   | 5 |   |   | 7 |   |
|   | 8 |   | 1 |   |   | 9 |   |   |
|   |   | 9 |   |   |   |   | 2 |   |

| | | 1 | | 9 | 4 | | 2 | 7 |
|---|---|---|---|---|---|---|---|---|
| | 8 | 4 | | | | | 3 | |
| | 5 | | 7 | | | 1 | | |
| | 7 | 5 | 6 | 2 | | | | |
| | | | | | | | | |
| | | | | 5 | 3 | 7 | 1 | |
| | | 3 | | | 5 | | 8 | |
| | 2 | | | | | 3 | 7 | |
| 4 | 6 | | 3 | 8 | | 9 | | |

| | | | | | 2 | | 1 | |
|---|---|---|---|---|---|---|---|---|
| | 1 | 2 | | 7 | | | | |
| 6 | | 9 | | | | | | 5 |
| 4 | | 1 | | | | | 2 | |
| | | 3 | 8 | | 5 | 9 | | |
| | 9 | | | | | 1 | | 3 |
| 9 | | | | | | 8 | | 7 |
| | | | | 8 | | 3 | 4 | |
| | 4 | | 2 | | | | | |

| | | | 2 | | 7 | | 5 | 1 |
|---|---|---|---|---|---|---|---|---|
| | | | 6 | 9 | 5 | 4 | | |
| | | 6 | | | | | | |
| | 3 | | | | 6 | 8 | 9 | |
| | | 9 | | | | 5 | | |
| | 6 | 4 | 7 | | | | 2 | |
| | | | | | | 7 | | |
| | | 1 | 5 | 3 | 2 | | | |
| 9 | 2 | | 4 | | 1 | | | |

| 8 | | | 6 | 3 | 7 | 4 | | |
|---|---|---|---|---|---|---|---|---|
| | | 4 | | | | 1 | | |
| | | 2 | | | 4 | | 6 | 8 |
| 3 | | | 9 | | 5 | | | |
| | 4 | | | | | | 2 | |
| | | | 4 | | 6 | | | 1 |
| 4 | 2 | | 7 | | | 9 | | |
| | | 9 | | | | 7 | | |
| | | 8 | 5 | 4 | 9 | | | 3 |

**135**

| | | 5 | 9 | 1 | | | 8 | |
|---|---|---|---|---|---|---|---|---|
| | | | | 3 | | 2 | 6 | 7 |
| | | | | 2 | | | | |
| 6 | 8 | | | | | | | |
| | | 4 | | | | 5 | | |
| | | | | | | | 1 | 9 |
| | | | 8 | | | | | |
| 2 | 1 | 6 | | 9 | | | | |
| | 9 | | | 6 | 4 | 3 | | |

**136**

| | | 8 | | | 3 | | | |
|---|---|---|---|---|---|---|---|---|
| | | 4 | 5 | 1 | 7 | | | 2 |
| 3 | 1 | | | | | | | |
| | 8 | 3 | | 2 | | | | |
| 4 | | | | | | | | 5 |
| | | | | 9 | | 3 | 7 | |
| | | | | | | | 2 | 7 |
| 2 | | | 7 | 3 | 6 | 5 | | |
| | | | 8 | | | 9 | | |

| | 3 | | 9 | | 2 | | | 1 |
|---|---|---|---|---|---|---|---|---|
| 1 | | | | | | 6 | | |
| | | | | 5 | | | 3 | 8 |
| | | 5 | | 1 | | | | |
| | | 2 | 8 | | 4 | 9 | | |
| | | | | 7 | | 3 | | |
| 4 | 6 | | | 2 | | | | |
| | | 1 | | | | | | 6 |
| 9 | | | 6 | | 7 | | 4 | |

| | 3 | | | 5 | 1 | 9 | | |
|---|---|---|---|---|---|---|---|---|
| | 7 | | | | | | | 8 |
| 8 | | 4 | | 6 | | | | |
| 6 | | | | | | 8 | | |
| | 4 | 3 | | 1 | | 5 | 6 | |
| | | 2 | | | | | | 9 |
| | | | | 9 | | 4 | | 3 |
| 4 | | | | | | | 9 | |
| | | 8 | 6 | 4 | | | 5 | |

Puzzle 139:

|   |   | 9 |   | 3 |   |   |   |   |
|---|---|---|---|---|---|---|---|---|
|   |   |   | 6 |   |   |   |   | 7 |
| 7 |   | 2 |   |   |   |   | 9 |   |
|   | 6 |   | 3 | 8 |   |   |   |   |
| 9 |   | 4 |   |   |   | 1 |   | 5 |
|   |   |   | 4 | 5 |   |   | 2 |   |
|   | 2 |   |   |   |   | 4 |   | 8 |
| 5 |   |   |   |   | 6 |   |   |   |
|   |   |   |   | 5 |   | 7 |   |   |

Puzzle 140:

|   |   |   | 3 |   |   |   |   | 7 |
|---|---|---|---|---|---|---|---|---|
| 9 |   |   |   |   | 5 | 1 |   |   |
| 1 | 8 |   | 7 |   |   |   | 9 |   |
|   | 1 |   |   | 7 | 8 |   | 4 | 3 |
|   |   |   |   |   |   |   |   |   |
| 2 | 7 |   | 9 | 4 |   |   | 8 |   |
|   | 4 |   |   |   | 6 |   | 2 | 9 |
|   |   | 2 | 4 |   |   |   |   | 8 |
| 8 |   |   |   |   | 7 |   |   |   |

Puzzle 141

| 7 |   |   | 1 | 5 |   |   |   |   |
|---|---|---|---|---|---|---|---|---|
|   | 9 |   |   |   |   |   |   |   |
| 2 |   | 6 | 4 |   |   |   | 3 |   |
| 1 |   | 9 |   |   |   | 8 |   |   |
| 8 | 6 |   | 7 |   | 9 |   | 5 | 3 |
|   |   | 3 |   |   |   | 2 |   | 6 |
|   | 8 |   |   |   | 1 | 3 |   | 5 |
|   |   |   |   |   |   |   | 2 |   |
|   |   |   |   | 8 | 3 |   |   | 9 |

Puzzle 142

| 9 |   | 8 | 5 |   |   |   |   |   |
|---|---|---|---|---|---|---|---|---|
|   |   | 3 |   | 4 | 1 |   | 8 |   |
| 6 | 2 |   |   |   |   |   | 7 |   |
|   |   |   |   | 1 |   |   | 2 |   |
| 1 |   |   |   |   |   |   |   | 6 |
|   | 5 |   |   | 9 |   |   |   |   |
|   | 6 |   |   |   |   |   | 9 | 3 |
|   | 8 |   | 3 | 5 |   | 6 |   |   |
|   |   |   |   |   | 9 | 8 |   | 4 |

75

| | | | 1 | 2 | 5 | 6 | | |
|---|---|---|---|---|---|---|---|---|
| | | 8 | 9 | | | | | 4 |
| | 2 | | | | | | | |
| 9 | 5 | | 8 | | | | 4 | |
| | | 7 | | 6 | | 1 | | |
| | 6 | | | | 1 | | 3 | 8 |
| | | | | | | | 5 | |
| 8 | | | | | 7 | 3 | | |
| | | 5 | 6 | 4 | 9 | | | |

| 4 | | 1 | 2 | | 7 | | | |
|---|---|---|---|---|---|---|---|---|
| | 5 | | | | | | | 8 |
| | | 9 | | | 1 | | | 3 |
| 9 | 1 | | | | 4 | 2 | | |
| | | | | | | | | |
| | | 3 | 1 | | | | 5 | 9 |
| 8 | | | 9 | | | 6 | | |
| 6 | | | | | | | 1 | |
| | | | 4 | | 6 | 9 | | 5 |

| 1 | 9 |   |   |   | 7 | 3 |   |   |
|---|---|---|---|---|---|---|---|---|
|   |   |   | 9 | 4 |   |   | 5 |   |
|   |   |   |   |   |   |   | 7 |   |
| 2 |   |   | 1 |   |   | 8 |   |   |
|   |   | 6 |   |   |   | 7 |   |   |
|   |   | 5 |   |   | 4 |   |   | 6 |
|   | 7 |   |   |   |   |   |   |   |
|   | 3 |   |   | 6 | 2 |   |   |   |
|   |   | 9 | 8 |   |   |   | 3 | 2 |

|   |   |   |   |   |   |   |   |   |
|---|---|---|---|---|---|---|---|---|
|   | 9 | 8 |   | 1 | 7 |   |   | 3 |
| 1 |   | 5 |   | 8 |   |   |   |   |
|   | 2 |   | 6 |   |   |   |   | 4 |
|   | 5 |   |   | 7 |   |   | 8 |   |
| 6 |   |   |   |   | 3 |   | 9 |   |
|   |   |   |   | 6 |   | 1 |   | 5 |
| 7 |   |   | 5 | 2 |   | 6 | 4 |   |
|   |   |   |   |   |   |   |   |   |

**147**

| | | 9 | | | | | | 5 |
|---|---|---|---|---|---|---|---|---|
| | | | 9 | | | 7 | 1 | |
| 5 | | | 7 | | 3 | | | |
| | 2 | | | | 8 | | | 3 |
| 9 | | 5 | 4 | | 2 | 1 | | 6 |
| 3 | | | 6 | | | | 2 | |
| | | | 2 | | 1 | | | 4 |
| | 1 | 8 | | | 9 | | | |
| 2 | | | | | | 9 | | |

**148**

| | | 6 | | 4 | | | | 5 |
|---|---|---|---|---|---|---|---|---|
| | | 5 | 9 | | 8 | | 1 | |
| 2 | | | | | 5 | | 4 | |
| 8 | | 3 | | | | 6 | | |
| | | | 8 | | 4 | | | |
| | | 9 | | | | 1 | | 8 |
| | 3 | | 7 | | | | | 9 |
| | 6 | | 5 | | 9 | 4 | | |
| 9 | | | | 8 | | 7 | | |

| | | | 3 | | | | | 7 |
|---|---|---|---|---|---|---|---|---|
| 7 | | 6 | 9 | | | 1 | 4 | |
| | 8 | | | 7 | | | | 2 |
| | | 2 | | 5 | | | | |
| 9 | | | | | | | | 1 |
| | | | | 8 | | 9 | | |
| 2 | | | | 3 | | | 7 | |
| | 4 | 8 | | | 7 | 5 | | 6 |
| 6 | | | | | 5 | | | |

| | | 5 | 7 | 1 | | | | |
|---|---|---|---|---|---|---|---|---|
| | 2 | | | | 3 | | | 8 |
| 3 | | 1 | 8 | | | | | |
| 2 | 4 | | | | | 3 | | |
| | | | 2 | | 7 | | | |
| | | 8 | | | | | 6 | 9 |
| | | | | | 2 | 7 | | 3 |
| 1 | | | 6 | | | | 2 | |
| | | | | 3 | 9 | 4 | | |

| | | | | 9 | 7 | 1 | | |
|---|---|---|---|---|---|---|---|---|
| | | | 4 | | | | | 2 |
| | 8 | 2 | | | | | | |
| | | | | | 6 | | 2 | 3 |
| | | 9 | | 4 | | 5 | | |
| 6 | 3 | | 1 | | | | | |
| | | | | | | 4 | 1 | |
| 9 | | | | | 2 | | | |
| | | 7 | 9 | 5 | | | | |

| | | 4 | | | 3 | | | 7 |
|---|---|---|---|---|---|---|---|---|
| | | | | | | 2 | | 9 |
| | | 9 | | 1 | 8 | | | |
| | 1 | 6 | | 4 | | | | 3 |
| | 4 | | | | | | 9 | |
| 9 | | | | 8 | | 4 | 2 | |
| | | | 5 | 2 | | 8 | | |
| 7 | | 2 | | | | | | |
| 5 | | | 8 | | | 9 | | |

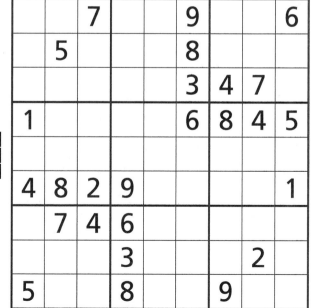

Puzzle 153

| | 7 | | 2 | | 9 | | | |
| 2 | 9 | | | 8 | | | 3 | |
| 6 | | | | 3 | | | | |
| | | 1 | | | | | 9 | |
| 4 | | | 1 | 9 | 3 | | | 7 |
| | 8 | | | | | 4 | | |
| | | | | 5 | | | | 1 |
| | 3 | | | 6 | | | 5 | 2 |
| | | | 8 | | 2 | | 7 | |

Puzzle 154

| | | 7 | | 9 | | | | 6 |
| | 5 | | | 8 | | | | |
| | | | | 3 | 4 | 7 | | |
| 1 | | | | 6 | 8 | 4 | | 5 |
| | | | | | | | | |
| 4 | 8 | 2 | 9 | | | | | 1 |
| | 7 | 4 | 6 | | | | | |
| | | | 3 | | | | 2 | |
| 5 | | | 8 | | | 9 | | |

| 3 |   | 7 |   | 5 |   |   |   |   |
|---|---|---|---|---|---|---|---|---|
|   |   |   | 3 |   |   |   |   | 2 |
|   |   |   | 2 | 6 | 8 |   |   |   |
| 7 |   | 1 | 9 |   |   |   | 4 |   |
|   | 3 |   |   |   |   |   | 6 |   |
|   | 4 |   |   |   | 2 | 1 |   | 3 |
|   |   | 4 | 6 | 8 |   |   |   |   |
| 1 |   |   |   |   | 7 |   |   |   |
|   |   |   |   | 1 |   | 7 |   | 5 |

|   | 5 |   | 9 | 8 |   | 4 |   | 6 |
|---|---|---|---|---|---|---|---|---|
|   |   |   |   |   |   | 2 |   |   |
|   |   |   | 3 | 2 |   |   | 5 |   |
| 6 |   | 5 |   |   |   | 8 | 4 |   |
| 7 |   |   |   |   |   |   |   | 2 |
|   | 8 | 4 |   |   |   | 5 |   | 9 |
|   | 2 |   | 3 | 6 |   |   |   |   |
|   |   | 6 |   |   |   |   |   |   |
| 4 |   | 1 |   | 2 | 5 |   | 6 |   |

Puzzle 157:

| 2 |   |   |   |   | 5 |   |   | 7 |
|---|---|---|---|---|---|---|---|---|
|   | 3 |   | 8 |   |   | 2 |   |   |
|   | 4 |   |   | 3 |   |   |   |   |
|   |   |   |   |   | 8 | 5 |   | 2 |
|   |   | 2 |   |   |   | 8 |   |   |
| 7 |   | 5 | 9 |   |   |   |   |   |
|   |   |   |   | 6 |   |   | 4 |   |
|   |   | 4 |   |   | 1 |   | 6 |   |
| 9 |   |   | 5 |   |   |   |   | 8 |

Puzzle 158:

| 5 |   |   |   |   | 9 |   |   | 6 |
|---|---|---|---|---|---|---|---|---|
|   |   |   |   | 8 |   |   | 4 |   |
|   |   |   | 6 | 4 |   | 9 | 5 |   |
|   |   | 2 | 9 |   |   | 1 |   | 5 |
|   |   |   |   |   |   |   |   |   |
| 9 |   | 5 |   |   | 7 | 4 |   |   |
|   | 6 | 3 |   | 2 | 4 |   |   |   |
|   | 5 |   |   | 6 |   |   |   |   |
| 1 |   |   | 3 |   |   |   |   | 4 |

159

160

| | 1 | 4 | | | | | | |
|---|---|---|---|---|---|---|---|---|
| 2 | | | | | 8 | | | 9 |
| | | | 6 | 4 | | | 3 | 5 |
| 9 | | 8 | | 3 | | | | |
| | | | 1 | | 9 | | | |
| | | | | 8 | | 5 | | 2 |
| 1 | 9 | | | 6 | 4 | | | |
| 4 | | | 8 | | | | | 3 |
| | | | | | | 2 | 6 | |

| 6 | 2 | | 1 | | | | | 4 |
|---|---|---|---|---|---|---|---|---|
| | 4 | | | 8 | | 9 | | |
| | | 9 | | | | | | 3 |
| | 6 | | 2 | | 1 | | | |
| | | | | 5 | | | | |
| | | | 9 | | 6 | | 1 | |
| 2 | | | | | | 7 | | |
| | | 5 | | 7 | | | 4 | |
| 7 | | | | | 3 | | 9 | 8 |

| | | | 7 | 5 | | | | |
|---|---|---|---|---|---|---|---|---|
| | | 5 | | 2 | | 1 | 7 | |
| | | | | | 9 | 6 | | 5 |
| | 3 | | | | | | 9 | 2 |
| | | 6 | | | | 7 | | |
| 2 | 1 | | | | | | 5 | |
| 7 | | 3 | 2 | | | | | |
| | 6 | 1 | | 8 | | 5 | | |
| | | | | 4 | 7 | | | |

| | | 7 | | | 8 | | | 4 |
|---|---|---|---|---|---|---|---|---|
| | 4 | | | | | | | |
| | 1 | 8 | 3 | 9 | | | | |
| | 5 | | | | 1 | | 4 | |
| 8 | | | | 3 | | | | 9 |
| | 7 | | 6 | | | | 2 | |
| | | | 5 | 9 | 4 | 3 | | |
| | | | | | | | 9 | |
| 2 | | | 7 | | | 1 | | |

| 6 |   |   |   |   |   | 3 |   | 4 |
|---|---|---|---|---|---|---|---|---|
|   |   | 3 |   | 1 |   | 5 |   |   |
|   | 7 |   |   |   | 9 |   |   |   |
|   |   |   | 1 |   |   |   | 7 | 3 |
|   |   | 7 |   | 5 |   | 6 |   |   |
| 1 | 3 |   |   |   | 2 |   |   |   |
|   |   |   | 4 |   |   |   | 2 |   |
|   |   | 8 |   | 3 |   | 9 |   |   |
| 7 |   | 6 |   |   |   |   |   | 8 |

|   | 5 | 4 |   | 3 |   | 2 |   |   |
|---|---|---|---|---|---|---|---|---|
|   | 1 |   | 7 |   |   |   |   |   |
| 3 |   | 2 |   |   | 8 |   |   |   |
| 9 |   |   |   | 5 |   |   |   |   |
| 2 |   | 3 |   |   |   | 4 |   | 8 |
|   |   |   |   | 2 |   |   |   | 3 |
|   |   |   | 2 |   |   | 5 |   | 1 |
|   |   |   |   |   | 9 |   | 7 |   |
|   |   | 8 |   | 1 |   | 6 | 2 |   |

| | | 1 | | | | | | |
|---|---|---|---|---|---|---|---|---|
| 6 | 3 | | | | | | | 5 |
| | 9 | | | | 4 | 2 | | 6 |
| | | | 6 | 1 | | | | 4 |
| 9 | 6 | | | 3 | | | 5 | 8 |
| 1 | | | | 9 | 5 | | | |
| 3 | | 4 | 8 | | | | 6 | |
| 2 | | | | | | | 4 | 9 |
| | | | | | | 5 | | |

| 8 | | 9 | | | | | | |
|---|---|---|---|---|---|---|---|---|
| | 5 | | 8 | 3 | | | | 2 |
| 7 | 3 | | | | 2 | | | 4 |
| | | 6 | | 5 | | | | |
| | 7 | | 9 | | 4 | | 1 | |
| | | | | 8 | | 7 | | |
| 2 | | | 4 | | | | 5 | 1 |
| 4 | | | | 1 | 8 | | 3 | |
| | | | | | | 4 | | 7 |

| | | | 6 | | 9 | | | 1 |
|---|---|---|---|---|---|---|---|---|
| | 4 | | 2 | | 8 | | 3 | 9 |
| | | | | 1 | | | | 2 |
| | 1 | 7 | | | | 9 | | |
| | | | 8 | | 1 | | | |
| | | 3 | | | | 4 | 1 | |
| 8 | | | | 9 | | | | |
| 7 | 3 | | 4 | | 6 | | 2 | |
| 6 | | | 7 | | 3 | | | |

| 5 | | | | | | | 9 | |
|---|---|---|---|---|---|---|---|---|
| 8 | | | | 6 | | | 2 | |
| | | 9 | | | 3 | 4 | | |
| 3 | | | 9 | | | 7 | 6 | |
| | | | | 1 | | | | |
| | 9 | 4 | | | 5 | | | 2 |
| | | 7 | 1 | | | 9 | | |
| | 2 | | | 3 | | | | 6 |
| | 8 | | | | | | | 7 |

| | | | | 2 | | | | |
|---|---|---|---|---|---|---|---|---|
| | 3 | | | | 5 | | 8 | 4 |
| | 5 | 4 | | | 3 | 2 | | |
| 5 | | 3 | 4 | | | | | |
| | | 1 | | | | 7 | | |
| | | | | | 7 | 8 | | 9 |
| | | 5 | 7 | | | 9 | 2 | |
| 8 | 2 | | 9 | | | | 3 | |
| | | | | 6 | | | | |

| 8 | 2 | | | | 1 | | 9 | 5 |
|---|---|---|---|---|---|---|---|---|
| 5 | | 9 | | | | 3 | | |
| | 6 | | | | | | | |
| | | | 9 | 5 | 6 | 8 | | |
| | | | 1 | | | | | |
| | 8 | 5 | 7 | 6 | | | | |
| | | | | | | | 3 | |
| | | 8 | | | | 1 | | 4 |
| 3 | 1 | | 4 | | | | 7 | 2 |

| | 4 | 2 | | | 5 | | | 1 |
|---|---|---|---|---|---|---|---|---|
| | | | | 4 | 2 | | | |
| | | | 2 | | 7 | 3 | | |
| | | | | 3 | | 6 | | |
| 8 | | | 9 | | | | | 5 |
| | 3 | | 5 | | | | | |
| | 1 | 4 | | 7 | | | | |
| | | 5 | 2 | | | | | |
| 6 | | | 1 | | | 4 | 8 | |

| 4 | | | 3 | | | 9 | 8 | |
|---|---|---|---|---|---|---|---|---|
| | | 5 | | | | 2 | | 1 |
| | | | | | 2 | | 3 | |
| | 7 | | | | 3 | 5 | | |
| | | 9 | 8 | | 1 | 4 | | |
| | | 4 | 6 | | | | 7 | |
| | 2 | | 7 | | | | | |
| 6 | | 8 | | | | 7 | | |
| | 4 | 1 | | | 8 | | | 6 |

| 8 |   |   |   |   | 9 | 4 |   |   |
|---|---|---|---|---|---|---|---|---|
| 4 |   |   |   |   | 7 |   |   |   |
|   |   | 2 | 8 | 1 |   | 9 |   |   |
|   | 8 |   | 2 |   |   |   |   |   |
| 1 |   | 9 |   | 7 |   | 6 |   | 5 |
|   |   |   |   |   | 3 |   | 8 |   |
|   |   | 1 |   | 8 | 2 | 5 |   |   |
|   |   |   | 1 |   |   |   |   | 4 |
|   |   | 8 | 9 |   |   |   |   | 6 |

|   |   |   |   | 3 | 9 |   |   |   |
|---|---|---|---|---|---|---|---|---|
| 6 |   |   | 2 |   |   | 8 |   | 1 |
|   | 8 | 3 |   |   |   | 2 |   |   |
|   |   |   |   |   |   |   | 5 | 2 |
| 9 |   |   | 3 |   | 6 |   |   | 7 |
| 3 | 4 |   |   |   |   |   |   |   |
|   |   | 1 |   |   |   | 5 | 2 |   |
| 5 |   | 7 |   |   | 2 |   |   | 6 |
|   |   |   | 4 | 5 |   |   |   |   |

| | | 1 | | | 3 | | 9 | |
|---|---|---|---|---|---|---|---|---|
| | | | | | 4 | 7 | 6 | |
| | | | 6 | | | | 3 | |
| | | 9 | | 6 | | 1 | | 2 |
| | | | | | | | | |
| 3 | | 5 | | 1 | | 4 | | |
| | 5 | | | | 6 | | | |
| | 1 | 6 | 2 | | | | | |
| | 7 | | 9 | | | 5 | | |

| | 6 | | 7 | 4 | 5 | | | 1 |
|---|---|---|---|---|---|---|---|---|
| | | | | | | 4 | 6 | |
| | | | | | 2 | 7 | 3 | |
| | | | | 5 | | 9 | 1 | |
| | | | 2 | | 4 | | | |
| | 5 | 4 | | 8 | | | | |
| | 3 | 5 | 1 | | | | | |
| | 7 | 8 | | | | | | |
| 2 | | | 5 | 3 | 9 | | 7 | |

179

| 6 |   | 8 |   |   |   |   |   |   |
|---|---|---|---|---|---|---|---|---|
|   | 2 |   |   | 6 | 1 |   | 9 |   |
|   |   | 4 | 2 |   |   | 6 |   |   |
|   |   |   | 9 |   |   |   |   | 5 |
|   | 8 |   | 7 | 4 | 2 |   | 1 |   |
| 1 |   |   |   |   | 8 |   |   |   |
|   |   | 1 |   |   | 5 | 7 |   |   |
|   | 3 |   | 4 | 8 |   |   | 2 |   |
|   |   |   |   |   |   | 9 |   | 3 |

180

|   |   | 4 |   |   |   |   | 9 |   |
|---|---|---|---|---|---|---|---|---|
| 7 | 1 |   |   |   |   |   | 3 | 6 |
|   |   | 9 | 1 | 8 |   |   |   | 5 |
| 8 |   | 1 | 3 |   |   |   |   |   |
|   | 6 |   |   | 4 |   |   | 8 |   |
|   |   |   |   |   | 5 | 6 |   | 7 |
| 1 |   |   |   | 9 | 8 | 3 |   |   |
| 9 | 7 |   |   |   |   |   | 6 | 8 |
|   | 2 |   |   |   |   | 7 |   |   |

| | 4 | | 8 | | 7 | | 5 | 6 |
|---|---|---|---|---|---|---|---|---|
| | | | | | | 1 | 8 | |
| 6 | | | | | 5 | | | |
| | | | 2 | | | 3 | | 4 |
| | 5 | | | | | | 2 | |
| 1 | | 9 | | | 8 | | | |
| | | | 1 | | | | | 2 |
| | 1 | 8 | | | | | | |
| 2 | 9 | | 5 | | 6 | | 1 | |

| | | | 1 | | | 6 | 9 | 4 |
|---|---|---|---|---|---|---|---|---|
| | 3 | | | | | | 2 | |
| | | | | 5 | 4 | | | |
| 7 | | | 4 | | | 2 | | |
| | 6 | 2 | | | | 4 | 8 | |
| | | 1 | | | 2 | | | 9 |
| | | | 9 | 6 | | | | |
| | 1 | | | | | | 5 | |
| 6 | 4 | 7 | | | 1 | | | |

| | | | | 1 | | | | |
|---|---|---|---|---|---|---|---|---|
| | 2 | 7 | | | 9 | | 6 | |
| | | | | 7 | | | 2 | 1 |
| | | 6 | | 8 | 1 | | 3 | |
| | 8 | 9 | | | | 2 | 1 | |
| | 5 | | 9 | 2 | | 6 | | |
| 7 | 3 | | | 6 | | | | |
| | 1 | | 5 | | | 3 | 8 | |
| | | | | 4 | | | | |

| | 5 | | 8 | | 6 | | | |
|---|---|---|---|---|---|---|---|---|
| | | 6 | | | 1 | 7 | | 5 |
| | | 4 | | 3 | | | | 6 |
| 1 | | 5 | | | | | | |
| | 4 | | | | | | 7 | |
| | | | | | | 3 | | 9 |
| 5 | | | | 6 | | 2 | | |
| 7 | | 1 | 2 | | | 9 | | |
| | | | 7 | | 8 | | 3 | |

| | 9 | | | | 5 | | 2 | |
|---|---|---|---|---|---|---|---|---|
| 7 | 6 | | | | 2 | | | 3 |
| | | | | 9 | | 8 | 7 | |
| 6 | | | | 5 | | | | 7 |
| | | 5 | | | | 3 | | |
| 3 | | | | 2 | | | | 5 |
| | 8 | 9 | | 4 | | | | |
| 4 | | | 2 | | | | 1 | 9 |
| | 3 | | 7 | | | | 8 | |

| 7 | | | 5 | | | | | |
|---|---|---|---|---|---|---|---|---|
| | | | | 1 | | | | 4 |
| | | 6 | | 2 | | 7 | | 9 |
| | 3 | | | | | 2 | | 7 |
| | 4 | | | 6 | | | 9 | |
| 2 | | 8 | | | | | 3 | |
| 5 | | 9 | | 3 | | 1 | | |
| 4 | | | | 7 | | | | |
| | | | | | 8 | | | 5 |

## 191

| | 4 | 1 | | | | 8 | | |
|---|---|---|---|---|---|---|---|---|
| | | 3 | | 9 | | | | 1 |
| 5 | | | | | 6 | | 4 | |
| | | | | 7 | 3 | | 2 | |
| | | | 8 | | 2 | | | |
| | 3 | | 1 | 5 | | | | |
| | 9 | | 7 | | | | | 4 |
| 1 | | | | 8 | | 6 | | |
| | | 6 | | | | 1 | 5 | |

## 192

| | 3 | | | | 9 | | 7 | |
|---|---|---|---|---|---|---|---|---|
| | | 2 | 4 | | | | | 9 |
| | 1 | | | | | | 3 | |
| | 2 | | 1 | | 7 | | | |
| | | 9 | | | | 7 | | |
| | | | 5 | | 3 | | 2 | |
| | 9 | | | | | | 4 | |
| 5 | | | | | 8 | 6 | | |
| | 7 | | 2 | | | | 8 | |

| | 8 | 6 | | | | 1 | | |
|---|---|---|---|---|---|---|---|---|
| | | | | | | | 3 | |
| 7 | 9 | | 8 | | 5 | | | |
| | 2 | 9 | | | 3 | | | |
| 8 | | | | 5 | | | | 3 |
| | | | 6 | | | 8 | 2 | |
| | | | 3 | | 9 | | 1 | 2 |
| | 1 | | | | | | | |
| | | 2 | | | | 7 | 9 | |

| | | | 8 | | 3 | | 7 | |
|---|---|---|---|---|---|---|---|---|
| | 2 | 8 | | | 1 | | | |
| 6 | | | | | | 4 | | |
| | 6 | | | | | | | 1 |
| 5 | 3 | | | 8 | | | 2 | 7 |
| 8 | | | | | | | 4 | |
| | | 9 | | | | | | 6 |
| | | | 6 | | | 2 | 5 | |
| | 7 | | 9 | | 2 | | | |

| 9 | | | | | | | | |
|---|---|---|---|---|---|---|---|---|
| 1 | | 5 | 7 | 6 | | | | |
| | | | 2 | | | | 7 | |
| | | 8 | | | 6 | | | 1 |
| 4 | 6 | | | | | | 5 | 2 |
| 7 | | | 1 | | | 9 | | |
| | 5 | | | | 9 | | | |
| | | | | 1 | 3 | 4 | | 8 |
| | | | | | | | | 9 |

| 9 | | | 2 | | | | | 4 |
|---|---|---|---|---|---|---|---|---|
| | 2 | | | | | | | 6 |
| | 4 | | 3 | | 6 | 5 | 2 | |
| | | | | 8 | 2 | | 7 | |
| | | 7 | | | | 2 | | |
| | 5 | | 4 | 7 | | | | |
| | 7 | 9 | 1 | | 5 | | 8 | |
| 4 | | | | | | | 5 | |
| 8 | | | | | 7 | | | 1 |

| 7 |   |   |   | 5 |   |   | 4 | 9 |
|---|---|---|---|---|---|---|---|---|
|   |   |   |   | 3 |   | 8 |   | 6 |
|   |   | 1 |   |   |   |   |   |   |
|   |   |   |   |   | 3 |   |   | 2 |
|   |   | 3 | 2 |   | 4 | 1 |   |   |
| 9 |   |   | 6 |   |   |   |   |   |
|   |   |   |   |   |   | 4 |   |   |
| 5 |   | 7 |   | 4 |   |   |   |   |
| 1 | 9 |   |   | 8 |   |   |   | 5 |

| | | 8 | 9 | | | 7 | 6 | |
|---|---|---|---|---|---|---|---|---|
| | 9 | | | | | 8 | 2 | |
| | | 2 | | | 5 | | | |
| 6 | | | | 5 | | | 1 | 3 |
| | 3 | 1 | | | | 5 | 8 | |
| 8 | 5 | | | 2 | | | | 7 |
| | | | 8 | | | 1 | | |
| | 8 | 3 | | | | | 7 | |
| | 6 | 7 | | | 4 | 3 | | |

Puzzle 199:

|   |   |   |   |   | 4 |   |   |   |
|---|---|---|---|---|---|---|---|---|
|   |   |   | 2 | 5 |   | 1 |   |   |
| 9 |   | 8 |   |   |   | 6 |   |   |
|   | 7 | 3 | 4 | 6 |   |   |   | 8 |
| 8 |   |   |   |   |   |   |   | 1 |
| 6 |   |   |   | 1 | 8 | 3 | 7 |   |
|   |   | 4 |   |   |   | 5 |   | 9 |
|   |   | 1 |   | 2 | 5 |   |   |   |
|   |   |   | 1 |   |   |   |   |   |

Puzzle 200:

|   |   |   |   | 2 | 3 | 4 |   | 1 |
|---|---|---|---|---|---|---|---|---|
|   |   |   | 1 |   | 9 |   |   |   |
|   | 1 |   | 4 |   |   | 9 | 8 |   |
|   |   | 2 | 5 |   |   | 1 | 3 |   |
|   |   |   |   | 9 |   |   |   |   |
|   | 8 | 4 |   |   | 2 | 5 |   |   |
|   | 5 | 3 |   |   | 1 |   | 9 |   |
|   |   |   | 9 |   | 4 |   |   |   |
| 4 |   | 7 | 2 | 5 |   |   |   |   |

| | | | 5 | | | 3 | | |
|---|---|---|---|---|---|---|---|---|
| | 8 | 4 | | 1 | | | | |
| 9 | 3 | | 4 | | | | | |
| 4 | 9 | | | | | 2 | | |
| | | | 9 | 2 | 7 | | | |
| | | 3 | | | | | 9 | 5 |
| | | | | | 1 | | 4 | 8 |
| | | | | 4 | | 7 | 1 | |
| | | 2 | | | 5 | | | |

| | | | | 7 | | | 4 | |
|---|---|---|---|---|---|---|---|---|
| | | 9 | 2 | 5 | | | 1 | |
| | | | | | 6 | 3 | | |
| | | | 7 | | | | 3 | 5 |
| 9 | | 6 | | | | 1 | | 4 |
| 3 | 7 | | | | 4 | | | |
| | | 8 | 3 | | | | | |
| | 3 | | | 4 | 9 | 5 | | |
| | 2 | | | 8 | | | | |

| 3 |   |   | 4 | 5 |   |   |   |   |
|---|---|---|---|---|---|---|---|---|
|   | 6 | 2 |   |   |   | 4 |   |   |
|   |   | 1 |   | 2 | 7 |   |   |   |
| 6 |   |   |   |   |   | 9 | 2 |   |
|   | 5 | 4 |   |   |   | 3 | 8 |   |
|   | 2 | 3 |   |   |   |   |   | 5 |
|   |   |   | 1 | 7 |   | 2 |   |   |
|   |   | 9 |   |   |   | 5 | 1 |   |
|   |   |   |   | 4 | 8 |   |   | 3 |

|   |   |   |   |   | 4 |   | 2 |   |
|---|---|---|---|---|---|---|---|---|
| 9 | 7 | 4 |   |   |   | 5 |   | 6 |
|   |   | 3 |   |   |   |   |   | 7 |
|   |   | 2 | 7 | 5 |   |   |   |   |
|   | 5 |   |   | 6 |   |   | 7 |   |
|   |   |   | 8 | 1 | 2 |   |   |   |
| 8 |   |   |   |   |   | 3 |   |   |
| 3 |   | 5 |   |   |   | 9 | 8 | 1 |
|   | 4 |   | 8 |   |   |   |   |   |

| | | 9 | | | | | 2 | |
|---|---|---|---|---|---|---|---|---|
| | | | 7 | | | 1 | | 3 |
| 3 | | | 6 | | | | 8 | |
| | 2 | | 1 | 9 | | | | |
| | 1 | | | | | | 5 | |
| | | | | 3 | 4 | | 6 | |
| | 8 | | | | 7 | | | 4 |
| 6 | | 5 | | | 2 | | | |
| | 9 | | | | | 5 | | |

| | | | | 9 | | | 5 | |
|---|---|---|---|---|---|---|---|---|
| 8 | 5 | | | 1 | | 3 | | |
| | 1 | 6 | | | | | | |
| 4 | | | | | 7 | | 8 | |
| | | | 8 | 6 | 3 | | | |
| | 8 | | 5 | | | | | 1 |
| | | | | | | 7 | 6 | |
| | | 9 | | 7 | | | 4 | 3 |
| | 4 | | | 8 | | | | |

Puzzle 207

| | | | | 2 | | 3 | 6 | |
|---|---|---|---|---|---|---|---|---|
| | | | 1 | 8 | | 2 | 5 | |
| | | | | | 7 | | 8 | |
| | 8 | | | 5 | | | 9 | 3 |
| | | 7 | | | | 5 | | |
| 5 | 1 | | 6 | | | 8 | | |
| | 5 | | 9 | | | | | |
| | 8 | 6 | | 1 | 3 | | | |
| | 4 | 3 | | 5 | | | | |

Puzzle 208

| | 8 | 2 | 7 | | | | | 4 |
|---|---|---|---|---|---|---|---|---|
| | 4 | | 2 | | 6 | 8 | | |
| 6 | | 9 | 4 | | | 7 | | |
| | | | 6 | | | 2 | | 8 |
| | | | | | | | | |
| 5 | | 6 | | | 7 | | | |
| | | 5 | | | 9 | 4 | | 7 |
| | | 7 | 8 | | 3 | | 9 | |
| 2 | | | | | 4 | 6 | 8 | |

| | 6 | | 4 | | | 5 | | |
|---|---|---|---|---|---|---|---|---|
| 4 | | | | | 1 | | | |
| 3 | | 5 | | | | | 4 | 7 |
| | 7 | | 6 | | | | 2 | 4 |
| | | | 8 | | | | | |
| 6 | 5 | | 2 | | | 7 | | |
| 5 | 2 | | | | | 4 | | 9 |
| | | 9 | | | | | | 1 |
| | | 1 | | | 8 | | 6 | |

| | 5 | 4 | 8 | | 1 | 7 | | 3 |
|---|---|---|---|---|---|---|---|---|
| | 6 | | | 3 | | | 9 | |
| | | | | | | 1 | | 4 |
| 8 | | 7 | 5 | | | | | |
| | | | 7 | | 4 | | | |
| | | | 8 | | | 6 | | 1 |
| 7 | | 6 | | | | | | |
| | 8 | | 1 | | | | 5 | |
| 5 | | 1 | 2 | | 8 | 9 | 4 | |

2 1 1

| | | 7 | | | 2 | | | |
|---|---|---|---|---|---|---|---|---|
| | 2 | 6 | | | 4 | | | 7 |
| 5 | | | 7 | 6 | | 9 | | |
| | | | | 5 | | | | 2 |
| | 9 | | | | | | 1 | |
| 4 | | | | 2 | | | | |
| | | 5 | | 7 | 6 | | | 4 |
| 2 | | | 9 | | | 3 | 6 | |
| | | | 1 | | | 2 | | |

2 1 2

| | 8 | 1 | | | 7 | 2 | | |
|---|---|---|---|---|---|---|---|---|
| | 7 | | 2 | 3 | | | 1 | |
| 9 | | | | | | | | |
| | 9 | 7 | | 2 | | | | 1 |
| 2 | | | 8 | | 6 | | | 7 |
| 1 | | | | 7 | | 3 | 2 | |
| | | | | | | | | 5 |
| | 3 | | | 8 | 5 | | 6 | |
| | | 4 | 6 | | | 1 | 7 | |

| 3 |   |   |   |   |   |   |   | 6 |
|---|---|---|---|---|---|---|---|---|
|   | 2 |   | 9 | 7 |   |   | 1 |   |
|   | 5 |   |   |   |   | 2 | 3 |   |
|   |   |   | 4 |   | 9 | 1 |   |   |
|   | 1 |   |   |   |   |   | 5 |   |
|   |   | 3 | 5 |   | 2 |   |   |   |
|   | 8 | 1 |   |   |   |   | 7 |   |
|   | 7 |   |   | 6 | 1 |   | 4 |   |
| 5 |   |   |   |   |   |   |   | 1 |

|   | 3 |   | 9 |   |   | 6 |   |   |
|---|---|---|---|---|---|---|---|---|
|   |   | 6 |   |   |   |   |   | 5 |
| 8 | 2 | 1 |   | 7 |   |   |   |   |
| 4 |   |   | 7 |   |   |   | 2 |   |
|   |   |   | 5 | 6 | 3 |   |   |   |
|   | 7 |   |   |   | 4 |   |   | 1 |
|   |   |   |   | 5 |   | 9 | 4 | 2 |
| 2 |   |   |   |   |   | 7 |   |   |
|   |   | 9 |   |   | 7 |   | 3 |   |

| 7 |   | 9 |   |   | 2 | 5 |   | 8 |
|---|---|---|---|---|---|---|---|---|
|   |   |   | 1 |   |   |   |   |   |
|   |   |   | 9 | 6 |   |   |   | 7 |
| 3 |   | 4 | 7 |   | 6 | 8 |   |   |
|   |   | 2 |   |   |   | 3 |   |   |
|   |   | 6 | 2 |   | 3 | 7 |   | 9 |
| 8 |   |   |   | 2 | 1 |   |   |   |
|   |   |   |   |   | 4 |   |   |   |
| 2 |   | 3 | 8 |   |   | 1 |   | 4 |

| 1 |   | 4 | 6 |   |   |   |   |   |
|---|---|---|---|---|---|---|---|---|
|   |   |   | 1 |   | 2 | 4 |   |   |
|   | 8 |   | 4 |   |   |   |   | 7 |
| 8 |   | 5 |   |   |   |   | 6 |   |
|   | 7 |   | 2 |   | 6 |   | 5 |   |
|   | 6 |   |   |   |   | 3 |   | 2 |
| 7 |   |   |   |   | 1 |   | 8 |   |
|   |   | 6 | 8 |   | 7 |   |   |   |
|   |   |   |   |   | 3 | 2 |   | 6 |

| 3 |   | 7 |   |   |   |   |   |   |
|---|---|---|---|---|---|---|---|---|
|   |   | 4 |   |   | 1 |   |   |   |
|   | 1 | 6 |   | 5 |   |   | 7 | 4 |
| 2 |   |   | 6 |   |   | 5 | 4 |   |
|   |   | 9 |   |   |   | 8 |   |   |
|   | 8 | 5 |   |   | 9 |   |   | 1 |
| 4 | 9 |   |   | 8 |   | 6 | 2 |   |
|   |   |   | 4 |   |   | 7 |   |   |
|   |   |   |   |   |   | 4 |   | 8 |

|   |   | 7 |   | 2 | 3 |   |   |   |
|---|---|---|---|---|---|---|---|---|
| 2 | 6 |   | 4 |   |   |   | 1 |   |
| 9 |   |   |   |   |   |   | 8 |   |
|   | 9 |   | 3 | 1 |   |   | 4 |   |
|   |   |   | 9 |   | 4 |   |   |   |
|   | 4 |   |   | 7 | 5 |   | 3 |   |
|   | 8 |   |   |   |   |   |   | 3 |
|   | 3 |   |   |   | 2 |   | 5 | 9 |
|   |   |   | 5 | 3 |   | 6 |   |   |

| | | 5 | 8 | | 6 | | | 7 |
|---|---|---|---|---|---|---|---|---|
| 9 | | | | | | | | |
| 2 | | | | 7 | | | 6 | |
| | | 4 | 9 | | | | 3 | |
| | | | 1 | | 5 | | | |
| | 3 | | | | | 8 | 1 | |
| | 5 | | | 8 | | | | 6 |
| | | | | | | | | 4 |
| 7 | | | 5 | | | 3 | 2 | |

| 8 | | | | | | | 5 | 1 |
|---|---|---|---|---|---|---|---|---|
| | | 2 | | | | 6 | | |
| | 7 | | 5 | | | 3 | | |
| | 1 | | | 7 | | 9 | | |
| | | | 9 | | 6 | | | |
| | | 3 | | 8 | | | 1 | |
| | | 5 | | | 3 | | 4 | |
| | | 6 | | | | 5 | | |
| 1 | 4 | | | | | | | 7 |

**Puzzle 221**

|   |   | 6 |   |   | 7 | 4 | 5 |   |
|---|---|---|---|---|---|---|---|---|
|   |   |   | 5 |   |   |   | 2 |   |
| 5 | 7 |   |   | 6 |   |   |   | 3 |
| 1 |   |   |   |   | 6 |   | 9 |   |
|   | 6 |   |   |   |   |   | 3 |   |
|   | 2 |   | 9 |   |   |   |   | 7 |
| 6 |   |   |   | 7 |   |   | 4 | 2 |
|   | 4 |   |   |   | 9 |   |   |   |
|   | 3 | 7 | 4 |   |   | 8 |   |   |

**Puzzle 222**

|   | 6 |   | 4 |   |   | 1 |   |   |
|---|---|---|---|---|---|---|---|---|
| 1 | 8 | 9 |   |   |   |   |   |   |
|   |   |   |   | 6 | 1 |   | 7 |   |
|   | 1 |   |   |   |   |   |   | 7 |
|   | 5 | 3 | 1 |   | 7 | 2 | 6 |   |
| 8 |   |   |   |   |   |   | 9 |   |
|   | 4 |   | 5 | 2 |   |   |   |   |
|   |   |   |   |   |   | 7 | 3 | 5 |
|   |   | 1 |   |   | 9 |   | 4 |   |

| 7 |   |   |   |   | 9 |   |   | 5 |
|---|---|---|---|---|---|---|---|---|
|   | 3 |   |   |   |   |   | 1 |   |
| 9 |   |   |   |   | 4 | 2 |   | 8 |
|   |   | 8 | 7 |   | 2 |   |   |   |
| 1 |   |   |   |   |   |   |   | 7 |
|   |   |   | 8 |   | 3 | 9 |   |   |
| 4 |   | 1 | 6 |   |   |   |   | 3 |
|   | 7 |   |   |   |   |   | 6 |   |
| 8 |   |   | 9 |   |   |   |   | 4 |

|   | 4 |   | 1 |   |   |   |   |   |
|---|---|---|---|---|---|---|---|---|
| 6 |   |   | 8 |   | 7 |   |   | 5 |
| 8 |   |   |   | 5 | 4 |   |   |   |
| 2 |   | 4 |   |   |   | 9 | 8 |   |
|   | 6 |   |   | 7 |   |   | 5 |   |
|   | 5 | 8 |   |   |   | 1 |   | 3 |
|   |   |   | 5 | 4 |   |   |   | 8 |
| 1 |   |   | 7 |   | 3 |   |   | 4 |
|   |   |   |   |   | 2 |   | 1 |   |

| | 1 | 3 | | 9 | | | | |
|---|---|---|---|---|---|---|---|---|
| | 2 | | | 1 | 7 | 9 | | 6 |
| | | | | | 8 | | 2 | 1 |
| | | 7 | | | | | 8 | 3 |
| | | | | | | | | |
| 1 | 3 | | | | | 7 | | |
| 5 | 6 | | 1 | | | | | |
| 3 | | 4 | 8 | 5 | | | 1 | |
| | | | | 3 | | 4 | 9 | |

| 3 | | | | | | 2 | | |
|---|---|---|---|---|---|---|---|---|
| | | | | 2 | | | 1 | |
| | | 1 | | | 8 | | 5 | |
| | | 6 | 7 | | | | 4 | |
| 9 | | | 8 | | 4 | | | 7 |
| | 1 | | | | 6 | 9 | | |
| | 8 | | 6 | | | 3 | | |
| | 6 | | | 4 | | | | |
| | | 5 | | | | | | 9 |

**227**

|   |   | 6 |   |   |   |   |   |   |
|---|---|---|---|---|---|---|---|---|
|   | 5 |   | 3 | 9 |   |   |   | 2 |
| 9 |   |   |   | 2 | 1 | 8 |   |   |
|   |   | 4 |   |   | 2 |   |   |   |
| 8 |   |   |   | 1 |   |   |   | 6 |
|   |   |   | 5 |   |   | 2 |   |   |
|   |   | 5 | 2 | 3 |   |   |   | 4 |
| 1 |   |   |   | 7 | 9 |   | 3 |   |
|   |   |   |   |   |   | 9 |   |   |

**228**

|   |   |   |   | 5 |   | 2 |   | 9 |
|---|---|---|---|---|---|---|---|---|
|   | 1 | 4 | 6 |   |   | 3 |   |   |
|   | 9 |   |   |   | 3 | 8 |   |   |
| 1 |   | 5 |   |   | 9 |   |   |   |
|   |   |   |   |   |   |   |   |   |
|   |   |   | 1 |   |   | 6 |   | 7 |
|   |   | 8 | 7 |   |   |   | 6 |   |
|   |   | 1 |   |   | 4 | 7 | 3 |   |
| 7 |   | 9 |   | 3 |   |   |   |   |

229

| 2 | 3 |   | 7 |   | 8 |   |   |   |
|---|---|---|---|---|---|---|---|---|
|   |   | 7 |   |   |   |   |   |   |
|   | 1 |   | 3 | 5 | 4 |   |   | 7 |
|   |   | 6 |   |   |   |   | 8 | 9 |
|   |   | 2 |   |   |   | 4 |   |   |
| 8 | 7 |   |   |   |   | 3 |   |   |
| 7 |   |   | 9 | 4 | 2 |   | 6 |   |
|   |   |   |   |   |   | 2 |   |   |
|   |   |   | 8 |   | 1 |   | 9 | 5 |

230

| 2 | 9 |   |   | 6 |   |   | 3 |   |
|---|---|---|---|---|---|---|---|---|
|   | 6 | 5 |   |   |   |   |   |   |
|   |   |   | 7 |   |   |   |   | 9 |
|   |   |   | 1 | 6 |   | 2 |   |   |
| 5 |   | 4 |   | 7 |   | 1 |   | 6 |
|   | 1 |   | 2 | 5 |   |   |   |   |
| 1 |   |   |   |   | 8 |   |   |   |
|   |   |   |   |   |   | 8 | 6 |   |
|   | 8 |   |   | 9 |   |   | 5 | 1 |

**231**

| | 4 | 3 | | 6 | | | | |
|---|---|---|---|---|---|---|---|---|
| | 8 | 5 | | | 4 | | 7 | |
| | | | 7 | 8 | | | | |
| 3 | | | | | 9 | 4 | | 8 |
| | | | | | | | | |
| 8 | | 4 | 1 | | | | | 2 |
| | | | | 1 | 6 | | | |
| | 9 | | 4 | | | 2 | 6 | |
| | | | | 3 | | 1 | 5 | |

**232**

| | 9 | | | | | 1 | | 7 |
|---|---|---|---|---|---|---|---|---|
| 6 | 5 | 1 | | | | | | |
| | | 8 | | 9 | | | 5 | |
| 1 | | | | | 7 | | | |
| | | 5 | 1 | | 4 | 8 | | |
| | | | 2 | | | | | 4 |
| | 1 | | | 6 | | 7 | | |
| | | | | | | 9 | 4 | 3 |
| 8 | | 7 | | | | | 6 | |

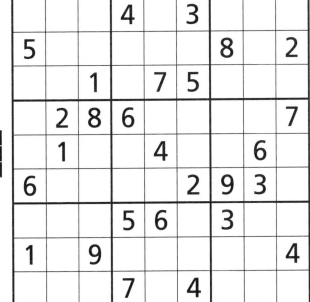

**233**

**234**

121

| 2 |   |   | 7 | 3 |   |   |   |   |
|---|---|---|---|---|---|---|---|---|
|   | 8 | 1 |   | 6 |   |   |   | 7 |
|   |   | 6 |   | 5 |   |   | 4 |   |
|   |   | 3 |   |   |   |   |   | 2 |
|   |   |   | 1 |   | 6 |   |   |   |
| 7 |   |   |   |   |   | 9 |   |   |
|   | 3 |   |   | 2 |   | 4 |   |   |
| 8 |   |   |   | 4 |   | 2 | 9 |   |
|   |   |   |   | 1 | 7 |   |   | 6 |

| 8 |   |   |   | 6 | 9 |   | 5 |   |
|---|---|---|---|---|---|---|---|---|
| 9 |   |   | 4 |   |   |   |   |   |
|   | 3 |   |   | 8 |   |   |   | 4 |
|   | 9 |   |   |   | 6 | 8 |   |   |
| 5 | 8 |   |   | 4 |   |   | 6 | 7 |
|   |   | 6 | 5 |   |   |   | 2 |   |
| 2 |   |   |   | 5 |   |   | 9 |   |
|   |   |   |   |   | 4 |   |   | 8 |
|   | 1 |   | 8 | 9 |   |   |   | 2 |

## Puzzle 1 (2 3 7)

| 5 |   | 4 |   | 1 |   |   |   | 9 |
|---|---|---|---|---|---|---|---|---|
|   |   | 2 |   |   | 9 |   | 7 |   |
| 3 |   |   |   |   | 2 | 1 |   |   |
|   |   |   |   |   | 7 | 8 |   | 6 |
|   |   |   |   |   |   |   |   |   |
| 7 |   | 3 | 8 |   |   |   |   |   |
|   |   | 9 | 2 |   |   |   |   | 7 |
|   | 2 |   | 9 |   |   | 6 |   |   |
| 1 |   |   |   | 5 |   | 2 |   | 4 |

## Puzzle 2 (2 3 8)

|   | 9 |   |   |   |   |   |   | 6 |
|---|---|---|---|---|---|---|---|---|
| 7 | 8 |   | 1 |   |   |   |   |   |
|   | 2 | 4 | 7 |   | 6 |   |   |   |
| 8 |   | 2 |   | 3 |   |   |   |   |
|   | 1 |   |   |   |   |   | 5 |   |
|   |   |   |   | 8 |   | 3 |   | 4 |
|   |   |   | 8 |   | 9 | 5 | 4 |   |
|   |   |   |   |   | 5 |   | 6 | 9 |
| 2 |   |   |   |   |   |   | 7 |   |

**239**

| 1 | 5 |   |   |   | 6 |   |   | 3 |
|---|---|---|---|---|---|---|---|---|
| 6 |   |   | 7 |   | 4 | 5 |   |   |
|   |   | 2 | 1 |   |   |   | 7 |   |
|   |   |   |   |   |   | 3 |   | 7 |
| 8 |   |   |   |   |   |   |   | 4 |
| 3 |   | 5 |   |   |   |   |   |   |
|   | 6 |   |   |   | 1 | 9 |   |   |
|   |   | 3 | 6 |   | 5 |   |   | 1 |
| 5 |   |   | 2 |   |   |   | 8 | 6 |

**240**

| | | 1 | 6 | | 2 | 8 | 4 | |
|---|---|---|---|---|---|---|---|---|
| 3 | | | | | | | | |
| | | | 7 | 5 | | | | 2 |
| 9 | | | 8 | | | | | |
| | 7 | | | | | | 6 | |
| | | | | | 1 | | | 4 |
| 5 | | | | 2 | 3 | | | |
| | | | | | | | | 9 |
| | 2 | 3 | 9 | | | 6 | 4 | |

241

| | 1 | | | 6 | | | 2 | 5 |
|---|---|---|---|---|---|---|---|---|
| | | | 3 | | | 1 | | |
| | | 9 | 5 | | | 3 | | |
| | | | 1 | | | 2 | 7 | |
| | | | | 3 | | | | |
| | 8 | 4 | | | 7 | | | |
| | | 1 | | | 9 | 8 | | |
| | | 3 | | | 5 | | | |
| 2 | 5 | | | 4 | | | 1 | |

242

| 2 | | 8 | | | | 7 | 6 | |
|---|---|---|---|---|---|---|---|---|
| 9 | | | | | 5 | | | |
| | | | | 4 | | 2 | | |
| 7 | | | | 8 | | | | 6 |
| | 9 | | | | | | 8 | |
| 5 | | | | 3 | | | | 2 |
| | 5 | | 1 | | | | | |
| | | 7 | | | | | | 3 |
| | 2 | 3 | | | | 4 | | 7 |

| 7 | 5 |   |   |   |   | 6 |   | 2 |
|---|---|---|---|---|---|---|---|---|
|   |   |   |   |   | 4 |   | 7 | 3 |
| 2 |   |   |   | 1 |   |   |   |   |
|   | 9 |   |   |   | 5 | 7 |   |   |
|   |   |   | 3 | 8 | 1 |   |   |   |
|   |   | 2 | 4 |   |   |   | 5 |   |
|   |   |   |   | 4 |   |   |   | 8 |
| 1 | 3 |   | 9 |   |   |   |   |   |
| 8 |   | 6 |   |   |   |   | 9 | 7 |

| 7 |   |   | 5 |   |   |   |   |   |
|---|---|---|---|---|---|---|---|---|
|   | 8 |   |   | 1 | 4 |   |   | 5 |
|   | 6 |   |   | 7 | 3 |   | 1 |   |
|   |   | 3 | 1 |   |   |   |   |   |
| 5 |   |   |   | 8 |   |   |   | 7 |
|   |   |   |   |   | 5 | 6 |   |   |
|   | 1 |   | 9 | 4 |   |   | 8 |   |
| 9 |   |   | 8 | 5 |   |   | 7 |   |
|   |   |   |   |   | 1 |   |   | 9 |

Puzzle 245:

| | 8 | | | 1 | | | | |
|---|---|---|---|---|---|---|---|---|
| 4 | 7 | | 8 | | 9 | | 5 | |
| | | 9 | 7 | | | | | |
| | | 8 | | | | | 1 | 5 |
| 2 | | 3 | | 6 | | 7 | | 9 |
| 9 | 1 | | | | | 3 | | |
| | | | | | 7 | 5 | | |
| | 5 | | 3 | | 1 | | 7 | 6 |
| | | | | 8 | | | 2 | |

Puzzle 246:

| | 9 | | | 1 | | 2 | | |
|---|---|---|---|---|---|---|---|---|
| | | | 4 | | | | | |
| | | 7 | | 6 | | 3 | 9 | 4 |
| 8 | | | 7 | | | | | |
| | 1 | | | 3 | | | 2 | |
| | | | | | 1 | | | 3 |
| 7 | 4 | 2 | | 5 | | 6 | | |
| | | | | | 9 | | | |
| | | 6 | | 2 | | | 1 | |

Puzzle 247

| | | | 7 | | | 2 | | 6 |
|---|---|---|---|---|---|---|---|---|
| | | | 9 | 4 | | | | |
| 2 | | 7 | 5 | | | | 8 | |
| | 9 | 3 | | | | 5 | | |
| 7 | | | | | | | | 4 |
| | | 8 | | | | 7 | 9 | |
| | 2 | | | | 4 | 6 | | 9 |
| | | | | 5 | 1 | | | |
| 8 | | 4 | | | 7 | | | |

Puzzle 248

| | | | | | | 7 | 8 | |
|---|---|---|---|---|---|---|---|---|
| | | | 5 | 8 | | | | |
| 8 | | 3 | | 4 | | | 9 | |
| | | | 7 | 5 | 9 | | | 3 |
| | | | | | | | | |
| 3 | | 4 | 1 | 2 | | | | |
| | 1 | | | 9 | | 2 | | 8 |
| | | | | 6 | 7 | | | |
| | 9 | 6 | | | | | | |

| | | | | 3 | 4 | 7 | | |
|---|---|---|---|---|---|---|---|---|
| | 1 | | | | | | 5 | 3 |
| | | 7 | | 5 | | | | |
| | 3 | 2 | | 8 | | | | |
| 7 | | 4 | | | | 8 | | 9 |
| | | | | 2 | | 4 | 3 | |
| | | | 6 | | | 5 | | |
| 6 | 2 | | | | | | 4 | |
| | | 8 | 7 | 1 | | | | |

| | | | 1 | 3 | | | | |
|---|---|---|---|---|---|---|---|---|
| | 5 | | | | 6 | 3 | | |
| | | | 2 | | | | 4 | 6 |
| | 3 | 9 | 6 | | | | 8 | |
| 8 | | | | | | | | 2 |
| | 1 | | | | 5 | 6 | 3 | |
| 7 | 6 | | | | 2 | | | |
| | | 8 | 3 | | | | 2 | |
| | | | | 8 | 4 | | | |

|   |   | 8 |   |   | 3 |   |   |   |
|---|---|---|---|---|---|---|---|---|
|   |   |   | 6 |   |   |   |   | 8 |
| 2 | 6 |   | 8 |   |   | 7 |   |   |
|   | 3 | 2 |   | 5 |   |   |   |   |
|   | 4 | 9 |   |   |   | 5 | 3 |   |
|   |   |   |   | 1 |   | 2 | 6 |   |
|   |   | 7 |   |   | 6 |   | 9 | 3 |
| 3 |   |   |   |   | 4 |   |   |   |
|   |   |   | 9 |   |   | 1 |   |   |

| 7 | 1 |   |   |   |   | 5 |   |   |
|---|---|---|---|---|---|---|---|---|
|   | 6 |   | 3 |   |   |   |   | 8 |
|   |   | 8 | 4 |   | 2 |   |   |   |
| 1 |   |   |   |   |   |   | 8 |   |
|   | 4 |   | 2 |   | 7 |   | 1 |   |
|   | 8 |   |   |   |   |   |   | 5 |
|   |   |   | 9 |   | 6 | 2 |   |   |
| 5 |   |   |   |   | 3 |   | 7 |   |
|   |   | 1 |   |   |   |   | 9 | 3 |

| | 9 | | | | 8 | | 2 | |
|---|---|---|---|---|---|---|---|---|
| | | 8 | 3 | 7 | | | | |
| 5 | 1 | | | | | 4 | | |
| 2 | | | 7 | | 4 | 9 | | |
| | | | | | | | | |
| | | 5 | 9 | | 3 | | | 7 |
| | | 2 | | | | | 4 | 8 |
| | | | 8 | 2 | 5 | | | |
| | 5 | | 4 | | | | 9 | |

| | | 7 | | | | | | 4 |
|---|---|---|---|---|---|---|---|---|
| 8 | | | 7 | 5 | | | | |
| | 1 | | | | 6 | | 7 | |
| | | | | | | 3 | 1 | 5 |
| | 3 | | | 2 | | | 4 | |
| 1 | 9 | 4 | | | | | | |
| | 4 | | 2 | | | | 8 | |
| | | | | 3 | 5 | | | 9 |
| 2 | | | | | | 1 | | |

**255**

| | | 7 | | | 1 | | 8 | |
|---|---|---|---|---|---|---|---|---|
| | | 2 | 5 | | | | | 1 |
| | 4 | | 6 | 2 | | | | |
| | | | | | | 5 | | 6 |
| | 7 | | | | | | 2 | |
| 5 | | 1 | | | | | | |
| | | | 3 | 9 | | | 7 | |
| 9 | | | | | 5 | 1 | | |
| | 8 | | 4 | | | 6 | | |

**256**

| 3 | | | | 6 | | | | |
|---|---|---|---|---|---|---|---|---|
| | 9 | 7 | | | | | | |
| | 5 | 2 | 1 | | 3 | | | |
| 8 | | | | | 1 | 6 | | |
| 2 | 1 | | | 7 | | | 4 | 3 |
| | | 4 | 2 | | | | | 8 |
| | | | 8 | | 4 | 9 | 6 | |
| | | | | | | 2 | 8 | |
| | | | 9 | | | | | 7 |

| | 1 | | | | 2 | | 7 | |
|---|---|---|---|---|---|---|---|---|
| 9 | | 3 | 7 | | | | | |
| | | | | 4 | 1 | 9 | | |
| 7 | | | 2 | | | | 4 | |
| 6 | | | | | | | | 5 |
| | 4 | | | | 9 | | | 3 |
| | | 1 | 6 | 2 | | | | |
| | | | | 8 | 4 | | | 9 |
| | 8 | | 3 | | | | 1 | |

| | | | | 1 | | 4 | | |
|---|---|---|---|---|---|---|---|---|
| 6 | | | | 3 | 4 | | | |
| | | 7 | | 2 | 9 | 8 | | |
| 8 | | | | | | 7 | 5 | |
| | | 2 | | | | 1 | | |
| | 7 | 3 | | | | | | 2 |
| | | 5 | 3 | 8 | | 2 | | |
| | | | 7 | 5 | | | | 1 |
| | | 1 | | 4 | | | | |

| | 6 | 1 | | 7 | 3 | | | |
|---|---|---|---|---|---|---|---|---|
| 4 | | | | 2 | | 3 | | |
| 7 | | | 1 | | | | | 4 |
| | | | | | | 9 | | |
| | 4 | | 9 | | 7 | | 3 | |
| | | 5 | | | | | | |
| 2 | | | | | 1 | | | 7 |
| | | 3 | | 6 | | | | 5 |
| | | | 7 | 8 | | 2 | 9 | |

| | 4 | | | | 1 | 5 | 9 | |
|---|---|---|---|---|---|---|---|---|
| | | | | | 5 | | | 6 |
| | | | 7 | | | | 4 | |
| | | | | 7 | 8 | | 5 | 3 |
| | | 2 | | | | 7 | | |
| 6 | 5 | | 2 | 4 | | | | |
| | 9 | | | | 4 | | | |
| 2 | | | 5 | | | | | |
| | 8 | 1 | 9 | | | | 3 | |

| | | | 5 | | | | 8 | |
|---|---|---|---|---|---|---|---|---|
| 6 | | 4 | | | 3 | | | 2 |
| | 9 | | | 8 | | | | |
| | | | | 4 | 8 | | 7 | |
| | | 2 | 7 | | 5 | 8 | | |
| | 7 | | 2 | 3 | | | | |
| | | | | 1 | | | 5 | |
| 8 | | | 4 | | | 9 | | 1 |
| | 6 | | | | 2 | | | |

| 9 | 1 | 5 | 2 | 7 | | | | |
|---|---|---|---|---|---|---|---|---|
| | 8 | | 6 | | 9 | | | |
| | | | | 1 | | | | |
| | 9 | | | | | 3 | | 4 |
| | 4 | | | | | | 6 | |
| 7 | | 8 | | | | | 9 | |
| | | | | 4 | | | | |
| | | | 8 | | 6 | | 5 | |
| | | | | 3 | 2 | 4 | 7 | 1 |

**263**

| | 2 | 3 | 8 | 6 | | | | 7 |
|---|---|---|---|---|---|---|---|---|
| | | 7 | | | 5 | | | |
| 8 | | | | 1 | | 2 | | |
| | 9 | | 6 | | | | | |
| | | 2 | | | | 1 | | |
| | | | | | 3 | | 2 | |
| | | 4 | | 7 | | | | 2 |
| | | | 4 | | | 3 | | |
| 3 | | | | 2 | 8 | 7 | 1 | |

**264**

| | | 6 | 1 | 5 | | | | |
|---|---|---|---|---|---|---|---|---|
| | | | | 7 | | | | 8 |
| | | | 6 | | 9 | 3 | | |
| | | 9 | | | | 5 | 7 | |
| | 4 | | | | | | 1 | |
| | 6 | 3 | | | | 2 | | |
| | | 5 | 8 | | 6 | | | |
| 3 | | | | 4 | | | | |
| | | | | 2 | 3 | 7 | | |

## 265

| | | | 8 | 4 | | | | 9 |
|---|---|---|---|---|---|---|---|---|
| | | | | 5 | | | 7 | |
| 8 | | | 3 | | | 6 | | |
| 9 | 2 | | | | | | 3 | |
| 5 | | 1 | | | | 9 | | 6 |
| | 7 | | | | | | 2 | 5 |
| | | 2 | | | 1 | | | 7 |
| | 5 | | | 6 | | | | |
| 6 | | | | 8 | 2 | | | |

## 266

| | | 3 | | 6 | 1 | | | |
|---|---|---|---|---|---|---|---|---|
| 8 | 4 | | | | | | | 1 |
| | | 6 | 8 | | | | 3 | |
| | 2 | | 5 | | | | | |
| 9 | | 5 | | | | 7 | | 2 |
| | | | | | 7 | | 8 | |
| | 1 | | | | 6 | 4 | | |
| 4 | | | | | | | 2 | 7 |
| | | | 4 | 9 | | 3 | | |

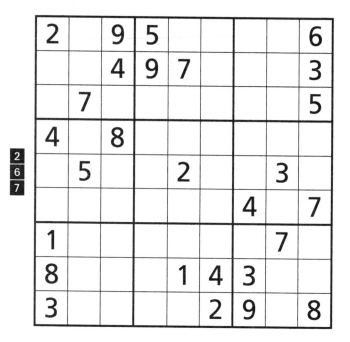

| 8 |   |   |   |   |   | 5 |   |   |
|---|---|---|---|---|---|---|---|---|
|   |   |   | 4 | 5 |   | 8 | 6 |   |
|   |   |   |   |   |   |   | 7 | 3 |
|   |   | 5 |   |   |   |   |   | 6 |
|   |   |   | 8 | 1 | 3 |   |   |   |
| 1 |   |   |   |   |   | 2 |   |   |
| 5 | 4 |   |   |   |   |   |   |   |
|   | 1 | 9 |   | 7 | 2 |   |   |   |
|   |   | 6 |   |   |   |   |   | 2 |

|   |   |   | 2 |   | 5 |   |   | 7 |
|---|---|---|---|---|---|---|---|---|
| 6 | 2 |   |   |   |   |   |   |   |
|   |   | 9 |   |   | 4 |   | 8 | 5 |
|   |   |   | 5 | 9 |   | 3 |   | 6 |
|   |   |   |   |   |   |   |   |   |
| 3 |   | 4 |   | 2 | 8 |   |   |   |
| 8 | 5 |   | 9 |   |   | 1 |   |   |
|   |   |   |   |   |   |   | 5 | 3 |
| 1 |   |   | 7 |   | 6 |   |   |   |

271

| | | | | 7 | | 1 | | |
|---|---|---|---|---|---|---|---|---|
| | | | | | 3 | | | |
| | 7 | | | | 8 | | 4 | 2 |
| | 4 | 3 | 9 | | | | | |
| | 9 | 5 | | | | 4 | 7 | |
| | | | | | 5 | 3 | 8 | |
| 7 | 5 | | 8 | | | | 6 | |
| | | | 4 | | | | | |
| | | 1 | | 3 | | | | |

272

| | | | | | | 4 | | |
|---|---|---|---|---|---|---|---|---|
| 4 | | | 9 | | 8 | | 3 | 1 |
| 6 | 3 | | 7 | | | | | |
| | 1 | 9 | | 5 | 2 | | | 8 |
| | | | | | | | | |
| 8 | | | 3 | 7 | | 1 | 4 | |
| | | | | | 3 | | 5 | 2 |
| 9 | 2 | | 1 | | 5 | | | 4 |
| | | 4 | | | | | | |

| | | | 7 | 4 | | | | |
|---|---|---|---|---|---|---|---|---|
| | 5 | | | | 1 | | 8 | |
| 9 | | | 5 | | | | | 3 |
| 7 | | | | 9 | | | 2 | 6 |
| | | 1 | | | | 3 | | |
| 6 | 4 | | | 8 | | | | 7 |
| 1 | | | | | 7 | | | 4 |
| | 3 | | 8 | | | | 5 | |
| | | | | 5 | 4 | | | |

| | | | | 2 | 8 | | | |
|---|---|---|---|---|---|---|---|---|
| | 4 | 6 | | | 7 | | | 2 |
| | 8 | 2 | 9 | | | | | |
| | | | | | | 3 | 1 | |
| | | 8 | 6 | | 2 | 9 | | |
| | 9 | 3 | | | | | | |
| | | | | | 6 | 8 | 7 | |
| 2 | | | 8 | | | 6 | 3 | |
| | | | 5 | 4 | | | | |

| | 7 | | | 4 | 8 | | | 2 |
|---|---|---|---|---|---|---|---|---|
| 2 | | | 3 | | | 4 | | |
| | 1 | 6 | | 7 | | | | |
| | | | | | | | 2 | |
| | 4 | 2 | | 1 | | 3 | 7 | |
| | 5 | | | | | | | |
| | | | 9 | | | 7 | 1 | |
| | | 8 | | | 4 | | | 9 |
| 5 | | | 2 | 3 | | | 4 | |

| | | 2 | | | 1 | | 6 | |
|---|---|---|---|---|---|---|---|---|
| | 1 | | 3 | | | | | 2 |
| 5 | 6 | | | | | | | |
| | 5 | | 2 | | 7 | 9 | | |
| 1 | | | | | | | | 3 |
| | | 8 | 4 | | 3 | | 5 | |
| | | | | | | | 3 | 9 |
| 3 | | | | | 5 | | 1 | |
| | 9 | | 8 | | | 4 | | |

277

| | 6 | | 5 | | | | 7 | |
|---|---|---|---|---|---|---|---|---|
| | | 3 | | | 4 | | 8 | |
| 4 | | | 9 | | | | | 2 |
| | | | | | | 3 | 1 | |
| | | 9 | | 7 | | 8 | | |
| | 3 | 5 | | | | | | |
| 5 | | | | | 1 | | | 8 |
| | 1 | | 7 | | | 2 | | |
| | 2 | | | | 3 | | 4 | |

278

| | | 8 | | | | | | 5 |
|---|---|---|---|---|---|---|---|---|
| 5 | | | 3 | | 7 | 9 | | |
| | 6 | | | | | | 4 | |
| | | | 7 | | | 5 | | |
| 9 | 3 | 6 | | | | 2 | 7 | 4 |
| | | 5 | | | 9 | | | |
| | 1 | | | | | | 2 | |
| | | 4 | 2 | | 6 | | | 8 |
| 6 | | | | | | 1 | | |

Puzzle 279

| | 8 | | | 3 | 7 | | | |
|---|---|---|---|---|---|---|---|---|
| | 2 | | 8 | | | 9 | | |
| 7 | 3 | 4 | | | 6 | 8 | | |
| 6 | | | | | | 4 | | |
| | | | | | | | | |
| | | 9 | | | | | | 3 |
| | | 8 | 7 | | | 3 | 5 | 4 |
| | | 7 | | | 4 | | 2 | |
| | | | 3 | 9 | | | 7 | |

Puzzle 280

| | 9 | | 5 | | | 3 | 1 | |
|---|---|---|---|---|---|---|---|---|
| | | | 8 | | | | 9 | |
| | | 4 | | | 3 | | | 2 |
| 1 | | | | 2 | | | | 9 |
| | | 9 | 1 | | 4 | 6 | | |
| 6 | | | | 9 | | | | 5 |
| 9 | | | 2 | | | 5 | | |
| | 3 | | | | 9 | | | |
| | 8 | 2 | | | 5 | | 6 | |

| | | 3 | | 4 | 8 | | | |
|---|---|---|---|---|---|---|---|---|
| | 6 | | | 9 | | | | |
| | 9 | | | | 3 | 6 | 1 | |
| | | | 4 | | | | | 6 |
| 3 | | 9 | | | | 4 | | 2 |
| 7 | | | | | 5 | | | |
| | 2 | 4 | 9 | | | | 6 | |
| | | | | 3 | | | 8 | |
| | | | 2 | 8 | | 1 | | |

| | 5 | | | 4 | 8 | | | 3 |
|---|---|---|---|---|---|---|---|---|
| 4 | | | | | 9 | | | |
| | 8 | | 3 | | | 4 | | |
| | | | 7 | | 2 | 8 | | 5 |
| | 7 | | | | | | 6 | |
| 5 | | 9 | 1 | | 6 | | | |
| | | 4 | | | 1 | | 8 | |
| | | | 8 | | | | | 1 |
| 1 | | | 4 | 6 | | | 2 | |

| | 1 | | | | 6 | | 7 | 5 |
|---|---|---|---|---|---|---|---|---|
| | | 8 | 4 | | | | | |
| | 2 | | | | | | | 1 |
| 7 | 6 | | 3 | | 5 | | | |
| | | | | 1 | | | | |
| | | | 6 | | 2 | | 8 | 7 |
| 6 | | | | | | | 3 | |
| | | | | | 8 | 2 | | |
| 8 | 3 | | 2 | | | | 4 | |

| | | 5 | | | | 8 | | 4 |
|---|---|---|---|---|---|---|---|---|
| 6 | 8 | | | 2 | | 5 | | |
| | | 7 | | | | | 9 | 6 |
| | | | 7 | | 5 | | 4 | 8 |
| | | | 6 | | 2 | | | |
| 8 | 5 | | 3 | | 4 | | | |
| 9 | 6 | | | | | 4 | | |
| | | 3 | | 4 | | | 8 | 2 |
| 1 | | 4 | | | | 7 | | |

**285**

| | | 4 | | | 5 | | 8 | |
|---|---|---|---|---|---|---|---|---|
| | | | 3 | 2 | | 6 | | |
| 1 | 3 | | 7 | | | | | |
| | | | | | 4 | | | 9 |
| | 4 | 5 | | | | 1 | 6 | |
| 3 | | | 5 | | | | | |
| | | | | | 2 | | 1 | 4 |
| | | 9 | | 5 | 1 | | | |
| | 7 | | 6 | | | 5 | | |

**286**

| | | | | | | | 6 | |
|---|---|---|---|---|---|---|---|---|
| | | 3 | | 8 | | | | 9 |
| 5 | | 7 | 9 | | | 3 | 1 | |
| | 2 | 8 | | | 4 | 1 | | |
| | | | | | | | | |
| | | 1 | 7 | | | 5 | 2 | |
| | 8 | 4 | | | 6 | 7 | | 1 |
| 2 | | | | 3 | | 8 | | |
| | 1 | | | | | | | |

| 4 | 1 |   | 9 |   |   |   | 6 |   |
|---|---|---|---|---|---|---|---|---|
|   |   |   |   |   |   | 1 |   |   |
| 6 | 9 | 3 |   |   |   |   | 8 | 4 |
| 9 |   |   | 4 | 6 |   |   | 2 |   |
|   |   |   | 1 |   | 9 |   |   |   |
|   | 3 |   |   | 5 | 2 |   |   | 6 |
| 7 | 4 |   |   |   |   | 6 | 3 | 8 |
|   |   | 6 |   |   |   |   |   |   |
|   | 2 |   |   |   | 4 |   | 1 | 9 |

|   |   | 8 | 6 |   |   |   |   | 4 |
|---|---|---|---|---|---|---|---|---|
|   | 5 |   |   | 7 |   |   |   |   |
| 2 |   | 4 |   |   | 9 | 1 |   |   |
|   |   |   |   |   | 7 | 9 | 3 | 5 |
|   |   |   |   |   |   |   |   |   |
| 9 | 3 | 7 | 5 |   |   |   |   |   |
|   |   | 6 | 8 |   |   | 2 |   | 9 |
|   |   |   |   | 3 |   |   | 8 |   |
| 8 |   |   |   |   | 1 | 5 |   |   |

**289**

| 6 |   |   |   |   |   |   | 3 | 9 |
|---|---|---|---|---|---|---|---|---|
|   |   |   | 6 |   | 8 |   |   |   |
|   |   |   |   | 9 |   | 7 | 8 |   |
| 5 |   | 9 |   | 3 |   |   |   | 4 |
|   |   |   | 1 |   | 2 |   |   |   |
| 7 |   |   |   | 5 |   | 1 |   | 3 |
|   | 3 | 5 |   | 6 |   |   |   |   |
|   |   |   | 4 |   | 5 |   |   |   |
| 9 | 4 |   |   |   |   |   |   | 2 |

**290**

| 2 |   |   | 3 |   |   |   |   |   |
|---|---|---|---|---|---|---|---|---|
|   |   |   | 6 | 8 |   | 7 |   |   |
|   | 1 | 3 |   |   | 2 |   | 4 |   |
|   | 2 |   |   |   | 6 | 3 |   |   |
|   |   | 1 |   |   |   | 9 |   |   |
|   |   | 5 | 1 |   |   |   | 7 |   |
|   | 3 |   | 7 |   |   | 1 | 9 |   |
|   |   | 4 |   | 6 | 3 |   |   |   |
|   |   |   |   |   | 8 |   |   | 4 |

| | | 6 | | | 1 | | 8 | |
|---|---|---|---|---|---|---|---|---|
| 3 | | | 6 | | | 2 | | |
| 8 | | | | 9 | | | | 5 |
| | 1 | | | | 6 | | | |
| | | 9 | | 2 | | 4 | | |
| | | | 4 | | | | 5 | |
| 1 | | | | 8 | | | | 4 |
| | | 2 | | | 7 | | | 8 |
| | 4 | | 1 | | | 9 | | |

| | 7 | | | | 2 | | 1 | |
|---|---|---|---|---|---|---|---|---|
| | 9 | 2 | 5 | | | | | |
| | | | 8 | 9 | | | | |
| 7 | | | | 5 | | 3 | | |
| 6 | | | | | | | | 7 |
| | | 5 | | 3 | | | | 8 |
| | | | | 6 | 8 | | | |
| | | | | | 5 | 9 | 3 | |
| | 4 | | 7 | | | | 6 | |

293

| | | | | | 2 | | | 3 |
|---|---|---|---|---|---|---|---|---|
| | | 3 | | | 4 | | 8 | |
| | | | | | 7 | 5 | 6 | |
| | 5 | 6 | | | | | 2 | |
| | | 2 | | 6 | | 4 | | |
| | 9 | | | | | 7 | 5 | |
| | 8 | 4 | 5 | | | | | |
| | 2 | | 1 | | | 9 | | |
| 6 | | | 2 | | | | | |

294

| | 1 | 4 | | 6 | | | | |
|---|---|---|---|---|---|---|---|---|
| | 8 | | | 4 | | 7 | | |
| | | | 3 | | 2 | | | |
| | 2 | 6 | | | 7 | 8 | | |
| | 9 | 7 | | | | 2 | 4 | |
| | | 1 | 8 | | | 6 | 7 | |
| | | | 9 | | 5 | | | |
| | | 2 | | 3 | | | 5 | |
| | | | | 8 | | 1 | 6 | |

|   | 1 | 9 | 8 |   |   | 4 |   |   |
|---|---|---|---|---|---|---|---|---|
|   |   |   | 6 |   |   |   | 1 |   |
| 3 |   |   |   |   | 9 |   | 2 |   |
| 2 | 6 |   |   |   |   |   |   | 5 |
|   | 3 | 4 |   |   |   | 1 | 8 |   |
| 1 |   |   |   |   |   |   | 4 | 2 |
|   | 8 |   | 5 |   |   |   |   | 1 |
|   | 5 |   |   |   | 4 |   |   |   |
|   |   | 3 |   |   | 1 | 9 | 5 |   |

|   |   |   |   |   |   | 4 |   |   |
|---|---|---|---|---|---|---|---|---|
|   |   |   | 1 | 5 | 9 | 6 |   |   |
| 6 |   |   | 7 |   |   |   | 1 | 3 |
| 8 |   | 1 |   |   |   |   | 5 |   |
|   | 2 |   |   | 9 |   |   | 4 |   |
|   | 5 |   |   |   |   | 7 |   | 2 |
| 5 | 3 |   |   |   | 1 |   |   | 4 |
|   |   | 8 | 6 | 4 | 3 |   |   |   |
|   |   | 9 |   |   |   |   |   |   |

| | 1 | | | | | 8 | | |
|---|---|---|---|---|---|---|---|---|
| | | | | | 8 | | 3 | 5 |
| | | | 1 | | | 2 | 4 | |
| | | | | 6 | | 9 | | |
| 5 | 3 | | | 4 | | | 7 | 1 |
| | | 7 | | 3 | | | | |
| | 4 | 5 | | | 7 | | | |
| 1 | 2 | | 4 | | | | | |
| | | 8 | | | | | 9 | |

| 5 | | 7 | 4 | | | 6 | | |
|---|---|---|---|---|---|---|---|---|
| 4 | 8 | | | | | | | 1 |
| | | | | | 6 | 9 | 4 | |
| | 3 | 5 | | 4 | | | | |
| | | | | 6 | | | | |
| | | | | 7 | | 3 | 2 | |
| | 6 | 9 | 1 | | | | | |
| 7 | | | | | | | 1 | 9 |
| | | 1 | | | 9 | 8 | | 6 |

| 6 | 8 |   |   |   |   |   | 5 |   |
|---|---|---|---|---|---|---|---|---|
| 9 |   |   | 8 |   |   |   | 4 | 2 |
|   |   | 2 |   | 7 |   |   |   |   |
|   |   |   |   | 2 |   | 3 |   |   |
| 8 |   |   |   |   |   |   |   | 1 |
|   |   | 7 |   | 5 |   |   |   |   |
|   |   |   |   | 4 |   | 2 |   |   |
| 2 | 3 |   |   |   | 5 |   |   | 8 |
|   | 9 |   |   |   |   |   | 7 | 4 |

|   |   | 4 |   | 5 | 9 |   |   |   |
|---|---|---|---|---|---|---|---|---|
|   |   |   | 4 |   |   | 2 |   |   |
|   | 2 |   |   |   | 7 |   |   | 3 |
| 9 | 3 |   |   |   |   | 1 |   | 6 |
|   |   | 5 |   |   |   | 4 |   |   |
| 2 |   | 6 |   |   |   |   | 3 | 5 |
| 1 |   |   | 9 |   |   |   | 2 |   |
|   |   | 2 |   |   | 5 |   |   |   |
|   |   |   | 1 | 6 |   | 9 |   |   |

**1**

| 9 | 8 | 6 | 1 | 4 | 2 | 3 | 5 | 7 |
|---|---|---|---|---|---|---|---|---|
| 3 | 5 | 1 | 9 | 6 | 7 | 2 | 8 | 4 |
| 4 | 2 | 7 | 5 | 8 | 3 | 9 | 6 | 1 |
| 5 | 6 | 2 | 7 | 1 | 9 | 8 | 4 | 3 |
| 7 | 1 | 3 | 4 | 5 | 8 | 6 | 2 | 9 |
| 8 | 4 | 9 | 3 | 2 | 6 | 7 | 1 | 5 |
| 2 | 9 | 4 | 6 | 3 | 1 | 5 | 7 | 8 |
| 1 | 7 | 8 | 2 | 9 | 5 | 4 | 3 | 6 |
| 6 | 3 | 5 | 8 | 7 | 4 | 1 | 9 | 2 |

**2**

| 5 | 6 | 9 | 8 | 1 | 4 | 7 | 3 | 2 |
|---|---|---|---|---|---|---|---|---|
| 1 | 4 | 3 | 6 | 2 | 7 | 9 | 8 | 5 |
| 7 | 2 | 8 | 3 | 5 | 9 | 1 | 6 | 4 |
| 3 | 8 | 7 | 9 | 6 | 2 | 5 | 4 | 1 |
| 9 | 1 | 2 | 5 | 4 | 3 | 6 | 7 | 8 |
| 4 | 5 | 6 | 1 | 7 | 8 | 2 | 9 | 3 |
| 2 | 3 | 1 | 4 | 9 | 6 | 8 | 5 | 7 |
| 8 | 9 | 5 | 7 | 3 | 1 | 4 | 2 | 6 |
| 6 | 7 | 4 | 2 | 8 | 5 | 3 | 1 | 9 |

**3**

| 4 | 6 | 7 | 9 | 1 | 5 | 8 | 2 | 3 |
|---|---|---|---|---|---|---|---|---|
| 8 | 3 | 5 | 4 | 2 | 7 | 1 | 9 | 6 |
| 9 | 2 | 1 | 6 | 3 | 8 | 4 | 5 | 7 |
| 2 | 7 | 6 | 5 | 9 | 4 | 3 | 8 | 1 |
| 5 | 8 | 9 | 3 | 7 | 1 | 2 | 6 | 4 |
| 3 | 1 | 4 | 8 | 6 | 2 | 9 | 7 | 5 |
| 6 | 9 | 8 | 7 | 4 | 3 | 5 | 1 | 2 |
| 7 | 4 | 2 | 1 | 5 | 9 | 6 | 3 | 8 |
| 1 | 5 | 3 | 2 | 8 | 6 | 7 | 4 | 9 |

**4**

| 8 | 4 | 7 | 3 | 2 | 1 | 6 | 5 | 9 |
|---|---|---|---|---|---|---|---|---|
| 3 | 6 | 2 | 7 | 9 | 5 | 4 | 8 | 1 |
| 5 | 9 | 1 | 8 | 4 | 6 | 3 | 7 | 2 |
| 7 | 3 | 8 | 1 | 6 | 2 | 5 | 9 | 4 |
| 4 | 1 | 5 | 9 | 3 | 7 | 8 | 2 | 6 |
| 6 | 2 | 9 | 4 | 5 | 8 | 1 | 3 | 7 |
| 9 | 8 | 3 | 6 | 7 | 4 | 2 | 1 | 5 |
| 1 | 5 | 4 | 2 | 8 | 9 | 7 | 6 | 3 |
| 2 | 7 | 6 | 5 | 1 | 3 | 9 | 4 | 8 |

**5**

| 1 | 2 | 7 | 9 | 5 | 8 | 4 | 6 | 3 |
|---|---|---|---|---|---|---|---|---|
| 3 | 9 | 4 | 1 | 2 | 6 | 7 | 5 | 8 |
| 6 | 8 | 5 | 3 | 4 | 7 | 1 | 9 | 2 |
| 9 | 6 | 8 | 4 | 3 | 2 | 5 | 7 | 1 |
| 5 | 1 | 2 | 8 | 7 | 9 | 3 | 4 | 6 |
| 7 | 4 | 3 | 5 | 6 | 1 | 8 | 2 | 9 |
| 4 | 5 | 9 | 2 | 1 | 3 | 6 | 8 | 7 |
| 2 | 7 | 1 | 6 | 8 | 5 | 9 | 3 | 4 |
| 8 | 3 | 6 | 7 | 9 | 4 | 2 | 1 | 5 |

**6**

| 3 | 5 | 6 | 2 | 4 | 8 | 9 | 1 | 7 |
|---|---|---|---|---|---|---|---|---|
| 4 | 7 | 1 | 5 | 6 | 9 | 8 | 3 | 2 |
| 8 | 9 | 2 | 7 | 3 | 1 | 5 | 4 | 6 |
| 2 | 8 | 5 | 4 | 7 | 6 | 1 | 9 | 3 |
| 6 | 4 | 3 | 9 | 1 | 2 | 7 | 5 | 8 |
| 7 | 1 | 9 | 8 | 5 | 3 | 2 | 6 | 4 |
| 5 | 6 | 8 | 3 | 9 | 7 | 4 | 2 | 1 |
| 1 | 2 | 4 | 6 | 8 | 5 | 3 | 7 | 9 |
| 9 | 3 | 7 | 1 | 2 | 4 | 6 | 8 | 5 |

**7**

| 6 | 9 | 4 | 3 | 7 | 8 | 1 | 2 | 5 |
|---|---|---|---|---|---|---|---|---|
| 8 | 2 | 7 | 1 | 5 | 9 | 4 | 3 | 6 |
| 3 | 5 | 1 | 4 | 6 | 2 | 9 | 8 | 7 |
| 9 | 6 | 2 | 5 | 1 | 7 | 8 | 4 | 3 |
| 5 | 1 | 8 | 2 | 3 | 4 | 6 | 7 | 9 |
| 7 | 4 | 3 | 9 | 8 | 6 | 2 | 5 | 1 |
| 2 | 7 | 5 | 6 | 4 | 1 | 3 | 9 | 8 |
| 1 | 8 | 9 | 7 | 2 | 3 | 5 | 6 | 4 |
| 4 | 3 | 6 | 8 | 9 | 5 | 7 | 1 | 2 |

**8**

| 9 | 8 | 3 | 6 | 5 | 2 | 4 | 1 | 7 |
|---|---|---|---|---|---|---|---|---|
| 6 | 4 | 7 | 8 | 3 | 1 | 9 | 5 | 2 |
| 1 | 2 | 5 | 4 | 9 | 7 | 6 | 3 | 8 |
| 5 | 6 | 4 | 3 | 8 | 9 | 7 | 2 | 1 |
| 8 | 3 | 2 | 7 | 1 | 4 | 5 | 9 | 6 |
| 7 | 9 | 1 | 5 | 2 | 6 | 3 | 8 | 4 |
| 3 | 5 | 6 | 2 | 4 | 8 | 1 | 7 | 9 |
| 4 | 1 | 8 | 9 | 7 | 5 | 2 | 6 | 3 |
| 2 | 7 | 9 | 1 | 6 | 3 | 8 | 4 | 5 |

**9**

| 7 | 3 | 9 | 5 | 1 | 6 | 8 | 2 | 4 |
| 6 | 8 | 5 | 3 | 2 | 4 | 7 | 1 | 9 |
| 1 | 4 | 2 | 9 | 8 | 7 | 5 | 3 | 6 |
| 2 | 6 | 1 | 8 | 3 | 9 | 4 | 7 | 5 |
| 8 | 9 | 4 | 1 | 7 | 5 | 3 | 6 | 2 |
| 3 | 5 | 7 | 6 | 4 | 2 | 9 | 8 | 1 |
| 5 | 2 | 6 | 7 | 9 | 3 | 1 | 4 | 8 |
| 4 | 7 | 8 | 2 | 5 | 1 | 6 | 9 | 3 |
| 9 | 1 | 3 | 4 | 6 | 8 | 2 | 5 | 7 |

**10**

| 9 | 2 | 6 | 3 | 4 | 7 | 8 | 5 | 1 |
| 3 | 4 | 1 | 8 | 6 | 5 | 7 | 9 | 2 |
| 5 | 7 | 8 | 1 | 9 | 2 | 6 | 3 | 4 |
| 6 | 5 | 4 | 9 | 1 | 3 | 2 | 7 | 8 |
| 8 | 9 | 3 | 2 | 7 | 6 | 4 | 1 | 5 |
| 2 | 1 | 7 | 5 | 8 | 4 | 9 | 6 | 3 |
| 1 | 6 | 9 | 4 | 5 | 8 | 3 | 2 | 7 |
| 4 | 3 | 5 | 7 | 2 | 9 | 1 | 8 | 6 |
| 7 | 8 | 2 | 6 | 3 | 1 | 5 | 4 | 9 |

**11**

| 3 | 7 | 6 | 1 | 4 | 2 | 8 | 9 | 5 |
| 4 | 8 | 1 | 7 | 9 | 5 | 2 | 6 | 3 |
| 9 | 2 | 5 | 3 | 8 | 6 | 4 | 7 | 1 |
| 5 | 1 | 2 | 4 | 7 | 3 | 9 | 8 | 6 |
| 6 | 9 | 4 | 8 | 2 | 1 | 5 | 3 | 7 |
| 7 | 3 | 8 | 5 | 6 | 9 | 1 | 2 | 4 |
| 2 | 6 | 3 | 9 | 5 | 4 | 7 | 1 | 8 |
| 8 | 5 | 9 | 6 | 1 | 7 | 3 | 4 | 2 |
| 1 | 4 | 7 | 2 | 3 | 8 | 6 | 5 | 9 |

**12**

| 9 | 1 | 2 | 6 | 5 | 4 | 3 | 8 | 7 |
| 3 | 4 | 8 | 1 | 2 | 7 | 9 | 5 | 6 |
| 7 | 6 | 5 | 3 | 8 | 9 | 2 | 1 | 4 |
| 8 | 2 | 3 | 7 | 9 | 1 | 4 | 6 | 5 |
| 5 | 7 | 6 | 2 | 4 | 8 | 1 | 3 | 9 |
| 4 | 9 | 1 | 5 | 6 | 3 | 7 | 2 | 8 |
| 2 | 3 | 9 | 8 | 7 | 6 | 5 | 4 | 1 |
| 1 | 8 | 4 | 9 | 3 | 5 | 6 | 7 | 2 |
| 6 | 5 | 7 | 4 | 1 | 2 | 8 | 9 | 3 |

**13**

| 5 | 3 | 7 | 1 | 8 | 4 | 6 | 2 | 9 |
| 9 | 8 | 4 | 5 | 2 | 6 | 1 | 3 | 7 |
| 6 | 1 | 2 | 3 | 7 | 9 | 4 | 8 | 5 |
| 2 | 6 | 8 | 9 | 4 | 5 | 7 | 1 | 3 |
| 3 | 5 | 9 | 6 | 1 | 7 | 8 | 4 | 2 |
| 7 | 4 | 1 | 8 | 3 | 2 | 5 | 9 | 6 |
| 1 | 7 | 3 | 2 | 5 | 8 | 9 | 6 | 4 |
| 4 | 2 | 6 | 7 | 9 | 1 | 3 | 5 | 8 |
| 8 | 9 | 5 | 4 | 6 | 3 | 2 | 7 | 1 |

**14**

| 8 | 6 | 9 | 4 | 2 | 1 | 3 | 5 | 7 |
| 3 | 4 | 7 | 5 | 9 | 8 | 2 | 6 | 1 |
| 2 | 1 | 5 | 7 | 6 | 3 | 8 | 9 | 4 |
| 5 | 3 | 8 | 6 | 1 | 4 | 7 | 2 | 9 |
| 4 | 7 | 1 | 2 | 3 | 9 | 5 | 8 | 6 |
| 9 | 2 | 6 | 8 | 7 | 5 | 1 | 4 | 3 |
| 1 | 8 | 2 | 3 | 4 | 6 | 9 | 7 | 5 |
| 6 | 5 | 3 | 9 | 8 | 7 | 4 | 1 | 2 |
| 7 | 9 | 4 | 1 | 5 | 2 | 6 | 3 | 8 |

**15**

| 2 | 9 | 3 | 8 | 7 | 5 | 6 | 4 | 1 |
| 4 | 8 | 5 | 6 | 2 | 1 | 9 | 7 | 3 |
| 7 | 1 | 6 | 9 | 3 | 4 | 8 | 2 | 5 |
| 5 | 3 | 7 | 1 | 6 | 2 | 4 | 9 | 8 |
| 8 | 4 | 2 | 5 | 9 | 3 | 7 | 1 | 6 |
| 1 | 6 | 9 | 4 | 8 | 7 | 5 | 3 | 2 |
| 9 | 5 | 1 | 3 | 4 | 8 | 2 | 6 | 7 |
| 6 | 2 | 8 | 7 | 1 | 9 | 3 | 5 | 4 |
| 3 | 7 | 4 | 2 | 5 | 6 | 1 | 8 | 9 |

**16**

| 4 | 1 | 8 | 9 | 3 | 2 | 6 | 7 | 5 |
| 9 | 5 | 2 | 8 | 6 | 7 | 3 | 1 | 4 |
| 7 | 6 | 3 | 4 | 1 | 5 | 8 | 2 | 9 |
| 5 | 2 | 7 | 1 | 8 | 6 | 4 | 9 | 3 |
| 3 | 4 | 6 | 7 | 5 | 9 | 1 | 8 | 2 |
| 8 | 9 | 1 | 2 | 4 | 3 | 7 | 5 | 6 |
| 6 | 3 | 9 | 5 | 7 | 8 | 2 | 4 | 1 |
| 1 | 8 | 5 | 3 | 2 | 4 | 9 | 6 | 7 |
| 2 | 7 | 4 | 6 | 9 | 1 | 5 | 3 | 8 |

## 17

| 7 | 3 | 6 | 8 | 2 | 9 | 4 | 1 | 5 |
|---|---|---|---|---|---|---|---|---|
| 1 | 5 | 4 | 6 | 3 | 7 | 9 | 8 | 2 |
| 8 | 9 | 2 | 4 | 1 | 5 | 3 | 6 | 7 |
| 2 | 7 | 3 | 5 | 8 | 6 | 1 | 4 | 9 |
| 4 | 1 | 8 | 7 | 9 | 3 | 2 | 5 | 6 |
| 5 | 6 | 9 | 1 | 4 | 2 | 7 | 3 | 8 |
| 6 | 4 | 1 | 9 | 7 | 8 | 5 | 2 | 3 |
| 9 | 2 | 5 | 3 | 6 | 4 | 8 | 7 | 1 |
| 3 | 8 | 7 | 2 | 5 | 1 | 6 | 9 | 4 |

## 18

| 1 | 8 | 4 | 5 | 2 | 7 | 3 | 9 | 6 |
|---|---|---|---|---|---|---|---|---|
| 5 | 7 | 6 | 8 | 3 | 9 | 2 | 4 | 1 |
| 9 | 3 | 2 | 6 | 1 | 4 | 5 | 7 | 8 |
| 3 | 5 | 8 | 9 | 4 | 1 | 6 | 2 | 7 |
| 4 | 9 | 1 | 2 | 7 | 6 | 8 | 5 | 3 |
| 6 | 2 | 7 | 3 | 8 | 5 | 4 | 1 | 9 |
| 2 | 4 | 3 | 1 | 9 | 8 | 7 | 6 | 5 |
| 7 | 1 | 5 | 4 | 6 | 3 | 9 | 8 | 2 |
| 8 | 6 | 9 | 7 | 5 | 2 | 1 | 3 | 4 |

## 19

| 6 | 2 | 3 | 4 | 8 | 9 | 7 | 1 | 5 |
|---|---|---|---|---|---|---|---|---|
| 5 | 8 | 9 | 3 | 7 | 1 | 6 | 2 | 4 |
| 1 | 7 | 4 | 6 | 2 | 5 | 9 | 3 | 8 |
| 3 | 4 | 7 | 5 | 6 | 2 | 1 | 8 | 9 |
| 9 | 1 | 6 | 7 | 4 | 8 | 2 | 5 | 3 |
| 8 | 5 | 2 | 9 | 1 | 3 | 4 | 7 | 6 |
| 4 | 9 | 1 | 8 | 3 | 7 | 5 | 6 | 2 |
| 7 | 6 | 8 | 2 | 5 | 4 | 3 | 9 | 1 |
| 2 | 3 | 5 | 1 | 9 | 6 | 8 | 4 | 7 |

## 20

| 8 | 7 | 4 | 3 | 9 | 6 | 1 | 2 | 5 |
|---|---|---|---|---|---|---|---|---|
| 1 | 2 | 9 | 7 | 5 | 8 | 3 | 6 | 4 |
| 3 | 5 | 6 | 1 | 2 | 4 | 7 | 9 | 8 |
| 9 | 6 | 8 | 4 | 7 | 2 | 5 | 1 | 3 |
| 5 | 1 | 2 | 9 | 8 | 3 | 4 | 7 | 6 |
| 4 | 3 | 7 | 6 | 1 | 5 | 9 | 8 | 2 |
| 2 | 4 | 1 | 8 | 3 | 7 | 6 | 5 | 9 |
| 6 | 9 | 5 | 2 | 4 | 1 | 8 | 3 | 7 |
| 7 | 8 | 3 | 5 | 6 | 9 | 2 | 4 | 1 |

## 21

| 2 | 8 | 6 | 1 | 5 | 9 | 4 | 3 | 7 |
|---|---|---|---|---|---|---|---|---|
| 9 | 7 | 5 | 6 | 4 | 3 | 2 | 1 | 8 |
| 4 | 3 | 1 | 8 | 2 | 7 | 9 | 6 | 5 |
| 3 | 6 | 4 | 5 | 8 | 2 | 7 | 9 | 1 |
| 5 | 2 | 9 | 3 | 7 | 1 | 6 | 8 | 4 |
| 7 | 1 | 8 | 4 | 9 | 6 | 5 | 2 | 3 |
| 8 | 5 | 2 | 9 | 3 | 4 | 1 | 7 | 6 |
| 6 | 4 | 7 | 2 | 1 | 8 | 3 | 5 | 9 |
| 1 | 9 | 3 | 7 | 6 | 5 | 8 | 4 | 2 |

## 22

| 5 | 6 | 8 | 2 | 9 | 7 | 3 | 4 | 1 |
|---|---|---|---|---|---|---|---|---|
| 9 | 1 | 3 | 4 | 8 | 5 | 7 | 2 | 6 |
| 2 | 4 | 7 | 6 | 3 | 1 | 5 | 8 | 9 |
| 8 | 3 | 6 | 5 | 4 | 9 | 2 | 1 | 7 |
| 7 | 2 | 5 | 1 | 6 | 8 | 4 | 9 | 3 |
| 1 | 9 | 4 | 3 | 7 | 2 | 6 | 5 | 8 |
| 3 | 5 | 2 | 8 | 1 | 6 | 9 | 7 | 4 |
| 6 | 8 | 9 | 7 | 2 | 4 | 1 | 3 | 5 |
| 4 | 7 | 1 | 9 | 5 | 3 | 8 | 6 | 2 |

## 23

| 4 | 2 | 7 | 9 | 3 | 1 | 6 | 5 | 8 |
|---|---|---|---|---|---|---|---|---|
| 8 | 5 | 9 | 6 | 7 | 2 | 1 | 4 | 3 |
| 1 | 3 | 6 | 8 | 4 | 5 | 9 | 7 | 2 |
| 5 | 8 | 4 | 3 | 1 | 9 | 2 | 6 | 7 |
| 7 | 6 | 1 | 2 | 5 | 4 | 3 | 8 | 9 |
| 2 | 9 | 3 | 7 | 6 | 8 | 4 | 1 | 5 |
| 6 | 7 | 2 | 4 | 8 | 3 | 5 | 9 | 1 |
| 3 | 1 | 8 | 5 | 9 | 6 | 7 | 2 | 4 |
| 9 | 4 | 5 | 1 | 2 | 7 | 8 | 3 | 6 |

## 24

| 9 | 7 | 5 | 1 | 8 | 3 | 6 | 4 | 2 |
|---|---|---|---|---|---|---|---|---|
| 3 | 6 | 2 | 4 | 9 | 5 | 8 | 1 | 7 |
| 4 | 8 | 1 | 7 | 6 | 2 | 3 | 5 | 9 |
| 7 | 5 | 3 | 2 | 1 | 8 | 9 | 6 | 4 |
| 1 | 2 | 4 | 6 | 3 | 9 | 7 | 8 | 5 |
| 6 | 9 | 8 | 5 | 7 | 4 | 2 | 3 | 1 |
| 2 | 1 | 9 | 3 | 4 | 6 | 5 | 7 | 8 |
| 8 | 3 | 7 | 9 | 5 | 1 | 4 | 2 | 6 |
| 5 | 4 | 6 | 8 | 2 | 7 | 1 | 9 | 3 |

**25**

| 3 | 1 | 5 | 2 | 6 | 8 | 9 | 4 | 7 |
|---|---|---|---|---|---|---|---|---|
| 8 | 2 | 4 | 5 | 9 | 7 | 3 | 6 | 1 |
| 6 | 7 | 9 | 1 | 3 | 4 | 2 | 5 | 8 |
| 4 | 5 | 3 | 7 | 1 | 9 | 6 | 8 | 2 |
| 2 | 9 | 1 | 8 | 5 | 6 | 4 | 7 | 3 |
| 7 | 6 | 8 | 4 | 2 | 3 | 5 | 1 | 9 |
| 1 | 3 | 7 | 6 | 4 | 2 | 8 | 9 | 5 |
| 5 | 4 | 2 | 9 | 8 | 1 | 7 | 3 | 6 |
| 9 | 8 | 6 | 3 | 7 | 5 | 1 | 2 | 4 |

**26**

| 7 | 6 | 1 | 8 | 4 | 9 | 3 | 2 | 5 |
|---|---|---|---|---|---|---|---|---|
| 9 | 2 | 3 | 5 | 6 | 7 | 4 | 8 | 1 |
| 8 | 4 | 5 | 3 | 2 | 1 | 6 | 7 | 9 |
| 3 | 1 | 6 | 7 | 8 | 2 | 5 | 9 | 4 |
| 5 | 9 | 2 | 1 | 3 | 4 | 8 | 6 | 7 |
| 4 | 8 | 7 | 9 | 5 | 6 | 1 | 3 | 2 |
| 6 | 5 | 4 | 2 | 9 | 8 | 7 | 1 | 3 |
| 2 | 7 | 8 | 4 | 1 | 3 | 9 | 5 | 6 |
| 1 | 3 | 9 | 6 | 7 | 5 | 2 | 4 | 8 |

**27**

| 8 | 9 | 3 | 4 | 1 | 5 | 7 | 2 | 6 |
|---|---|---|---|---|---|---|---|---|
| 4 | 1 | 6 | 3 | 7 | 2 | 5 | 9 | 8 |
| 5 | 7 | 2 | 6 | 8 | 9 | 4 | 3 | 1 |
| 2 | 5 | 4 | 1 | 6 | 3 | 8 | 7 | 9 |
| 9 | 8 | 1 | 7 | 2 | 4 | 6 | 5 | 3 |
| 6 | 3 | 7 | 9 | 5 | 8 | 2 | 1 | 4 |
| 7 | 4 | 5 | 8 | 3 | 1 | 9 | 6 | 2 |
| 1 | 2 | 8 | 5 | 9 | 6 | 3 | 4 | 7 |
| 3 | 6 | 9 | 2 | 4 | 7 | 1 | 8 | 5 |

**28**

| 4 | 5 | 9 | 3 | 6 | 8 | 1 | 2 | 7 |
|---|---|---|---|---|---|---|---|---|
| 1 | 8 | 6 | 4 | 7 | 2 | 3 | 9 | 5 |
| 3 | 7 | 2 | 1 | 9 | 5 | 4 | 8 | 6 |
| 7 | 2 | 5 | 9 | 1 | 6 | 8 | 3 | 4 |
| 6 | 9 | 3 | 5 | 8 | 4 | 2 | 7 | 1 |
| 8 | 4 | 1 | 2 | 3 | 7 | 5 | 6 | 9 |
| 5 | 3 | 7 | 8 | 4 | 9 | 6 | 1 | 2 |
| 9 | 1 | 4 | 6 | 2 | 3 | 7 | 5 | 8 |
| 2 | 6 | 8 | 7 | 5 | 1 | 9 | 4 | 3 |

**29**

| 9 | 6 | 2 | 4 | 3 | 7 | 8 | 1 | 5 |
|---|---|---|---|---|---|---|---|---|
| 8 | 5 | 1 | 9 | 6 | 2 | 4 | 7 | 3 |
| 4 | 7 | 3 | 8 | 1 | 5 | 9 | 2 | 6 |
| 3 | 2 | 4 | 1 | 8 | 9 | 5 | 6 | 7 |
| 1 | 9 | 6 | 5 | 7 | 3 | 2 | 8 | 4 |
| 7 | 8 | 5 | 2 | 4 | 6 | 1 | 3 | 9 |
| 5 | 1 | 7 | 3 | 2 | 4 | 6 | 9 | 8 |
| 2 | 3 | 9 | 6 | 5 | 8 | 7 | 4 | 1 |
| 6 | 4 | 8 | 7 | 9 | 1 | 3 | 5 | 2 |

**30**

| 9 | 5 | 8 | 6 | 7 | 2 | 4 | 1 | 3 |
|---|---|---|---|---|---|---|---|---|
| 1 | 6 | 7 | 4 | 8 | 3 | 9 | 5 | 2 |
| 2 | 3 | 4 | 1 | 5 | 9 | 6 | 8 | 7 |
| 5 | 2 | 3 | 8 | 4 | 6 | 7 | 9 | 1 |
| 7 | 1 | 6 | 2 | 9 | 5 | 3 | 4 | 8 |
| 4 | 8 | 9 | 3 | 1 | 7 | 2 | 6 | 5 |
| 3 | 7 | 1 | 9 | 6 | 8 | 5 | 2 | 4 |
| 8 | 9 | 5 | 7 | 2 | 4 | 1 | 3 | 6 |
| 6 | 4 | 2 | 5 | 3 | 1 | 8 | 7 | 9 |

**31**

| 2 | 4 | 7 | 6 | 5 | 1 | 9 | 3 | 8 |
|---|---|---|---|---|---|---|---|---|
| 3 | 1 | 6 | 8 | 2 | 9 | 4 | 7 | 5 |
| 8 | 5 | 9 | 3 | 7 | 4 | 1 | 6 | 2 |
| 1 | 3 | 4 | 2 | 8 | 6 | 7 | 5 | 9 |
| 6 | 9 | 5 | 1 | 4 | 7 | 2 | 8 | 3 |
| 7 | 8 | 2 | 9 | 3 | 5 | 6 | 4 | 1 |
| 5 | 6 | 3 | 7 | 1 | 2 | 8 | 9 | 4 |
| 4 | 7 | 1 | 5 | 9 | 8 | 3 | 2 | 6 |
| 9 | 2 | 8 | 4 | 6 | 3 | 5 | 1 | 7 |

**32**

| 6 | 1 | 4 | 3 | 5 | 9 | 2 | 8 | 7 |
|---|---|---|---|---|---|---|---|---|
| 2 | 8 | 5 | 4 | 1 | 7 | 9 | 3 | 6 |
| 3 | 7 | 9 | 6 | 8 | 2 | 4 | 1 | 5 |
| 5 | 6 | 7 | 9 | 4 | 1 | 8 | 2 | 3 |
| 8 | 3 | 1 | 7 | 2 | 5 | 6 | 9 | 4 |
| 9 | 4 | 2 | 8 | 3 | 6 | 7 | 5 | 1 |
| 1 | 9 | 8 | 5 | 7 | 4 | 3 | 6 | 2 |
| 4 | 5 | 6 | 2 | 9 | 3 | 1 | 7 | 8 |
| 7 | 2 | 3 | 1 | 6 | 8 | 5 | 4 | 9 |

| 6 | 2 | 9 | 3 | 8 | 7 | 1 | 4 | 5 |
|---|---|---|---|---|---|---|---|---|
| 3 | 7 | 1 | 9 | 5 | 4 | 8 | 6 | 2 |
| 5 | 4 | 8 | 1 | 6 | 2 | 7 | 9 | 3 |
| 7 | 9 | 2 | 6 | 1 | 3 | 5 | 8 | 4 |
| 1 | 6 | 5 | 4 | 9 | 8 | 2 | 3 | 7 |
| 4 | 8 | 3 | 7 | 2 | 5 | 9 | 1 | 6 |
| 8 | 3 | 6 | 2 | 7 | 1 | 4 | 5 | 9 |
| 2 | 1 | 4 | 5 | 3 | 9 | 6 | 7 | 8 |
| 9 | 5 | 7 | 8 | 4 | 6 | 3 | 2 | 1 |

| 6 | 7 | 3 | 8 | 5 | 4 | 9 | 2 | 1 |
|---|---|---|---|---|---|---|---|---|
| 5 | 8 | 2 | 9 | 7 | 1 | 3 | 4 | 6 |
| 9 | 1 | 4 | 3 | 2 | 6 | 8 | 5 | 7 |
| 1 | 6 | 7 | 5 | 9 | 2 | 4 | 8 | 3 |
| 8 | 4 | 5 | 7 | 6 | 3 | 1 | 9 | 2 |
| 3 | 2 | 9 | 4 | 1 | 8 | 6 | 7 | 5 |
| 7 | 3 | 6 | 2 | 4 | 9 | 5 | 1 | 8 |
| 4 | 5 | 8 | 1 | 3 | 7 | 2 | 6 | 9 |
| 2 | 9 | 1 | 6 | 8 | 5 | 7 | 3 | 4 |

| 7 | 8 | 1 | 9 | 6 | 5 | 3 | 4 | 2 |
|---|---|---|---|---|---|---|---|---|
| 9 | 5 | 3 | 4 | 8 | 2 | 7 | 6 | 1 |
| 6 | 2 | 4 | 1 | 7 | 3 | 5 | 8 | 9 |
| 2 | 7 | 6 | 8 | 4 | 1 | 9 | 5 | 3 |
| 5 | 1 | 9 | 2 | 3 | 6 | 4 | 7 | 8 |
| 3 | 4 | 8 | 5 | 9 | 7 | 2 | 1 | 6 |
| 8 | 6 | 7 | 3 | 2 | 4 | 1 | 9 | 5 |
| 4 | 3 | 5 | 6 | 1 | 9 | 8 | 2 | 7 |
| 1 | 9 | 2 | 7 | 5 | 8 | 6 | 3 | 4 |

| 7 | 5 | 9 | 4 | 2 | 3 | 1 | 8 | 6 |
|---|---|---|---|---|---|---|---|---|
| 3 | 2 | 4 | 8 | 1 | 6 | 9 | 7 | 5 |
| 1 | 6 | 8 | 9 | 5 | 7 | 3 | 2 | 4 |
| 5 | 9 | 3 | 2 | 8 | 1 | 4 | 6 | 7 |
| 8 | 4 | 1 | 6 | 7 | 9 | 2 | 5 | 3 |
| 2 | 7 | 6 | 3 | 4 | 5 | 8 | 1 | 9 |
| 9 | 1 | 5 | 7 | 3 | 2 | 6 | 4 | 8 |
| 6 | 8 | 7 | 1 | 9 | 4 | 5 | 3 | 2 |
| 4 | 3 | 2 | 5 | 6 | 8 | 7 | 9 | 1 |

| 5 | 2 | 3 | 9 | 1 | 4 | 8 | 6 | 7 |
|---|---|---|---|---|---|---|---|---|
| 1 | 6 | 9 | 8 | 7 | 3 | 5 | 4 | 2 |
| 7 | 8 | 4 | 2 | 5 | 6 | 9 | 1 | 3 |
| 4 | 9 | 6 | 1 | 3 | 2 | 7 | 5 | 8 |
| 8 | 3 | 1 | 7 | 9 | 5 | 6 | 2 | 4 |
| 2 | 7 | 5 | 4 | 6 | 8 | 1 | 3 | 9 |
| 3 | 1 | 8 | 5 | 4 | 9 | 2 | 7 | 6 |
| 6 | 5 | 2 | 3 | 8 | 7 | 4 | 9 | 1 |
| 9 | 4 | 7 | 6 | 2 | 1 | 3 | 8 | 5 |

| 9 | 2 | 8 | 1 | 5 | 3 | 4 | 6 | 7 |
|---|---|---|---|---|---|---|---|---|
| 7 | 3 | 6 | 2 | 4 | 9 | 8 | 1 | 5 |
| 4 | 1 | 5 | 6 | 8 | 7 | 3 | 2 | 9 |
| 6 | 7 | 1 | 5 | 9 | 4 | 2 | 3 | 8 |
| 2 | 5 | 9 | 3 | 6 | 8 | 7 | 4 | 1 |
| 8 | 4 | 3 | 7 | 1 | 2 | 9 | 5 | 6 |
| 5 | 8 | 7 | 4 | 2 | 1 | 6 | 9 | 3 |
| 1 | 9 | 2 | 8 | 3 | 6 | 5 | 7 | 4 |
| 3 | 6 | 4 | 9 | 7 | 5 | 1 | 8 | 2 |

| 2 | 7 | 6 | 3 | 9 | 5 | 1 | 8 | 4 |
|---|---|---|---|---|---|---|---|---|
| 5 | 8 | 9 | 7 | 4 | 1 | 6 | 3 | 2 |
| 3 | 1 | 4 | 6 | 8 | 2 | 5 | 9 | 7 |
| 9 | 3 | 7 | 4 | 2 | 6 | 8 | 5 | 1 |
| 6 | 5 | 8 | 9 | 1 | 7 | 2 | 4 | 3 |
| 1 | 4 | 2 | 8 | 5 | 3 | 7 | 6 | 9 |
| 8 | 6 | 1 | 2 | 3 | 9 | 4 | 7 | 5 |
| 4 | 9 | 5 | 1 | 7 | 8 | 3 | 2 | 6 |
| 7 | 2 | 3 | 5 | 6 | 4 | 9 | 1 | 8 |

| 6 | 4 | 3 | 2 | 7 | 9 | 1 | 8 | 5 |
|---|---|---|---|---|---|---|---|---|
| 5 | 2 | 1 | 4 | 8 | 3 | 9 | 7 | 6 |
| 9 | 7 | 8 | 1 | 6 | 5 | 3 | 4 | 2 |
| 4 | 6 | 9 | 8 | 3 | 1 | 5 | 2 | 7 |
| 7 | 3 | 2 | 6 | 5 | 4 | 8 | 1 | 9 |
| 1 | 8 | 5 | 7 | 9 | 2 | 4 | 6 | 3 |
| 8 | 9 | 7 | 3 | 1 | 6 | 2 | 5 | 4 |
| 3 | 1 | 4 | 5 | 2 | 7 | 6 | 9 | 8 |
| 2 | 5 | 6 | 9 | 4 | 8 | 7 | 3 | 1 |

## 4/1

| 7 | 9 | 3 | 1 | 5 | 6 | 2 | 4 | 8 |
| 2 | 4 | 8 | 9 | 7 | 3 | 5 | 6 | 1 |
| 1 | 6 | 5 | 4 | 2 | 8 | 9 | 3 | 7 |
| 8 | 1 | 9 | 6 | 3 | 7 | 4 | 5 | 2 |
| 6 | 5 | 4 | 8 | 9 | 2 | 7 | 1 | 3 |
| 3 | 2 | 7 | 5 | 1 | 4 | 6 | 8 | 9 |
| 4 | 8 | 2 | 7 | 6 | 1 | 3 | 9 | 5 |
| 9 | 7 | 6 | 3 | 8 | 5 | 1 | 2 | 4 |
| 5 | 3 | 1 | 2 | 4 | 9 | 8 | 7 | 6 |

## 4/2

| 5 | 4 | 6 | 2 | 8 | 1 | 9 | 7 | 3 |
| 2 | 1 | 9 | 7 | 6 | 3 | 8 | 4 | 5 |
| 7 | 8 | 3 | 9 | 4 | 5 | 1 | 6 | 2 |
| 3 | 2 | 1 | 5 | 9 | 7 | 6 | 8 | 4 |
| 8 | 5 | 4 | 6 | 1 | 2 | 7 | 3 | 9 |
| 6 | 9 | 7 | 4 | 3 | 8 | 2 | 5 | 1 |
| 1 | 6 | 5 | 8 | 2 | 4 | 3 | 9 | 7 |
| 4 | 3 | 8 | 1 | 7 | 9 | 5 | 2 | 6 |
| 9 | 7 | 2 | 3 | 5 | 6 | 4 | 1 | 8 |

## 4/3

| 3 | 5 | 4 | 8 | 9 | 7 | 1 | 6 | 2 |
| 2 | 8 | 9 | 5 | 6 | 1 | 4 | 7 | 3 |
| 1 | 6 | 7 | 4 | 3 | 2 | 8 | 5 | 9 |
| 7 | 2 | 8 | 1 | 4 | 3 | 5 | 9 | 6 |
| 5 | 1 | 6 | 2 | 7 | 9 | 3 | 8 | 4 |
| 9 | 4 | 3 | 6 | 5 | 8 | 7 | 2 | 1 |
| 4 | 3 | 2 | 7 | 8 | 6 | 9 | 1 | 5 |
| 6 | 7 | 5 | 9 | 1 | 4 | 2 | 3 | 8 |
| 8 | 9 | 1 | 3 | 2 | 5 | 6 | 4 | 7 |

## 4/4

| 8 | 7 | 3 | 4 | 1 | 5 | 2 | 6 | 9 |
| 5 | 6 | 4 | 2 | 9 | 8 | 3 | 1 | 7 |
| 1 | 2 | 9 | 6 | 3 | 7 | 5 | 8 | 4 |
| 6 | 8 | 2 | 9 | 5 | 1 | 7 | 4 | 3 |
| 4 | 9 | 1 | 3 | 7 | 6 | 8 | 5 | 2 |
| 3 | 5 | 7 | 8 | 4 | 2 | 6 | 9 | 1 |
| 2 | 4 | 8 | 1 | 6 | 3 | 9 | 7 | 5 |
| 9 | 3 | 5 | 7 | 8 | 4 | 1 | 2 | 6 |
| 7 | 1 | 6 | 5 | 2 | 9 | 4 | 3 | 8 |

## 4/5

| 4 | 3 | 6 | 8 | 9 | 1 | 7 | 2 | 5 |
| 2 | 7 | 5 | 3 | 4 | 6 | 9 | 1 | 8 |
| 8 | 9 | 1 | 7 | 5 | 2 | 3 | 4 | 6 |
| 5 | 8 | 4 | 1 | 2 | 9 | 6 | 7 | 3 |
| 9 | 1 | 7 | 6 | 3 | 4 | 5 | 8 | 2 |
| 3 | 6 | 2 | 5 | 7 | 8 | 4 | 9 | 1 |
| 7 | 2 | 8 | 4 | 6 | 3 | 1 | 5 | 9 |
| 1 | 4 | 3 | 9 | 8 | 5 | 2 | 6 | 7 |
| 6 | 5 | 9 | 2 | 1 | 7 | 8 | 3 | 4 |

## 4/6

| 1 | 6 | 7 | 3 | 9 | 5 | 8 | 2 | 4 |
| 2 | 4 | 5 | 1 | 6 | 8 | 7 | 9 | 3 |
| 3 | 9 | 8 | 7 | 4 | 2 | 1 | 6 | 5 |
| 5 | 3 | 4 | 8 | 1 | 9 | 6 | 7 | 2 |
| 6 | 8 | 9 | 5 | 2 | 7 | 3 | 4 | 1 |
| 7 | 2 | 1 | 6 | 3 | 4 | 5 | 8 | 9 |
| 9 | 7 | 6 | 4 | 5 | 1 | 2 | 3 | 8 |
| 8 | 5 | 2 | 9 | 7 | 3 | 4 | 1 | 6 |
| 4 | 1 | 3 | 2 | 8 | 6 | 9 | 5 | 7 |

## 4/7

| 2 | 8 | 3 | 4 | 5 | 6 | 9 | 7 | 1 |
| 1 | 4 | 7 | 3 | 8 | 9 | 6 | 2 | 5 |
| 9 | 6 | 5 | 7 | 2 | 1 | 8 | 4 | 3 |
| 7 | 9 | 1 | 5 | 3 | 2 | 4 | 6 | 8 |
| 8 | 5 | 4 | 6 | 1 | 7 | 2 | 3 | 9 |
| 6 | 3 | 2 | 9 | 4 | 8 | 1 | 5 | 7 |
| 4 | 1 | 8 | 2 | 7 | 5 | 3 | 9 | 6 |
| 5 | 2 | 9 | 1 | 6 | 3 | 7 | 8 | 4 |
| 3 | 7 | 6 | 8 | 9 | 4 | 5 | 1 | 2 |

## 4/8

| 4 | 6 | 1 | 3 | 2 | 5 | 8 | 9 | 7 |
| 5 | 3 | 8 | 9 | 7 | 4 | 1 | 2 | 6 |
| 7 | 2 | 9 | 1 | 8 | 6 | 3 | 5 | 4 |
| 9 | 7 | 3 | 8 | 6 | 2 | 4 | 1 | 5 |
| 8 | 4 | 2 | 5 | 9 | 1 | 6 | 7 | 3 |
| 6 | 1 | 5 | 7 | 4 | 3 | 2 | 8 | 9 |
| 1 | 9 | 7 | 6 | 3 | 8 | 5 | 4 | 2 |
| 3 | 8 | 4 | 2 | 5 | 9 | 7 | 6 | 1 |
| 2 | 5 | 6 | 4 | 1 | 7 | 9 | 3 | 8 |

**49**

| 1 | 3 | 9 | 4 | 8 | 6 | 2 | 7 | 5 |
| 5 | 7 | 6 | 2 | 1 | 3 | 9 | 4 | 8 |
| 2 | 8 | 4 | 7 | 5 | 9 | 6 | 1 | 3 |
| 3 | 6 | 2 | 1 | 9 | 7 | 8 | 5 | 4 |
| 7 | 9 | 1 | 8 | 4 | 5 | 3 | 2 | 6 |
| 8 | 4 | 5 | 3 | 6 | 2 | 1 | 9 | 7 |
| 9 | 2 | 7 | 6 | 3 | 4 | 5 | 8 | 1 |
| 4 | 1 | 3 | 5 | 2 | 8 | 7 | 6 | 9 |
| 6 | 5 | 8 | 9 | 7 | 1 | 4 | 3 | 2 |

**50**

| 7 | 2 | 8 | 6 | 1 | 5 | 3 | 4 | 9 |
| 9 | 6 | 1 | 4 | 2 | 3 | 7 | 8 | 5 |
| 4 | 5 | 3 | 9 | 8 | 7 | 6 | 2 | 1 |
| 5 | 4 | 2 | 3 | 9 | 1 | 8 | 7 | 6 |
| 8 | 3 | 6 | 7 | 5 | 4 | 9 | 1 | 2 |
| 1 | 9 | 7 | 2 | 6 | 8 | 5 | 3 | 4 |
| 6 | 1 | 5 | 8 | 7 | 2 | 4 | 9 | 3 |
| 2 | 8 | 4 | 5 | 3 | 9 | 1 | 6 | 7 |
| 3 | 7 | 9 | 1 | 4 | 6 | 2 | 5 | 8 |

**51**

| 2 | 5 | 4 | 7 | 9 | 8 | 1 | 6 | 3 |
| 8 | 7 | 3 | 4 | 1 | 6 | 5 | 9 | 2 |
| 6 | 9 | 1 | 5 | 2 | 3 | 4 | 8 | 7 |
| 4 | 1 | 7 | 3 | 5 | 9 | 6 | 2 | 8 |
| 9 | 6 | 5 | 2 | 8 | 1 | 7 | 3 | 4 |
| 3 | 2 | 8 | 6 | 7 | 4 | 9 | 5 | 1 |
| 1 | 8 | 2 | 9 | 6 | 7 | 3 | 4 | 5 |
| 5 | 4 | 9 | 1 | 3 | 2 | 8 | 7 | 6 |
| 7 | 3 | 6 | 8 | 4 | 5 | 2 | 1 | 9 |

**52**

| 4 | 1 | 5 | 3 | 9 | 7 | 6 | 2 | 8 |
| 2 | 6 | 7 | 1 | 5 | 8 | 3 | 4 | 9 |
| 8 | 3 | 9 | 6 | 2 | 4 | 1 | 5 | 7 |
| 3 | 9 | 2 | 4 | 1 | 6 | 7 | 8 | 5 |
| 7 | 5 | 1 | 2 | 8 | 9 | 4 | 6 | 3 |
| 6 | 4 | 8 | 7 | 3 | 5 | 9 | 1 | 2 |
| 9 | 8 | 3 | 5 | 6 | 1 | 2 | 7 | 4 |
| 1 | 2 | 4 | 8 | 7 | 3 | 5 | 9 | 6 |
| 5 | 7 | 6 | 9 | 4 | 2 | 8 | 3 | 1 |

**53**

| 8 | 2 | 7 | 6 | 1 | 5 | 3 | 4 | 9 |
| 6 | 9 | 3 | 7 | 4 | 8 | 5 | 2 | 1 |
| 1 | 5 | 4 | 2 | 3 | 9 | 8 | 6 | 7 |
| 3 | 7 | 6 | 8 | 9 | 2 | 1 | 5 | 4 |
| 9 | 1 | 2 | 5 | 6 | 4 | 7 | 3 | 8 |
| 4 | 8 | 5 | 3 | 7 | 1 | 2 | 9 | 6 |
| 5 | 3 | 1 | 4 | 8 | 6 | 9 | 7 | 2 |
| 7 | 6 | 9 | 1 | 2 | 3 | 4 | 8 | 5 |
| 2 | 4 | 8 | 9 | 5 | 7 | 6 | 1 | 3 |

**54**

| 1 | 8 | 5 | 6 | 9 | 3 | 7 | 2 | 4 |
| 9 | 7 | 2 | 4 | 5 | 1 | 6 | 3 | 8 |
| 6 | 4 | 3 | 7 | 8 | 2 | 1 | 9 | 5 |
| 7 | 3 | 1 | 9 | 6 | 5 | 4 | 8 | 2 |
| 8 | 5 | 6 | 3 | 2 | 4 | 9 | 7 | 1 |
| 2 | 9 | 4 | 8 | 1 | 7 | 5 | 6 | 3 |
| 4 | 1 | 8 | 2 | 7 | 9 | 3 | 5 | 6 |
| 3 | 6 | 9 | 5 | 4 | 8 | 2 | 1 | 7 |
| 5 | 2 | 7 | 1 | 3 | 6 | 8 | 4 | 9 |

**55**

| 9 | 3 | 2 | 8 | 1 | 5 | 7 | 6 | 4 |
| 1 | 4 | 5 | 3 | 6 | 7 | 8 | 2 | 9 |
| 6 | 7 | 8 | 9 | 4 | 2 | 1 | 3 | 5 |
| 4 | 6 | 1 | 5 | 3 | 8 | 2 | 9 | 7 |
| 2 | 9 | 3 | 4 | 7 | 6 | 5 | 8 | 1 |
| 5 | 8 | 7 | 1 | 2 | 9 | 6 | 4 | 3 |
| 8 | 1 | 4 | 6 | 5 | 3 | 9 | 7 | 2 |
| 7 | 5 | 9 | 2 | 8 | 4 | 3 | 1 | 6 |
| 3 | 2 | 6 | 7 | 9 | 1 | 4 | 5 | 8 |

**56**

| 8 | 2 | 9 | 6 | 3 | 4 | 7 | 1 | 5 |
| 4 | 3 | 7 | 1 | 9 | 5 | 6 | 2 | 8 |
| 5 | 1 | 6 | 8 | 2 | 7 | 9 | 3 | 4 |
| 6 | 9 | 5 | 4 | 8 | 1 | 3 | 7 | 2 |
| 3 | 4 | 8 | 7 | 6 | 2 | 1 | 5 | 9 |
| 1 | 7 | 2 | 9 | 5 | 3 | 8 | 4 | 6 |
| 7 | 8 | 1 | 5 | 4 | 6 | 2 | 9 | 3 |
| 9 | 5 | 3 | 2 | 1 | 8 | 4 | 6 | 7 |
| 2 | 6 | 4 | 3 | 7 | 9 | 5 | 8 | 1 |

**5 / 7**

| 8 | 4 | 5 | 2 | 7 | 6 | 9 | 3 | 1 |
|---|---|---|---|---|---|---|---|---|
| 2 | 9 | 7 | 1 | 8 | 3 | 6 | 4 | 5 |
| 3 | 1 | 6 | 5 | 4 | 9 | 2 | 8 | 7 |
| 5 | 6 | 2 | 7 | 9 | 8 | 3 | 1 | 4 |
| 4 | 3 | 1 | 6 | 5 | 2 | 7 | 9 | 8 |
| 7 | 8 | 9 | 4 | 3 | 1 | 5 | 6 | 2 |
| 6 | 7 | 3 | 8 | 1 | 5 | 4 | 2 | 9 |
| 9 | 5 | 8 | 3 | 2 | 4 | 1 | 7 | 6 |
| 1 | 2 | 4 | 9 | 6 | 7 | 8 | 5 | 3 |

**5 / 8**

| 3 | 5 | 6 | 7 | 4 | 2 | 8 | 1 | 9 |
|---|---|---|---|---|---|---|---|---|
| 4 | 9 | 8 | 5 | 6 | 1 | 2 | 3 | 7 |
| 1 | 2 | 7 | 9 | 3 | 8 | 4 | 5 | 6 |
| 2 | 6 | 9 | 1 | 7 | 4 | 5 | 8 | 3 |
| 5 | 7 | 1 | 8 | 2 | 3 | 6 | 9 | 4 |
| 8 | 4 | 3 | 6 | 5 | 9 | 7 | 2 | 1 |
| 9 | 8 | 4 | 2 | 1 | 6 | 3 | 7 | 5 |
| 7 | 3 | 2 | 4 | 9 | 5 | 1 | 6 | 8 |
| 6 | 1 | 5 | 3 | 8 | 7 | 9 | 4 | 2 |

**5 / 9**

| 6 | 8 | 9 | 7 | 2 | 1 | 5 | 4 | 3 |
|---|---|---|---|---|---|---|---|---|
| 2 | 5 | 3 | 6 | 9 | 4 | 1 | 8 | 7 |
| 4 | 1 | 7 | 8 | 3 | 5 | 2 | 9 | 6 |
| 1 | 6 | 8 | 2 | 7 | 3 | 9 | 5 | 4 |
| 9 | 4 | 5 | 1 | 6 | 8 | 7 | 3 | 2 |
| 3 | 7 | 2 | 5 | 4 | 9 | 6 | 1 | 8 |
| 8 | 9 | 6 | 4 | 5 | 7 | 3 | 2 | 1 |
| 5 | 2 | 4 | 3 | 1 | 6 | 8 | 7 | 9 |
| 7 | 3 | 1 | 9 | 8 | 2 | 4 | 6 | 5 |

**6 / 0**

| 8 | 2 | 1 | 5 | 9 | 7 | 6 | 4 | 3 |
|---|---|---|---|---|---|---|---|---|
| 5 | 7 | 6 | 4 | 1 | 3 | 8 | 2 | 9 |
| 3 | 4 | 9 | 6 | 8 | 2 | 5 | 1 | 7 |
| 1 | 9 | 4 | 3 | 6 | 5 | 2 | 7 | 8 |
| 6 | 5 | 7 | 9 | 2 | 8 | 4 | 3 | 1 |
| 2 | 8 | 3 | 7 | 4 | 1 | 9 | 5 | 6 |
| 7 | 6 | 5 | 2 | 3 | 9 | 1 | 8 | 4 |
| 4 | 3 | 8 | 1 | 5 | 6 | 7 | 9 | 2 |
| 9 | 1 | 2 | 8 | 7 | 4 | 3 | 6 | 5 |

**6 / 1**

| 7 | 3 | 6 | 1 | 2 | 8 | 5 | 4 | 9 |
|---|---|---|---|---|---|---|---|---|
| 5 | 4 | 8 | 7 | 6 | 9 | 1 | 3 | 2 |
| 9 | 1 | 2 | 4 | 3 | 5 | 6 | 7 | 8 |
| 2 | 9 | 4 | 3 | 5 | 1 | 8 | 6 | 7 |
| 6 | 8 | 1 | 2 | 7 | 4 | 3 | 9 | 5 |
| 3 | 7 | 5 | 9 | 8 | 6 | 2 | 1 | 4 |
| 1 | 5 | 3 | 8 | 4 | 7 | 9 | 2 | 6 |
| 4 | 6 | 9 | 5 | 1 | 2 | 7 | 8 | 3 |
| 8 | 2 | 7 | 6 | 9 | 3 | 4 | 5 | 1 |

**6 / 2**

| 4 | 9 | 1 | 3 | 6 | 2 | 7 | 5 | 8 |
|---|---|---|---|---|---|---|---|---|
| 6 | 8 | 2 | 5 | 7 | 9 | 4 | 1 | 3 |
| 3 | 5 | 7 | 1 | 4 | 8 | 2 | 6 | 9 |
| 9 | 3 | 8 | 2 | 1 | 6 | 5 | 4 | 7 |
| 7 | 2 | 5 | 8 | 9 | 4 | 6 | 3 | 1 |
| 1 | 6 | 4 | 7 | 5 | 3 | 9 | 8 | 2 |
| 8 | 7 | 6 | 4 | 2 | 1 | 3 | 9 | 5 |
| 2 | 1 | 9 | 6 | 3 | 5 | 8 | 7 | 4 |
| 5 | 4 | 3 | 9 | 8 | 7 | 1 | 2 | 6 |

**6 / 3**

| 5 | 8 | 4 | 1 | 3 | 7 | 2 | 6 | 9 |
|---|---|---|---|---|---|---|---|---|
| 7 | 9 | 1 | 2 | 6 | 8 | 3 | 5 | 4 |
| 6 | 2 | 3 | 4 | 5 | 9 | 1 | 8 | 7 |
| 2 | 6 | 8 | 3 | 4 | 1 | 9 | 7 | 5 |
| 4 | 5 | 7 | 9 | 8 | 2 | 6 | 1 | 3 |
| 1 | 3 | 9 | 5 | 7 | 6 | 8 | 4 | 2 |
| 3 | 7 | 6 | 8 | 9 | 4 | 5 | 2 | 1 |
| 8 | 1 | 5 | 7 | 2 | 3 | 4 | 9 | 6 |
| 9 | 4 | 2 | 6 | 1 | 5 | 7 | 3 | 8 |

**6 / 4**

| 2 | 8 | 3 | 4 | 1 | 5 | 6 | 9 | 7 |
|---|---|---|---|---|---|---|---|---|
| 1 | 6 | 9 | 7 | 8 | 2 | 5 | 3 | 4 |
| 7 | 5 | 4 | 9 | 6 | 3 | 2 | 8 | 1 |
| 6 | 9 | 8 | 1 | 7 | 4 | 3 | 5 | 2 |
| 5 | 1 | 2 | 3 | 9 | 8 | 4 | 7 | 6 |
| 4 | 3 | 7 | 2 | 5 | 6 | 9 | 1 | 8 |
| 9 | 4 | 1 | 6 | 3 | 7 | 8 | 2 | 5 |
| 8 | 7 | 6 | 5 | 2 | 9 | 1 | 4 | 3 |
| 3 | 2 | 5 | 8 | 4 | 1 | 7 | 6 | 9 |

**65**

| 2 | 8 | 4 | 5 | 9 | 7 | 1 | 3 | 6 |
|---|---|---|---|---|---|---|---|---|
| 1 | 3 | 9 | 8 | 2 | 6 | 4 | 5 | 7 |
| 7 | 6 | 5 | 4 | 3 | 1 | 8 | 9 | 2 |
| 9 | 2 | 3 | 6 | 8 | 5 | 7 | 4 | 1 |
| 4 | 1 | 6 | 9 | 7 | 3 | 5 | 2 | 8 |
| 5 | 7 | 8 | 2 | 1 | 4 | 3 | 6 | 9 |
| 3 | 9 | 1 | 7 | 4 | 2 | 6 | 8 | 5 |
| 6 | 4 | 2 | 1 | 5 | 8 | 9 | 7 | 3 |
| 8 | 5 | 7 | 3 | 6 | 9 | 2 | 1 | 4 |

**66**

| 5 | 6 | 1 | 7 | 4 | 9 | 2 | 8 | 3 |
|---|---|---|---|---|---|---|---|---|
| 4 | 7 | 8 | 1 | 3 | 2 | 6 | 9 | 5 |
| 9 | 3 | 2 | 5 | 6 | 8 | 4 | 1 | 7 |
| 6 | 4 | 5 | 9 | 8 | 7 | 3 | 2 | 1 |
| 1 | 8 | 3 | 2 | 5 | 4 | 7 | 6 | 9 |
| 7 | 2 | 9 | 6 | 1 | 3 | 8 | 5 | 4 |
| 3 | 9 | 7 | 8 | 2 | 5 | 1 | 4 | 6 |
| 8 | 1 | 4 | 3 | 9 | 6 | 5 | 7 | 2 |
| 2 | 5 | 6 | 4 | 7 | 1 | 9 | 3 | 8 |

**67**

| 5 | 8 | 4 | 9 | 3 | 2 | 6 | 1 | 7 |
|---|---|---|---|---|---|---|---|---|
| 3 | 1 | 9 | 4 | 6 | 7 | 5 | 2 | 8 |
| 2 | 7 | 6 | 1 | 8 | 5 | 4 | 9 | 3 |
| 4 | 9 | 8 | 2 | 1 | 3 | 7 | 5 | 6 |
| 7 | 6 | 3 | 8 | 5 | 9 | 1 | 4 | 2 |
| 1 | 2 | 5 | 7 | 4 | 6 | 8 | 3 | 9 |
| 9 | 4 | 1 | 6 | 2 | 8 | 3 | 7 | 5 |
| 6 | 3 | 7 | 5 | 9 | 1 | 2 | 8 | 4 |
| 8 | 5 | 2 | 3 | 7 | 4 | 9 | 6 | 1 |

**68**

| 2 | 9 | 1 | 7 | 3 | 4 | 5 | 6 | 8 |
|---|---|---|---|---|---|---|---|---|
| 6 | 8 | 5 | 1 | 9 | 2 | 3 | 4 | 7 |
| 3 | 4 | 7 | 6 | 8 | 5 | 2 | 1 | 9 |
| 7 | 6 | 3 | 2 | 5 | 1 | 8 | 9 | 4 |
| 9 | 1 | 8 | 3 | 4 | 7 | 6 | 5 | 2 |
| 4 | 5 | 2 | 9 | 6 | 8 | 1 | 7 | 3 |
| 1 | 7 | 4 | 8 | 2 | 6 | 9 | 3 | 5 |
| 5 | 2 | 9 | 4 | 1 | 3 | 7 | 8 | 6 |
| 8 | 3 | 6 | 5 | 7 | 9 | 4 | 2 | 1 |

**69**

| 5 | 6 | 3 | 4 | 9 | 8 | 1 | 7 | 2 |
|---|---|---|---|---|---|---|---|---|
| 7 | 1 | 9 | 3 | 6 | 2 | 5 | 4 | 8 |
| 4 | 2 | 8 | 5 | 1 | 7 | 3 | 6 | 9 |
| 9 | 8 | 7 | 1 | 2 | 5 | 6 | 3 | 4 |
| 1 | 3 | 2 | 9 | 4 | 6 | 8 | 5 | 7 |
| 6 | 4 | 5 | 7 | 8 | 3 | 9 | 2 | 1 |
| 8 | 5 | 1 | 6 | 7 | 4 | 2 | 9 | 3 |
| 3 | 9 | 4 | 2 | 5 | 1 | 7 | 8 | 6 |
| 2 | 7 | 6 | 8 | 3 | 9 | 4 | 1 | 5 |

**70**

| 3 | 7 | 8 | 2 | 9 | 1 | 4 | 6 | 5 |
|---|---|---|---|---|---|---|---|---|
| 2 | 5 | 1 | 3 | 4 | 6 | 7 | 9 | 8 |
| 9 | 6 | 4 | 8 | 7 | 5 | 2 | 1 | 3 |
| 6 | 8 | 5 | 1 | 2 | 7 | 9 | 3 | 4 |
| 7 | 1 | 2 | 9 | 3 | 4 | 5 | 8 | 6 |
| 4 | 9 | 3 | 5 | 6 | 8 | 1 | 2 | 7 |
| 5 | 4 | 9 | 6 | 8 | 2 | 3 | 7 | 1 |
| 8 | 2 | 7 | 4 | 1 | 3 | 6 | 5 | 9 |
| 1 | 3 | 6 | 7 | 5 | 9 | 8 | 4 | 2 |

**71**

| 7 | 5 | 3 | 1 | 4 | 2 | 6 | 9 | 8 |
|---|---|---|---|---|---|---|---|---|
| 1 | 6 | 8 | 9 | 3 | 7 | 4 | 5 | 2 |
| 4 | 2 | 9 | 6 | 8 | 5 | 7 | 1 | 3 |
| 9 | 4 | 6 | 7 | 2 | 3 | 1 | 8 | 5 |
| 2 | 1 | 5 | 4 | 9 | 8 | 3 | 7 | 6 |
| 3 | 8 | 7 | 5 | 6 | 1 | 2 | 4 | 9 |
| 6 | 3 | 1 | 8 | 7 | 9 | 5 | 2 | 4 |
| 8 | 7 | 2 | 3 | 5 | 4 | 9 | 6 | 1 |
| 5 | 9 | 4 | 2 | 1 | 6 | 8 | 3 | 7 |

**72**

| 6 | 4 | 5 | 3 | 2 | 7 | 9 | 8 | 1 |
|---|---|---|---|---|---|---|---|---|
| 2 | 9 | 3 | 4 | 8 | 1 | 6 | 7 | 5 |
| 8 | 1 | 7 | 6 | 9 | 5 | 4 | 2 | 3 |
| 9 | 8 | 6 | 7 | 1 | 4 | 3 | 5 | 2 |
| 5 | 2 | 1 | 8 | 6 | 3 | 7 | 9 | 4 |
| 7 | 3 | 4 | 2 | 5 | 9 | 8 | 1 | 6 |
| 4 | 6 | 9 | 5 | 7 | 2 | 1 | 3 | 8 |
| 3 | 7 | 2 | 1 | 4 | 8 | 5 | 6 | 9 |
| 1 | 5 | 8 | 9 | 3 | 6 | 2 | 4 | 7 |

## 73

| 1 | 6 | 8 | 2 | 9 | 3 | 5 | 4 | 7 |
| 7 | 2 | 3 | 8 | 5 | 4 | 1 | 6 | 9 |
| 4 | 9 | 5 | 7 | 6 | 1 | 8 | 2 | 3 |
| 5 | 1 | 6 | 3 | 8 | 7 | 2 | 9 | 4 |
| 2 | 4 | 7 | 9 | 1 | 6 | 3 | 5 | 8 |
| 8 | 3 | 9 | 5 | 4 | 2 | 6 | 7 | 1 |
| 9 | 7 | 2 | 1 | 3 | 5 | 4 | 8 | 6 |
| 3 | 5 | 4 | 6 | 7 | 8 | 9 | 1 | 2 |
| 6 | 8 | 1 | 4 | 2 | 9 | 7 | 3 | 5 |

## 74

| 7 | 1 | 5 | 6 | 4 | 2 | 8 | 9 | 3 |
| 3 | 8 | 9 | 7 | 5 | 1 | 2 | 6 | 4 |
| 2 | 4 | 6 | 8 | 3 | 9 | 7 | 5 | 1 |
| 1 | 9 | 2 | 5 | 6 | 3 | 4 | 7 | 8 |
| 8 | 3 | 4 | 9 | 1 | 7 | 6 | 2 | 5 |
| 6 | 5 | 7 | 4 | 2 | 8 | 3 | 1 | 9 |
| 9 | 2 | 1 | 3 | 8 | 6 | 5 | 4 | 7 |
| 4 | 7 | 3 | 2 | 9 | 5 | 1 | 8 | 6 |
| 5 | 6 | 8 | 1 | 7 | 4 | 9 | 3 | 2 |

## 75

| 8 | 1 | 5 | 3 | 7 | 6 | 2 | 9 | 4 |
| 4 | 3 | 7 | 1 | 2 | 9 | 8 | 6 | 5 |
| 9 | 6 | 2 | 8 | 4 | 5 | 7 | 1 | 3 |
| 6 | 5 | 3 | 9 | 1 | 7 | 4 | 8 | 2 |
| 7 | 8 | 1 | 2 | 5 | 4 | 9 | 3 | 6 |
| 2 | 4 | 9 | 6 | 8 | 3 | 5 | 7 | 1 |
| 3 | 7 | 6 | 5 | 9 | 2 | 1 | 4 | 8 |
| 1 | 2 | 4 | 7 | 3 | 8 | 6 | 5 | 9 |
| 5 | 9 | 8 | 4 | 6 | 1 | 3 | 2 | 7 |

## 76

| 6 | 1 | 8 | 4 | 9 | 3 | 2 | 7 | 5 |
| 7 | 2 | 9 | 6 | 1 | 5 | 3 | 8 | 4 |
| 3 | 4 | 5 | 7 | 8 | 2 | 6 | 1 | 9 |
| 9 | 6 | 2 | 1 | 5 | 4 | 8 | 3 | 7 |
| 8 | 3 | 1 | 9 | 2 | 7 | 4 | 5 | 6 |
| 4 | 5 | 7 | 8 | 3 | 6 | 1 | 9 | 2 |
| 1 | 8 | 6 | 2 | 7 | 9 | 5 | 4 | 3 |
| 2 | 7 | 3 | 5 | 4 | 8 | 9 | 6 | 1 |
| 5 | 9 | 4 | 3 | 6 | 1 | 7 | 2 | 8 |

## 77

| 4 | 1 | 9 | 8 | 3 | 2 | 6 | 5 | 7 |
| 8 | 5 | 2 | 6 | 4 | 7 | 1 | 3 | 9 |
| 6 | 3 | 7 | 9 | 5 | 1 | 2 | 8 | 4 |
| 5 | 7 | 3 | 4 | 9 | 6 | 8 | 1 | 2 |
| 2 | 6 | 8 | 1 | 7 | 5 | 4 | 9 | 3 |
| 9 | 4 | 1 | 3 | 2 | 8 | 7 | 6 | 5 |
| 7 | 2 | 6 | 5 | 8 | 9 | 3 | 4 | 1 |
| 1 | 9 | 4 | 2 | 6 | 3 | 5 | 7 | 8 |
| 3 | 8 | 5 | 7 | 1 | 4 | 9 | 2 | 6 |

## 78

| 5 | 6 | 1 | 3 | 2 | 7 | 9 | 4 | 8 |
| 4 | 2 | 7 | 9 | 6 | 8 | 3 | 5 | 1 |
| 9 | 3 | 8 | 4 | 5 | 1 | 2 | 7 | 6 |
| 2 | 8 | 3 | 7 | 9 | 6 | 4 | 1 | 5 |
| 6 | 5 | 4 | 2 | 1 | 3 | 8 | 9 | 7 |
| 1 | 7 | 9 | 5 | 8 | 4 | 6 | 3 | 2 |
| 3 | 9 | 6 | 8 | 7 | 5 | 1 | 2 | 4 |
| 7 | 1 | 2 | 6 | 4 | 9 | 5 | 8 | 3 |
| 8 | 4 | 5 | 1 | 3 | 2 | 7 | 6 | 9 |

## 79

| 6 | 1 | 5 | 9 | 4 | 3 | 7 | 8 | 2 |
| 8 | 7 | 2 | 5 | 6 | 1 | 9 | 4 | 3 |
| 4 | 3 | 9 | 2 | 7 | 8 | 1 | 6 | 5 |
| 1 | 8 | 7 | 3 | 2 | 5 | 6 | 9 | 4 |
| 3 | 5 | 6 | 4 | 8 | 9 | 2 | 7 | 1 |
| 9 | 2 | 4 | 7 | 1 | 6 | 5 | 3 | 8 |
| 2 | 6 | 1 | 8 | 3 | 7 | 4 | 5 | 9 |
| 7 | 9 | 3 | 1 | 5 | 4 | 8 | 2 | 6 |
| 5 | 4 | 8 | 6 | 9 | 2 | 3 | 1 | 7 |

## 80

| 7 | 1 | 2 | 6 | 8 | 5 | 4 | 9 | 3 |
| 4 | 3 | 5 | 7 | 9 | 1 | 6 | 2 | 8 |
| 6 | 8 | 9 | 4 | 2 | 3 | 7 | 1 | 5 |
| 8 | 2 | 4 | 3 | 6 | 7 | 1 | 5 | 9 |
| 3 | 7 | 6 | 1 | 5 | 9 | 8 | 4 | 2 |
| 9 | 5 | 1 | 2 | 4 | 8 | 3 | 6 | 7 |
| 2 | 9 | 3 | 8 | 1 | 4 | 5 | 7 | 6 |
| 5 | 4 | 7 | 9 | 3 | 6 | 2 | 8 | 1 |
| 1 | 6 | 8 | 5 | 7 | 2 | 9 | 3 | 4 |

**8-1**

| 9 | 6 | 4 | 2 | 8 | 1 | 7 | 5 | 3 |
|---|---|---|---|---|---|---|---|---|
| 7 | 1 | 2 | 3 | 9 | 5 | 4 | 6 | 8 |
| 8 | 3 | 5 | 4 | 7 | 6 | 1 | 2 | 9 |
| 4 | 8 | 3 | 5 | 2 | 9 | 6 | 1 | 7 |
| 1 | 7 | 9 | 8 | 6 | 4 | 5 | 3 | 2 |
| 5 | 2 | 6 | 7 | 1 | 3 | 8 | 9 | 4 |
| 6 | 9 | 8 | 1 | 4 | 2 | 3 | 7 | 5 |
| 2 | 5 | 7 | 6 | 3 | 8 | 9 | 4 | 1 |
| 3 | 4 | 1 | 9 | 5 | 7 | 2 | 8 | 6 |

**8-2**

| 7 | 4 | 6 | 8 | 1 | 3 | 5 | 2 | 9 |
|---|---|---|---|---|---|---|---|---|
| 8 | 5 | 9 | 7 | 6 | 2 | 3 | 4 | 1 |
| 1 | 2 | 3 | 9 | 4 | 5 | 8 | 6 | 7 |
| 9 | 8 | 1 | 5 | 2 | 6 | 4 | 7 | 3 |
| 5 | 6 | 7 | 3 | 8 | 4 | 9 | 1 | 2 |
| 2 | 3 | 4 | 1 | 9 | 7 | 6 | 8 | 5 |
| 6 | 9 | 8 | 2 | 5 | 1 | 7 | 3 | 4 |
| 3 | 1 | 5 | 4 | 7 | 8 | 2 | 9 | 6 |
| 4 | 7 | 2 | 6 | 3 | 9 | 1 | 5 | 8 |

**8-3**

| 5 | 8 | 4 | 6 | 9 | 2 | 1 | 3 | 7 |
|---|---|---|---|---|---|---|---|---|
| 2 | 3 | 9 | 1 | 7 | 4 | 8 | 5 | 6 |
| 1 | 6 | 7 | 5 | 8 | 3 | 4 | 9 | 2 |
| 7 | 1 | 3 | 8 | 5 | 9 | 2 | 6 | 4 |
| 6 | 2 | 5 | 3 | 4 | 1 | 7 | 8 | 9 |
| 4 | 9 | 8 | 7 | 2 | 6 | 5 | 1 | 3 |
| 8 | 5 | 6 | 4 | 3 | 7 | 9 | 2 | 1 |
| 3 | 4 | 2 | 9 | 1 | 8 | 6 | 7 | 5 |
| 9 | 7 | 1 | 2 | 6 | 5 | 3 | 4 | 8 |

**8-4**

| 5 | 9 | 3 | 6 | 2 | 7 | 1 | 8 | 4 |
|---|---|---|---|---|---|---|---|---|
| 6 | 8 | 7 | 4 | 1 | 9 | 2 | 3 | 5 |
| 4 | 1 | 2 | 8 | 5 | 3 | 9 | 7 | 6 |
| 9 | 7 | 8 | 3 | 4 | 1 | 5 | 6 | 2 |
| 1 | 3 | 4 | 5 | 6 | 2 | 8 | 9 | 7 |
| 2 | 5 | 6 | 7 | 9 | 8 | 3 | 4 | 1 |
| 3 | 6 | 1 | 9 | 7 | 5 | 4 | 2 | 8 |
| 8 | 4 | 5 | 2 | 3 | 6 | 7 | 1 | 9 |
| 7 | 2 | 9 | 1 | 8 | 4 | 6 | 5 | 3 |

**8-5**

| 4 | 1 | 3 | 6 | 9 | 7 | 8 | 2 | 5 |
|---|---|---|---|---|---|---|---|---|
| 6 | 2 | 9 | 8 | 4 | 5 | 3 | 7 | 1 |
| 5 | 8 | 7 | 2 | 3 | 1 | 6 | 4 | 9 |
| 9 | 7 | 1 | 5 | 8 | 4 | 2 | 6 | 3 |
| 2 | 5 | 8 | 1 | 6 | 3 | 4 | 9 | 7 |
| 3 | 6 | 4 | 7 | 2 | 9 | 5 | 1 | 8 |
| 7 | 3 | 5 | 4 | 1 | 6 | 9 | 8 | 2 |
| 8 | 9 | 6 | 3 | 7 | 2 | 1 | 5 | 4 |
| 1 | 4 | 2 | 9 | 5 | 8 | 7 | 3 | 6 |

**8-6**

| 4 | 2 | 1 | 9 | 6 | 7 | 3 | 8 | 5 |
|---|---|---|---|---|---|---|---|---|
| 5 | 8 | 7 | 3 | 4 | 2 | 9 | 6 | 1 |
| 3 | 6 | 9 | 1 | 8 | 5 | 7 | 2 | 4 |
| 1 | 9 | 5 | 8 | 3 | 6 | 2 | 4 | 7 |
| 7 | 4 | 6 | 2 | 1 | 9 | 8 | 5 | 3 |
| 2 | 3 | 8 | 5 | 7 | 4 | 1 | 9 | 6 |
| 6 | 7 | 3 | 4 | 2 | 8 | 5 | 1 | 9 |
| 9 | 1 | 2 | 6 | 5 | 3 | 4 | 7 | 8 |
| 8 | 5 | 4 | 7 | 9 | 1 | 6 | 3 | 2 |

**8-7**

| 7 | 8 | 6 | 4 | 2 | 3 | 9 | 1 | 5 |
|---|---|---|---|---|---|---|---|---|
| 2 | 1 | 5 | 6 | 9 | 8 | 3 | 7 | 4 |
| 4 | 3 | 9 | 1 | 7 | 5 | 8 | 6 | 2 |
| 3 | 7 | 8 | 2 | 6 | 4 | 5 | 9 | 1 |
| 9 | 2 | 1 | 8 | 5 | 7 | 6 | 4 | 3 |
| 5 | 6 | 4 | 9 | 3 | 1 | 2 | 8 | 7 |
| 8 | 9 | 3 | 7 | 1 | 2 | 4 | 5 | 6 |
| 6 | 5 | 7 | 3 | 4 | 9 | 1 | 2 | 8 |
| 1 | 4 | 2 | 5 | 8 | 6 | 7 | 3 | 9 |

**8-8**

| 4 | 7 | 3 | 8 | 1 | 6 | 5 | 2 | 9 |
|---|---|---|---|---|---|---|---|---|
| 8 | 1 | 9 | 5 | 2 | 4 | 3 | 7 | 6 |
| 5 | 2 | 6 | 7 | 9 | 3 | 1 | 4 | 8 |
| 6 | 9 | 7 | 4 | 3 | 5 | 8 | 1 | 2 |
| 2 | 5 | 4 | 9 | 8 | 1 | 7 | 6 | 3 |
| 3 | 8 | 1 | 2 | 6 | 7 | 9 | 5 | 4 |
| 1 | 6 | 5 | 3 | 4 | 9 | 2 | 8 | 7 |
| 7 | 3 | 2 | 6 | 5 | 8 | 4 | 9 | 1 |
| 9 | 4 | 8 | 1 | 7 | 2 | 6 | 3 | 5 |

**89**

| 4 | 5 | 6 | 1 | 8 | 2 | 7 | 3 | 9 |
|---|---|---|---|---|---|---|---|---|
| 2 | 7 | 3 | 4 | 9 | 5 | 8 | 6 | 1 |
| 8 | 1 | 9 | 7 | 3 | 6 | 2 | 4 | 5 |
| 1 | 2 | 4 | 5 | 6 | 7 | 3 | 9 | 8 |
| 3 | 6 | 8 | 2 | 4 | 9 | 1 | 5 | 7 |
| 7 | 9 | 5 | 8 | 1 | 3 | 4 | 2 | 6 |
| 5 | 3 | 1 | 9 | 2 | 8 | 6 | 7 | 4 |
| 9 | 4 | 2 | 6 | 7 | 1 | 5 | 8 | 3 |
| 6 | 8 | 7 | 3 | 5 | 4 | 9 | 1 | 2 |

**90**

| 1 | 3 | 5 | 6 | 7 | 2 | 9 | 4 | 8 |
|---|---|---|---|---|---|---|---|---|
| 8 | 4 | 6 | 1 | 3 | 9 | 2 | 5 | 7 |
| 7 | 2 | 9 | 5 | 8 | 4 | 1 | 3 | 6 |
| 3 | 7 | 8 | 4 | 9 | 6 | 5 | 1 | 2 |
| 2 | 9 | 1 | 7 | 5 | 8 | 3 | 6 | 4 |
| 6 | 5 | 4 | 3 | 2 | 1 | 7 | 8 | 9 |
| 5 | 8 | 7 | 9 | 6 | 3 | 4 | 2 | 1 |
| 4 | 6 | 3 | 2 | 1 | 7 | 8 | 9 | 5 |
| 9 | 1 | 2 | 8 | 4 | 5 | 6 | 7 | 3 |

**91**

| 6 | 1 | 4 | 5 | 8 | 7 | 3 | 9 | 2 |
|---|---|---|---|---|---|---|---|---|
| 3 | 2 | 5 | 6 | 1 | 9 | 7 | 4 | 8 |
| 9 | 8 | 7 | 4 | 3 | 2 | 6 | 1 | 5 |
| 2 | 4 | 3 | 1 | 6 | 5 | 9 | 8 | 7 |
| 5 | 7 | 1 | 3 | 9 | 8 | 4 | 2 | 6 |
| 8 | 9 | 6 | 7 | 2 | 4 | 1 | 5 | 3 |
| 4 | 3 | 8 | 9 | 5 | 6 | 2 | 7 | 1 |
| 7 | 6 | 2 | 8 | 4 | 1 | 5 | 3 | 9 |
| 1 | 5 | 9 | 2 | 7 | 3 | 8 | 6 | 4 |

**92**

| 3 | 2 | 6 | 4 | 9 | 5 | 7 | 8 | 1 |
|---|---|---|---|---|---|---|---|---|
| 9 | 5 | 8 | 3 | 7 | 1 | 4 | 2 | 6 |
| 4 | 7 | 1 | 8 | 6 | 2 | 3 | 5 | 9 |
| 5 | 1 | 4 | 6 | 3 | 7 | 8 | 9 | 2 |
| 7 | 3 | 2 | 1 | 8 | 9 | 6 | 4 | 5 |
| 6 | 8 | 9 | 5 | 2 | 4 | 1 | 3 | 7 |
| 1 | 4 | 3 | 9 | 5 | 6 | 2 | 7 | 8 |
| 8 | 9 | 7 | 2 | 1 | 3 | 5 | 6 | 4 |
| 2 | 6 | 5 | 7 | 4 | 8 | 9 | 1 | 3 |

**93**

| 1 | 2 | 8 | 6 | 7 | 3 | 9 | 5 | 4 |
|---|---|---|---|---|---|---|---|---|
| 7 | 4 | 5 | 9 | 1 | 8 | 6 | 3 | 2 |
| 9 | 6 | 3 | 4 | 5 | 2 | 7 | 8 | 1 |
| 3 | 5 | 1 | 7 | 8 | 4 | 2 | 6 | 9 |
| 8 | 7 | 6 | 5 | 2 | 9 | 4 | 1 | 3 |
| 2 | 9 | 4 | 1 | 3 | 6 | 8 | 7 | 5 |
| 5 | 8 | 2 | 3 | 9 | 7 | 1 | 4 | 6 |
| 6 | 1 | 9 | 8 | 4 | 5 | 3 | 2 | 7 |
| 4 | 3 | 7 | 2 | 6 | 1 | 5 | 9 | 8 |

**94**

| 3 | 5 | 6 | 9 | 1 | 7 | 2 | 4 | 8 |
|---|---|---|---|---|---|---|---|---|
| 7 | 9 | 1 | 4 | 2 | 8 | 5 | 6 | 3 |
| 4 | 8 | 2 | 5 | 3 | 6 | 1 | 9 | 7 |
| 5 | 2 | 4 | 6 | 9 | 3 | 8 | 7 | 1 |
| 8 | 7 | 3 | 1 | 4 | 5 | 9 | 2 | 6 |
| 1 | 6 | 9 | 7 | 8 | 2 | 3 | 5 | 4 |
| 2 | 3 | 5 | 8 | 7 | 4 | 6 | 1 | 9 |
| 9 | 4 | 8 | 2 | 6 | 1 | 7 | 3 | 5 |
| 6 | 1 | 7 | 3 | 5 | 9 | 4 | 8 | 2 |

**95**

| 1 | 5 | 4 | 6 | 7 | 9 | 2 | 3 | 8 |
|---|---|---|---|---|---|---|---|---|
| 7 | 6 | 8 | 2 | 1 | 3 | 9 | 5 | 4 |
| 9 | 3 | 2 | 4 | 8 | 5 | 1 | 6 | 7 |
| 4 | 2 | 1 | 5 | 9 | 8 | 6 | 7 | 3 |
| 6 | 9 | 3 | 7 | 4 | 2 | 5 | 8 | 1 |
| 5 | 8 | 7 | 3 | 6 | 1 | 4 | 2 | 9 |
| 8 | 4 | 6 | 9 | 2 | 7 | 3 | 1 | 5 |
| 2 | 7 | 5 | 1 | 3 | 4 | 8 | 9 | 6 |
| 3 | 1 | 9 | 8 | 5 | 6 | 7 | 4 | 2 |

**96**

| 3 | 8 | 9 | 4 | 7 | 6 | 5 | 1 | 2 |
|---|---|---|---|---|---|---|---|---|
| 4 | 1 | 7 | 8 | 5 | 2 | 6 | 3 | 9 |
| 6 | 2 | 5 | 3 | 9 | 1 | 4 | 8 | 7 |
| 5 | 3 | 8 | 7 | 2 | 9 | 1 | 4 | 6 |
| 1 | 7 | 2 | 6 | 8 | 4 | 3 | 9 | 5 |
| 9 | 4 | 6 | 5 | 1 | 3 | 7 | 2 | 8 |
| 7 | 5 | 1 | 2 | 3 | 8 | 9 | 6 | 4 |
| 2 | 9 | 4 | 1 | 6 | 7 | 8 | 5 | 3 |
| 8 | 6 | 3 | 9 | 4 | 5 | 2 | 7 | 1 |

**97**

| 7 | 8 | 1 | 4 | 3 | 2 | 9 | 5 | 6 |
|---|---|---|---|---|---|---|---|---|
| 4 | 3 | 2 | 6 | 5 | 9 | 8 | 7 | 1 |
| 9 | 5 | 6 | 8 | 7 | 1 | 3 | 4 | 2 |
| 3 | 6 | 9 | 1 | 4 | 7 | 2 | 8 | 5 |
| 5 | 4 | 7 | 3 | 2 | 8 | 6 | 1 | 9 |
| 1 | 2 | 8 | 9 | 6 | 5 | 7 | 3 | 4 |
| 6 | 1 | 5 | 2 | 8 | 3 | 4 | 9 | 7 |
| 2 | 7 | 3 | 5 | 9 | 4 | 1 | 6 | 8 |
| 8 | 9 | 4 | 7 | 1 | 6 | 5 | 2 | 3 |

**98**

| 2 | 6 | 4 | 7 | 3 | 5 | 9 | 8 | 1 |
|---|---|---|---|---|---|---|---|---|
| 1 | 5 | 8 | 9 | 4 | 2 | 3 | 6 | 7 |
| 9 | 3 | 7 | 1 | 8 | 6 | 4 | 2 | 5 |
| 5 | 8 | 9 | 6 | 2 | 3 | 7 | 1 | 4 |
| 7 | 1 | 3 | 4 | 9 | 8 | 2 | 5 | 6 |
| 4 | 2 | 6 | 5 | 7 | 1 | 8 | 9 | 3 |
| 6 | 9 | 2 | 3 | 1 | 7 | 5 | 4 | 8 |
| 8 | 7 | 5 | 2 | 6 | 4 | 1 | 3 | 9 |
| 3 | 4 | 1 | 8 | 5 | 9 | 6 | 7 | 2 |

**99**

| 8 | 5 | 6 | 7 | 9 | 2 | 3 | 4 | 1 |
|---|---|---|---|---|---|---|---|---|
| 7 | 1 | 9 | 5 | 3 | 4 | 2 | 8 | 6 |
| 2 | 3 | 4 | 8 | 6 | 1 | 9 | 7 | 5 |
| 9 | 2 | 1 | 3 | 4 | 5 | 8 | 6 | 7 |
| 5 | 6 | 7 | 9 | 2 | 8 | 4 | 1 | 3 |
| 4 | 8 | 3 | 6 | 1 | 7 | 5 | 9 | 2 |
| 6 | 4 | 5 | 1 | 8 | 3 | 7 | 2 | 9 |
| 1 | 7 | 2 | 4 | 5 | 9 | 6 | 3 | 8 |
| 3 | 9 | 8 | 2 | 7 | 6 | 1 | 5 | 4 |

**100**

| 7 | 8 | 3 | 9 | 6 | 2 | 4 | 5 | 1 |
|---|---|---|---|---|---|---|---|---|
| 4 | 6 | 2 | 5 | 1 | 3 | 9 | 8 | 7 |
| 5 | 1 | 9 | 7 | 8 | 4 | 2 | 6 | 3 |
| 2 | 9 | 5 | 3 | 4 | 7 | 6 | 1 | 8 |
| 8 | 4 | 6 | 2 | 5 | 1 | 3 | 7 | 9 |
| 1 | 3 | 7 | 6 | 9 | 8 | 5 | 4 | 2 |
| 3 | 5 | 8 | 4 | 7 | 9 | 1 | 2 | 6 |
| 9 | 7 | 4 | 1 | 2 | 6 | 8 | 3 | 5 |
| 6 | 2 | 1 | 8 | 3 | 5 | 7 | 9 | 4 |

**101**

| 4 | 1 | 2 | 6 | 3 | 5 | 9 | 7 | 8 |
|---|---|---|---|---|---|---|---|---|
| 9 | 5 | 3 | 8 | 4 | 7 | 2 | 1 | 6 |
| 6 | 8 | 7 | 2 | 1 | 9 | 5 | 3 | 4 |
| 1 | 6 | 8 | 7 | 9 | 4 | 3 | 2 | 5 |
| 5 | 2 | 9 | 1 | 6 | 3 | 8 | 4 | 7 |
| 7 | 3 | 4 | 5 | 2 | 8 | 6 | 9 | 1 |
| 3 | 4 | 1 | 9 | 5 | 6 | 7 | 8 | 2 |
| 2 | 7 | 5 | 3 | 8 | 1 | 4 | 6 | 9 |
| 8 | 9 | 6 | 4 | 7 | 2 | 1 | 5 | 3 |

**102**

| 8 | 9 | 3 | 4 | 6 | 5 | 1 | 7 | 2 |
|---|---|---|---|---|---|---|---|---|
| 7 | 2 | 4 | 9 | 3 | 1 | 6 | 8 | 5 |
| 1 | 6 | 5 | 8 | 2 | 7 | 3 | 9 | 4 |
| 5 | 7 | 1 | 3 | 4 | 2 | 9 | 6 | 8 |
| 6 | 8 | 2 | 1 | 7 | 9 | 5 | 4 | 3 |
| 4 | 3 | 9 | 5 | 8 | 6 | 7 | 2 | 1 |
| 3 | 4 | 7 | 6 | 5 | 8 | 2 | 1 | 9 |
| 2 | 1 | 8 | 7 | 9 | 3 | 4 | 5 | 6 |
| 9 | 5 | 6 | 2 | 1 | 4 | 8 | 3 | 7 |

**103**

| 6 | 4 | 5 | 9 | 1 | 7 | 2 | 3 | 8 |
|---|---|---|---|---|---|---|---|---|
| 9 | 8 | 1 | 4 | 2 | 3 | 6 | 7 | 5 |
| 3 | 7 | 2 | 5 | 8 | 6 | 1 | 9 | 4 |
| 5 | 6 | 3 | 2 | 9 | 8 | 4 | 1 | 7 |
| 4 | 1 | 9 | 3 | 7 | 5 | 8 | 6 | 2 |
| 8 | 2 | 7 | 1 | 6 | 4 | 3 | 5 | 9 |
| 7 | 3 | 6 | 8 | 5 | 2 | 9 | 4 | 1 |
| 1 | 5 | 8 | 6 | 4 | 9 | 7 | 2 | 3 |
| 2 | 9 | 4 | 7 | 3 | 1 | 5 | 8 | 6 |

**104**

| 3 | 9 | 1 | 6 | 8 | 7 | 5 | 2 | 4 |
|---|---|---|---|---|---|---|---|---|
| 6 | 5 | 4 | 1 | 9 | 2 | 3 | 8 | 7 |
| 8 | 2 | 7 | 4 | 5 | 3 | 9 | 6 | 1 |
| 5 | 1 | 3 | 2 | 4 | 8 | 7 | 9 | 6 |
| 2 | 6 | 9 | 5 | 7 | 1 | 8 | 4 | 3 |
| 7 | 4 | 8 | 3 | 6 | 9 | 2 | 1 | 5 |
| 1 | 3 | 6 | 9 | 2 | 5 | 4 | 7 | 8 |
| 4 | 7 | 2 | 8 | 3 | 6 | 1 | 5 | 9 |
| 9 | 8 | 5 | 7 | 1 | 4 | 6 | 3 | 2 |

**105**

| 5 | 8 | 6 | 9 | 7 | 2 | 4 | 3 | 1 |
| 3 | 4 | 9 | 1 | 6 | 5 | 8 | 2 | 7 |
| 2 | 7 | 1 | 4 | 3 | 8 | 9 | 6 | 5 |
| 4 | 9 | 2 | 5 | 1 | 7 | 6 | 8 | 3 |
| 8 | 3 | 7 | 2 | 9 | 6 | 1 | 5 | 4 |
| 1 | 6 | 5 | 3 | 8 | 4 | 7 | 9 | 2 |
| 6 | 5 | 3 | 7 | 4 | 9 | 2 | 1 | 8 |
| 9 | 2 | 4 | 8 | 5 | 1 | 3 | 7 | 6 |
| 7 | 1 | 8 | 6 | 2 | 3 | 5 | 4 | 9 |

**106**

| 2 | 7 | 4 | 5 | 6 | 9 | 3 | 8 | 1 |
| 6 | 9 | 3 | 7 | 8 | 1 | 5 | 2 | 4 |
| 5 | 8 | 1 | 3 | 2 | 4 | 6 | 7 | 9 |
| 9 | 1 | 6 | 8 | 7 | 3 | 2 | 4 | 5 |
| 4 | 2 | 8 | 1 | 9 | 5 | 7 | 6 | 3 |
| 7 | 3 | 5 | 2 | 4 | 6 | 9 | 1 | 8 |
| 8 | 5 | 7 | 4 | 3 | 2 | 1 | 9 | 6 |
| 3 | 6 | 2 | 9 | 1 | 8 | 4 | 5 | 7 |
| 1 | 4 | 9 | 6 | 5 | 7 | 8 | 3 | 2 |

**107**

| 3 | 7 | 2 | 8 | 5 | 9 | 4 | 1 | 6 |
| 6 | 5 | 8 | 7 | 1 | 4 | 3 | 2 | 9 |
| 9 | 4 | 1 | 2 | 6 | 3 | 5 | 7 | 8 |
| 8 | 9 | 4 | 6 | 7 | 5 | 1 | 3 | 2 |
| 5 | 3 | 7 | 1 | 9 | 2 | 6 | 8 | 4 |
| 2 | 1 | 6 | 3 | 4 | 8 | 9 | 5 | 7 |
| 1 | 6 | 3 | 9 | 2 | 7 | 8 | 4 | 5 |
| 7 | 8 | 5 | 4 | 3 | 6 | 2 | 9 | 1 |
| 4 | 2 | 9 | 5 | 8 | 1 | 7 | 6 | 3 |

**108**

| 2 | 1 | 7 | 9 | 5 | 3 | 4 | 8 | 6 |
| 9 | 8 | 4 | 2 | 7 | 6 | 3 | 1 | 5 |
| 6 | 3 | 5 | 8 | 1 | 4 | 7 | 9 | 2 |
| 3 | 4 | 9 | 6 | 2 | 1 | 5 | 7 | 8 |
| 1 | 7 | 2 | 5 | 9 | 8 | 6 | 4 | 3 |
| 5 | 6 | 8 | 3 | 4 | 7 | 9 | 2 | 1 |
| 7 | 5 | 6 | 4 | 8 | 2 | 1 | 3 | 9 |
| 4 | 2 | 3 | 1 | 6 | 9 | 8 | 5 | 7 |
| 8 | 9 | 1 | 7 | 3 | 5 | 2 | 6 | 4 |

**109**

| 9 | 3 | 1 | 6 | 7 | 5 | 4 | 8 | 2 |
| 8 | 4 | 2 | 1 | 3 | 9 | 6 | 5 | 7 |
| 7 | 6 | 5 | 4 | 2 | 8 | 3 | 1 | 9 |
| 6 | 7 | 8 | 5 | 1 | 3 | 9 | 2 | 4 |
| 4 | 2 | 9 | 8 | 6 | 7 | 1 | 3 | 5 |
| 5 | 1 | 3 | 2 | 9 | 4 | 7 | 6 | 8 |
| 2 | 5 | 6 | 9 | 4 | 1 | 8 | 7 | 3 |
| 1 | 9 | 7 | 3 | 8 | 2 | 5 | 4 | 6 |
| 3 | 8 | 4 | 7 | 5 | 6 | 2 | 9 | 1 |

**110**

| 2 | 1 | 6 | 4 | 8 | 5 | 7 | 3 | 9 |
| 7 | 9 | 8 | 1 | 2 | 3 | 5 | 6 | 4 |
| 4 | 5 | 3 | 9 | 6 | 7 | 2 | 8 | 1 |
| 5 | 3 | 9 | 7 | 1 | 6 | 4 | 2 | 8 |
| 8 | 6 | 7 | 5 | 4 | 2 | 1 | 9 | 3 |
| 1 | 2 | 4 | 3 | 9 | 8 | 6 | 7 | 5 |
| 3 | 7 | 1 | 6 | 5 | 9 | 8 | 4 | 2 |
| 6 | 4 | 2 | 8 | 3 | 1 | 9 | 5 | 7 |
| 9 | 8 | 5 | 2 | 7 | 4 | 3 | 1 | 6 |

**111**

| 9 | 5 | 6 | 3 | 4 | 1 | 7 | 8 | 2 |
| 4 | 3 | 2 | 8 | 5 | 7 | 9 | 6 | 1 |
| 8 | 1 | 7 | 9 | 6 | 2 | 3 | 5 | 4 |
| 5 | 9 | 8 | 4 | 7 | 6 | 2 | 1 | 3 |
| 7 | 4 | 1 | 2 | 8 | 3 | 5 | 9 | 6 |
| 2 | 6 | 3 | 1 | 9 | 5 | 4 | 7 | 8 |
| 6 | 8 | 9 | 5 | 2 | 4 | 1 | 3 | 7 |
| 3 | 2 | 5 | 7 | 1 | 8 | 6 | 4 | 9 |
| 1 | 7 | 4 | 6 | 3 | 9 | 8 | 2 | 5 |

**112**

| 1 | 6 | 7 | 5 | 3 | 9 | 4 | 8 | 2 |
| 4 | 5 | 9 | 8 | 6 | 2 | 3 | 7 | 1 |
| 8 | 3 | 2 | 7 | 4 | 1 | 5 | 9 | 6 |
| 3 | 1 | 4 | 2 | 9 | 7 | 8 | 6 | 5 |
| 6 | 9 | 5 | 4 | 1 | 8 | 2 | 3 | 7 |
| 7 | 2 | 8 | 6 | 5 | 3 | 1 | 4 | 9 |
| 5 | 4 | 3 | 9 | 2 | 6 | 7 | 1 | 8 |
| 2 | 7 | 6 | 1 | 8 | 4 | 9 | 5 | 3 |
| 9 | 8 | 1 | 3 | 7 | 5 | 6 | 2 | 4 |

**113**

| 5 | 4 | 9 | 7 | 8 | 1 | 3 | 2 | 6 |
|---|---|---|---|---|---|---|---|---|
| 2 | 8 | 1 | 4 | 6 | 3 | 7 | 9 | 5 |
| 7 | 6 | 3 | 2 | 5 | 9 | 1 | 8 | 4 |
| 9 | 5 | 6 | 8 | 4 | 7 | 2 | 3 | 1 |
| 8 | 1 | 2 | 9 | 3 | 6 | 4 | 5 | 7 |
| 3 | 7 | 4 | 5 | 1 | 2 | 9 | 6 | 8 |
| 4 | 9 | 5 | 3 | 7 | 8 | 6 | 1 | 2 |
| 1 | 2 | 8 | 6 | 9 | 4 | 5 | 7 | 3 |
| 6 | 3 | 7 | 1 | 2 | 5 | 8 | 4 | 9 |

**114**

| 3 | 6 | 5 | 9 | 7 | 2 | 8 | 1 | 4 |
|---|---|---|---|---|---|---|---|---|
| 2 | 1 | 9 | 8 | 4 | 6 | 3 | 5 | 7 |
| 4 | 7 | 8 | 5 | 1 | 3 | 9 | 2 | 6 |
| 1 | 8 | 7 | 6 | 2 | 4 | 5 | 9 | 3 |
| 5 | 3 | 6 | 1 | 9 | 8 | 7 | 4 | 2 |
| 9 | 2 | 4 | 7 | 3 | 5 | 6 | 8 | 1 |
| 7 | 9 | 2 | 3 | 8 | 1 | 4 | 6 | 5 |
| 6 | 4 | 3 | 2 | 5 | 9 | 1 | 7 | 8 |
| 8 | 5 | 1 | 4 | 6 | 7 | 2 | 3 | 9 |

**115**

| 2 | 3 | 9 | 6 | 4 | 5 | 7 | 1 | 8 |
|---|---|---|---|---|---|---|---|---|
| 8 | 1 | 5 | 7 | 3 | 2 | 9 | 4 | 6 |
| 7 | 6 | 4 | 1 | 8 | 9 | 2 | 5 | 3 |
| 9 | 5 | 8 | 2 | 7 | 6 | 4 | 3 | 1 |
| 1 | 7 | 2 | 3 | 5 | 4 | 6 | 8 | 9 |
| 3 | 4 | 6 | 8 | 9 | 1 | 5 | 2 | 7 |
| 5 | 8 | 3 | 9 | 2 | 7 | 1 | 6 | 4 |
| 4 | 9 | 1 | 5 | 6 | 8 | 3 | 7 | 2 |
| 6 | 2 | 7 | 4 | 1 | 3 | 8 | 9 | 5 |

**116**

| 5 | 9 | 3 | 2 | 7 | 8 | 4 | 6 | 1 |
|---|---|---|---|---|---|---|---|---|
| 6 | 4 | 7 | 3 | 9 | 1 | 8 | 5 | 2 |
| 1 | 2 | 8 | 5 | 6 | 4 | 9 | 7 | 3 |
| 4 | 6 | 5 | 7 | 8 | 3 | 2 | 1 | 9 |
| 3 | 8 | 2 | 9 | 1 | 6 | 5 | 4 | 7 |
| 9 | 7 | 1 | 4 | 5 | 2 | 6 | 3 | 8 |
| 2 | 3 | 9 | 6 | 4 | 7 | 1 | 8 | 5 |
| 7 | 1 | 4 | 8 | 2 | 5 | 3 | 9 | 6 |
| 8 | 5 | 6 | 1 | 3 | 9 | 7 | 2 | 4 |

**117**

| 4 | 6 | 2 | 1 | 8 | 5 | 3 | 9 | 7 |
|---|---|---|---|---|---|---|---|---|
| 8 | 9 | 7 | 2 | 6 | 3 | 4 | 1 | 5 |
| 5 | 1 | 3 | 7 | 4 | 9 | 8 | 2 | 6 |
| 6 | 2 | 1 | 3 | 9 | 4 | 7 | 5 | 8 |
| 9 | 3 | 5 | 6 | 7 | 8 | 1 | 4 | 2 |
| 7 | 8 | 4 | 5 | 2 | 1 | 9 | 6 | 3 |
| 2 | 4 | 9 | 8 | 3 | 6 | 5 | 7 | 1 |
| 1 | 7 | 8 | 4 | 5 | 2 | 6 | 3 | 9 |
| 3 | 5 | 6 | 9 | 1 | 7 | 2 | 8 | 4 |

**118**

| 8 | 6 | 2 | 7 | 9 | 5 | 4 | 1 | 3 |
|---|---|---|---|---|---|---|---|---|
| 7 | 4 | 1 | 3 | 8 | 2 | 5 | 9 | 6 |
| 3 | 5 | 9 | 6 | 1 | 4 | 7 | 8 | 2 |
| 5 | 2 | 7 | 1 | 6 | 3 | 8 | 4 | 9 |
| 4 | 9 | 6 | 8 | 5 | 7 | 3 | 2 | 1 |
| 1 | 8 | 3 | 2 | 4 | 9 | 6 | 7 | 5 |
| 2 | 1 | 8 | 4 | 3 | 6 | 9 | 5 | 7 |
| 6 | 7 | 5 | 9 | 2 | 8 | 1 | 3 | 4 |
| 9 | 3 | 4 | 5 | 7 | 1 | 2 | 6 | 8 |

**119**

| 9 | 7 | 1 | 4 | 5 | 2 | 8 | 6 | 3 |
|---|---|---|---|---|---|---|---|---|
| 2 | 8 | 3 | 9 | 1 | 6 | 5 | 4 | 7 |
| 5 | 4 | 6 | 3 | 7 | 8 | 9 | 1 | 2 |
| 3 | 5 | 4 | 2 | 6 | 1 | 7 | 9 | 8 |
| 1 | 2 | 9 | 7 | 8 | 3 | 4 | 5 | 6 |
| 8 | 6 | 7 | 5 | 9 | 4 | 3 | 2 | 1 |
| 7 | 9 | 8 | 1 | 2 | 5 | 6 | 3 | 4 |
| 4 | 1 | 5 | 6 | 3 | 7 | 2 | 8 | 9 |
| 6 | 3 | 2 | 8 | 4 | 9 | 1 | 7 | 5 |

**120**

| 3 | 8 | 9 | 5 | 6 | 2 | 7 | 4 | 1 |
|---|---|---|---|---|---|---|---|---|
| 5 | 2 | 4 | 1 | 9 | 7 | 3 | 6 | 8 |
| 6 | 7 | 1 | 8 | 4 | 3 | 9 | 2 | 5 |
| 9 | 1 | 6 | 4 | 3 | 8 | 5 | 7 | 2 |
| 4 | 3 | 8 | 2 | 7 | 5 | 1 | 9 | 6 |
| 2 | 5 | 7 | 6 | 1 | 9 | 8 | 3 | 4 |
| 8 | 4 | 3 | 9 | 5 | 6 | 2 | 1 | 7 |
| 1 | 9 | 2 | 7 | 8 | 4 | 6 | 5 | 3 |
| 7 | 6 | 5 | 3 | 2 | 1 | 4 | 8 | 9 |

**121**

| 5 | 9 | 3 | 1 | 2 | 7 | 4 | 8 | 6 |
| 1 | 7 | 8 | 9 | 4 | 6 | 5 | 3 | 2 |
| 6 | 4 | 2 | 5 | 8 | 3 | 1 | 7 | 9 |
| 7 | 8 | 4 | 3 | 6 | 1 | 9 | 2 | 5 |
| 9 | 6 | 1 | 2 | 5 | 8 | 7 | 4 | 3 |
| 3 | 2 | 5 | 7 | 9 | 4 | 6 | 1 | 8 |
| 2 | 5 | 7 | 8 | 1 | 9 | 3 | 6 | 4 |
| 8 | 3 | 6 | 4 | 7 | 5 | 2 | 9 | 1 |
| 4 | 1 | 9 | 6 | 3 | 2 | 8 | 5 | 7 |

**122**

| 7 | 8 | 2 | 6 | 1 | 5 | 4 | 3 | 9 |
| 5 | 4 | 9 | 2 | 3 | 8 | 6 | 7 | 1 |
| 6 | 3 | 1 | 7 | 9 | 4 | 8 | 2 | 5 |
| 1 | 6 | 4 | 9 | 5 | 2 | 3 | 8 | 7 |
| 3 | 5 | 8 | 1 | 7 | 6 | 2 | 9 | 4 |
| 2 | 9 | 7 | 8 | 4 | 3 | 5 | 1 | 6 |
| 9 | 2 | 6 | 5 | 8 | 7 | 1 | 4 | 3 |
| 4 | 1 | 5 | 3 | 2 | 9 | 7 | 6 | 8 |
| 8 | 7 | 3 | 4 | 6 | 1 | 9 | 5 | 2 |

**123**

| 6 | 4 | 2 | 9 | 3 | 8 | 5 | 7 | 1 |
| 3 | 5 | 9 | 6 | 7 | 1 | 2 | 8 | 4 |
| 8 | 7 | 1 | 5 | 2 | 4 | 6 | 9 | 3 |
| 5 | 2 | 3 | 8 | 1 | 7 | 4 | 6 | 9 |
| 4 | 6 | 7 | 2 | 5 | 9 | 3 | 1 | 8 |
| 9 | 1 | 8 | 3 | 4 | 6 | 7 | 5 | 2 |
| 1 | 8 | 5 | 4 | 6 | 2 | 9 | 3 | 7 |
| 2 | 9 | 6 | 7 | 8 | 3 | 1 | 4 | 5 |
| 7 | 3 | 4 | 1 | 9 | 5 | 8 | 2 | 6 |

**124**

| 1 | 6 | 2 | 5 | 3 | 9 | 7 | 8 | 4 |
| 9 | 7 | 5 | 6 | 8 | 4 | 3 | 1 | 2 |
| 8 | 4 | 3 | 2 | 7 | 1 | 6 | 5 | 9 |
| 5 | 9 | 4 | 1 | 6 | 3 | 2 | 7 | 8 |
| 7 | 3 | 6 | 8 | 5 | 2 | 4 | 9 | 1 |
| 2 | 8 | 1 | 9 | 4 | 7 | 5 | 6 | 3 |
| 6 | 1 | 7 | 4 | 2 | 8 | 9 | 3 | 5 |
| 3 | 2 | 9 | 7 | 1 | 5 | 8 | 4 | 6 |
| 4 | 5 | 8 | 3 | 9 | 6 | 1 | 2 | 7 |

**125**

| 2 | 8 | 4 | 1 | 3 | 6 | 7 | 5 | 9 |
| 5 | 6 | 3 | 9 | 7 | 4 | 1 | 2 | 8 |
| 7 | 1 | 9 | 2 | 8 | 5 | 3 | 4 | 6 |
| 3 | 5 | 2 | 7 | 9 | 8 | 4 | 6 | 1 |
| 6 | 4 | 8 | 3 | 5 | 1 | 2 | 9 | 7 |
| 1 | 9 | 7 | 4 | 6 | 2 | 5 | 8 | 3 |
| 8 | 7 | 5 | 6 | 4 | 3 | 9 | 1 | 2 |
| 9 | 2 | 6 | 5 | 1 | 7 | 8 | 3 | 4 |
| 4 | 3 | 1 | 8 | 2 | 9 | 6 | 7 | 5 |

**126**

| 9 | 4 | 8 | 5 | 7 | 1 | 6 | 3 | 2 |
| 7 | 2 | 6 | 8 | 3 | 4 | 9 | 1 | 5 |
| 1 | 3 | 5 | 2 | 9 | 6 | 8 | 7 | 4 |
| 8 | 6 | 7 | 1 | 5 | 3 | 4 | 2 | 9 |
| 4 | 9 | 1 | 6 | 2 | 7 | 5 | 8 | 3 |
| 2 | 5 | 3 | 9 | 4 | 8 | 7 | 6 | 1 |
| 6 | 8 | 2 | 4 | 1 | 9 | 3 | 5 | 7 |
| 5 | 7 | 9 | 3 | 6 | 2 | 1 | 4 | 8 |
| 3 | 1 | 4 | 7 | 8 | 5 | 2 | 9 | 6 |

**127**

| 9 | 4 | 2 | 6 | 7 | 8 | 1 | 5 | 3 |
| 6 | 1 | 3 | 9 | 2 | 5 | 8 | 4 | 7 |
| 5 | 8 | 7 | 1 | 3 | 4 | 9 | 6 | 2 |
| 2 | 7 | 1 | 3 | 4 | 6 | 5 | 9 | 8 |
| 8 | 5 | 9 | 2 | 1 | 7 | 4 | 3 | 6 |
| 3 | 6 | 4 | 8 | 5 | 9 | 7 | 2 | 1 |
| 4 | 2 | 5 | 7 | 6 | 1 | 3 | 8 | 9 |
| 7 | 3 | 8 | 4 | 9 | 2 | 6 | 1 | 5 |
| 1 | 9 | 6 | 5 | 8 | 3 | 2 | 7 | 4 |

**128**

| 7 | 2 | 4 | 1 | 6 | 9 | 5 | 8 | 3 |
| 9 | 6 | 5 | 3 | 4 | 8 | 1 | 2 | 7 |
| 3 | 8 | 1 | 5 | 7 | 2 | 9 | 6 | 4 |
| 6 | 4 | 2 | 8 | 3 | 5 | 7 | 9 | 1 |
| 5 | 7 | 3 | 6 | 9 | 1 | 2 | 4 | 8 |
| 8 | 1 | 9 | 4 | 2 | 7 | 6 | 3 | 5 |
| 2 | 9 | 8 | 7 | 5 | 3 | 4 | 1 | 6 |
| 1 | 5 | 6 | 9 | 8 | 4 | 3 | 7 | 2 |
| 4 | 3 | 7 | 2 | 1 | 6 | 8 | 5 | 9 |

**129**

| 2 | 5 | 7 | 6 | 1 | 8 | 3 | 9 | 4 |
|---|---|---|---|---|---|---|---|---|
| 3 | 6 | 4 | 9 | 5 | 2 | 7 | 1 | 8 |
| 1 | 9 | 8 | 3 | 7 | 4 | 2 | 5 | 6 |
| 7 | 8 | 3 | 2 | 6 | 1 | 5 | 4 | 9 |
| 9 | 1 | 5 | 8 | 4 | 7 | 6 | 3 | 2 |
| 4 | 2 | 6 | 5 | 3 | 9 | 1 | 8 | 7 |
| 5 | 4 | 1 | 7 | 9 | 6 | 8 | 2 | 3 |
| 6 | 3 | 2 | 4 | 8 | 5 | 9 | 7 | 1 |
| 8 | 7 | 9 | 1 | 2 | 3 | 4 | 6 | 5 |

**130**

| 4 | 2 | 8 | 5 | 1 | 3 | 6 | 9 | 7 |
|---|---|---|---|---|---|---|---|---|
| 9 | 6 | 1 | 8 | 2 | 7 | 5 | 4 | 3 |
| 3 | 7 | 5 | 4 | 9 | 6 | 1 | 8 | 2 |
| 1 | 5 | 6 | 9 | 8 | 2 | 7 | 3 | 4 |
| 7 | 3 | 2 | 6 | 4 | 1 | 8 | 5 | 9 |
| 8 | 9 | 4 | 3 | 7 | 5 | 2 | 1 | 6 |
| 6 | 1 | 3 | 2 | 5 | 9 | 4 | 7 | 8 |
| 2 | 8 | 7 | 1 | 3 | 4 | 9 | 6 | 5 |
| 5 | 4 | 9 | 7 | 6 | 8 | 3 | 2 | 1 |

**131**

| 6 | 3 | 1 | 5 | 9 | 4 | 8 | 2 | 7 |
|---|---|---|---|---|---|---|---|---|
| 7 | 8 | 4 | 2 | 1 | 6 | 5 | 3 | 9 |
| 9 | 5 | 2 | 7 | 3 | 8 | 1 | 4 | 6 |
| 8 | 7 | 5 | 6 | 2 | 1 | 4 | 9 | 3 |
| 3 | 1 | 9 | 8 | 4 | 7 | 2 | 6 | 5 |
| 2 | 4 | 6 | 9 | 5 | 3 | 7 | 1 | 8 |
| 1 | 9 | 3 | 4 | 7 | 5 | 6 | 8 | 2 |
| 5 | 2 | 8 | 1 | 6 | 9 | 3 | 7 | 4 |
| 4 | 6 | 7 | 3 | 8 | 2 | 9 | 5 | 1 |

**132**

| 8 | 3 | 4 | 5 | 6 | 2 | 7 | 1 | 9 |
|---|---|---|---|---|---|---|---|---|
| 5 | 1 | 2 | 3 | 7 | 9 | 4 | 6 | 8 |
| 6 | 7 | 9 | 1 | 4 | 8 | 2 | 3 | 5 |
| 4 | 8 | 1 | 7 | 9 | 3 | 5 | 2 | 6 |
| 2 | 6 | 3 | 8 | 1 | 5 | 9 | 7 | 4 |
| 7 | 9 | 5 | 6 | 2 | 4 | 1 | 8 | 3 |
| 9 | 2 | 6 | 4 | 3 | 1 | 8 | 5 | 7 |
| 1 | 5 | 7 | 9 | 8 | 6 | 3 | 4 | 2 |
| 3 | 4 | 8 | 2 | 5 | 7 | 6 | 9 | 1 |

**133**

| 4 | 9 | 3 | 2 | 8 | 7 | 6 | 5 | 1 |
|---|---|---|---|---|---|---|---|---|
| 1 | 8 | 2 | 6 | 9 | 5 | 4 | 3 | 7 |
| 7 | 5 | 6 | 3 | 1 | 4 | 2 | 8 | 9 |
| 5 | 3 | 7 | 1 | 2 | 6 | 8 | 9 | 4 |
| 2 | 1 | 9 | 8 | 4 | 3 | 5 | 7 | 6 |
| 8 | 6 | 4 | 7 | 5 | 9 | 1 | 2 | 3 |
| 3 | 4 | 5 | 9 | 6 | 8 | 7 | 1 | 2 |
| 6 | 7 | 1 | 5 | 3 | 2 | 9 | 4 | 8 |
| 9 | 2 | 8 | 4 | 7 | 1 | 3 | 6 | 5 |

**134**

| 8 | 1 | 5 | 6 | 3 | 7 | 4 | 9 | 2 |
|---|---|---|---|---|---|---|---|---|
| 6 | 3 | 4 | 8 | 9 | 2 | 1 | 7 | 5 |
| 9 | 7 | 2 | 1 | 5 | 4 | 3 | 6 | 8 |
| 3 | 8 | 1 | 9 | 2 | 5 | 6 | 4 | 7 |
| 5 | 4 | 6 | 3 | 7 | 1 | 8 | 2 | 9 |
| 2 | 9 | 7 | 4 | 8 | 6 | 5 | 3 | 1 |
| 4 | 2 | 3 | 7 | 1 | 8 | 9 | 5 | 6 |
| 1 | 5 | 9 | 2 | 6 | 3 | 7 | 8 | 4 |
| 7 | 6 | 8 | 5 | 4 | 9 | 2 | 1 | 3 |

**135**

| 7 | 2 | 5 | 9 | 1 | 6 | 4 | 8 | 3 |
|---|---|---|---|---|---|---|---|---|
| 9 | 4 | 1 | 5 | 3 | 8 | 2 | 6 | 7 |
| 3 | 6 | 8 | 7 | 4 | 2 | 1 | 9 | 5 |
| 6 | 8 | 9 | 1 | 5 | 3 | 7 | 4 | 2 |
| 1 | 7 | 4 | 6 | 2 | 9 | 5 | 3 | 8 |
| 5 | 3 | 2 | 4 | 8 | 7 | 6 | 1 | 9 |
| 4 | 5 | 3 | 8 | 7 | 1 | 9 | 2 | 6 |
| 2 | 1 | 6 | 3 | 9 | 5 | 8 | 7 | 4 |
| 8 | 9 | 7 | 2 | 6 | 4 | 3 | 5 | 1 |

**136**

| 5 | 2 | 8 | 4 | 6 | 3 | 7 | 1 | 9 |
|---|---|---|---|---|---|---|---|---|
| 9 | 6 | 4 | 5 | 1 | 7 | 8 | 3 | 2 |
| 3 | 1 | 7 | 2 | 8 | 9 | 4 | 5 | 6 |
| 7 | 8 | 3 | 6 | 2 | 5 | 1 | 9 | 4 |
| 4 | 9 | 1 | 3 | 7 | 8 | 2 | 6 | 5 |
| 6 | 5 | 2 | 1 | 9 | 4 | 3 | 7 | 8 |
| 8 | 3 | 5 | 9 | 4 | 1 | 6 | 2 | 7 |
| 2 | 4 | 9 | 7 | 3 | 6 | 5 | 8 | 1 |
| 1 | 7 | 6 | 8 | 5 | 2 | 9 | 4 | 3 |

**137**

| 8 | 3 | 6 | 9 | 4 | 2 | 5 | 7 | 1 |
| 1 | 5 | 4 | 7 | 3 | 8 | 6 | 2 | 9 |
| 2 | 9 | 7 | 1 | 5 | 6 | 4 | 3 | 8 |
| 7 | 4 | 5 | 3 | 1 | 9 | 8 | 6 | 2 |
| 3 | 1 | 2 | 8 | 6 | 4 | 9 | 5 | 7 |
| 6 | 8 | 9 | 2 | 7 | 5 | 3 | 1 | 4 |
| 4 | 6 | 8 | 5 | 2 | 1 | 7 | 9 | 3 |
| 5 | 7 | 1 | 4 | 9 | 3 | 2 | 8 | 6 |
| 9 | 2 | 3 | 6 | 8 | 7 | 1 | 4 | 5 |

**138**

| 2 | 3 | 6 | 8 | 5 | 1 | 9 | 7 | 4 |
| 5 | 7 | 9 | 4 | 2 | 3 | 6 | 1 | 8 |
| 8 | 1 | 4 | 7 | 6 | 9 | 2 | 3 | 5 |
| 6 | 5 | 7 | 9 | 3 | 4 | 8 | 2 | 1 |
| 9 | 4 | 3 | 2 | 1 | 8 | 5 | 6 | 7 |
| 1 | 8 | 2 | 5 | 7 | 6 | 3 | 4 | 9 |
| 7 | 6 | 5 | 1 | 9 | 2 | 4 | 8 | 3 |
| 4 | 2 | 1 | 3 | 8 | 5 | 7 | 9 | 6 |
| 3 | 9 | 8 | 6 | 4 | 7 | 1 | 5 | 2 |

**139**

| 6 | 5 | 9 | 7 | 3 | 4 | 2 | 8 | 1 |
| 8 | 1 | 3 | 6 | 9 | 2 | 5 | 4 | 7 |
| 7 | 4 | 2 | 5 | 1 | 8 | 6 | 9 | 3 |
| 2 | 6 | 5 | 3 | 8 | 1 | 9 | 7 | 4 |
| 9 | 8 | 4 | 2 | 6 | 7 | 1 | 3 | 5 |
| 1 | 3 | 7 | 9 | 4 | 5 | 8 | 2 | 6 |
| 3 | 2 | 6 | 1 | 7 | 9 | 4 | 5 | 8 |
| 5 | 7 | 8 | 4 | 2 | 6 | 3 | 1 | 9 |
| 4 | 9 | 1 | 8 | 5 | 3 | 7 | 6 | 2 |

**140**

| 6 | 2 | 4 | 3 | 1 | 9 | 8 | 5 | 7 |
| 9 | 3 | 7 | 2 | 8 | 5 | 1 | 6 | 4 |
| 1 | 8 | 5 | 7 | 6 | 4 | 3 | 9 | 2 |
| 5 | 1 | 9 | 6 | 7 | 8 | 2 | 4 | 3 |
| 4 | 6 | 8 | 5 | 3 | 2 | 9 | 7 | 1 |
| 2 | 7 | 3 | 9 | 4 | 1 | 5 | 8 | 6 |
| 3 | 4 | 1 | 8 | 5 | 6 | 7 | 2 | 9 |
| 7 | 5 | 2 | 4 | 9 | 3 | 6 | 1 | 8 |
| 8 | 9 | 6 | 1 | 2 | 7 | 4 | 3 | 5 |

**141**

| 7 | 3 | 8 | 1 | 5 | 6 | 9 | 4 | 2 |
| 4 | 9 | 5 | 3 | 7 | 2 | 6 | 8 | 1 |
| 2 | 1 | 6 | 4 | 9 | 8 | 5 | 3 | 7 |
| 1 | 2 | 9 | 6 | 3 | 5 | 8 | 7 | 4 |
| 8 | 6 | 4 | 7 | 2 | 9 | 1 | 5 | 3 |
| 5 | 7 | 3 | 8 | 1 | 4 | 2 | 9 | 6 |
| 9 | 8 | 7 | 2 | 4 | 1 | 3 | 6 | 5 |
| 3 | 5 | 1 | 9 | 6 | 7 | 4 | 2 | 8 |
| 6 | 4 | 2 | 5 | 8 | 3 | 7 | 1 | 9 |

**142**

| 9 | 4 | 8 | 5 | 2 | 7 | 3 | 6 | 1 |
| 5 | 7 | 3 | 6 | 4 | 1 | 9 | 8 | 2 |
| 6 | 2 | 1 | 9 | 8 | 3 | 4 | 7 | 5 |
| 8 | 3 | 4 | 7 | 1 | 6 | 5 | 2 | 9 |
| 1 | 9 | 2 | 8 | 3 | 5 | 7 | 4 | 6 |
| 7 | 5 | 6 | 4 | 9 | 2 | 1 | 3 | 8 |
| 4 | 6 | 5 | 1 | 7 | 8 | 2 | 9 | 3 |
| 2 | 8 | 9 | 3 | 5 | 4 | 6 | 1 | 7 |
| 3 | 1 | 7 | 2 | 6 | 9 | 8 | 5 | 4 |

**143**

| 4 | 9 | 3 | 1 | 2 | 5 | 6 | 8 | 7 |
| 7 | 1 | 8 | 9 | 3 | 6 | 5 | 2 | 4 |
| 5 | 2 | 6 | 7 | 8 | 4 | 9 | 1 | 3 |
| 9 | 5 | 1 | 8 | 7 | 3 | 2 | 4 | 6 |
| 3 | 8 | 7 | 4 | 6 | 2 | 1 | 9 | 5 |
| 2 | 6 | 4 | 5 | 9 | 1 | 7 | 3 | 8 |
| 6 | 7 | 2 | 3 | 1 | 8 | 4 | 5 | 9 |
| 8 | 4 | 9 | 2 | 5 | 7 | 3 | 6 | 1 |
| 1 | 3 | 5 | 6 | 4 | 9 | 8 | 7 | 2 |

**144**

| 4 | 8 | 1 | 2 | 3 | 7 | 5 | 9 | 6 |
| 3 | 5 | 7 | 6 | 4 | 9 | 1 | 2 | 8 |
| 2 | 6 | 9 | 5 | 8 | 1 | 4 | 7 | 3 |
| 9 | 1 | 8 | 3 | 5 | 4 | 2 | 6 | 7 |
| 5 | 2 | 6 | 7 | 9 | 8 | 3 | 4 | 1 |
| 7 | 4 | 3 | 1 | 6 | 2 | 8 | 5 | 9 |
| 8 | 7 | 4 | 9 | 1 | 5 | 6 | 3 | 2 |
| 6 | 9 | 5 | 8 | 2 | 3 | 7 | 1 | 4 |
| 1 | 3 | 2 | 4 | 7 | 6 | 9 | 8 | 5 |

**145**

| 1 | 9 | 4 | 6 | 5 | 7 | 3 | 2 | 8 |
| 7 | 2 | 8 | 9 | 4 | 3 | 6 | 5 | 1 |
| 6 | 5 | 3 | 2 | 8 | 1 | 4 | 7 | 9 |
| 2 | 4 | 7 | 1 | 3 | 6 | 8 | 9 | 5 |
| 9 | 1 | 6 | 5 | 2 | 8 | 7 | 4 | 3 |
| 3 | 8 | 5 | 7 | 9 | 4 | 2 | 1 | 6 |
| 8 | 7 | 2 | 3 | 1 | 9 | 5 | 6 | 4 |
| 5 | 3 | 1 | 4 | 6 | 2 | 9 | 8 | 7 |
| 4 | 6 | 9 | 8 | 7 | 5 | 1 | 3 | 2 |

**146**

| 2 | 6 | 3 | 9 | 4 | 5 | 8 | 1 | 7 |
| 4 | 9 | 8 | 2 | 1 | 7 | 5 | 6 | 3 |
| 1 | 7 | 5 | 3 | 8 | 6 | 4 | 2 | 9 |
| 3 | 2 | 1 | 6 | 9 | 8 | 7 | 5 | 4 |
| 9 | 5 | 4 | 1 | 7 | 2 | 3 | 8 | 6 |
| 6 | 8 | 7 | 4 | 5 | 3 | 2 | 9 | 1 |
| 8 | 4 | 2 | 7 | 6 | 9 | 1 | 3 | 5 |
| 7 | 3 | 9 | 5 | 2 | 1 | 6 | 4 | 8 |
| 5 | 1 | 6 | 8 | 3 | 4 | 9 | 7 | 2 |

**147**

| 1 | 7 | 9 | 8 | 2 | 4 | 3 | 6 | 5 |
| 8 | 3 | 4 | 9 | 5 | 6 | 7 | 1 | 2 |
| 5 | 6 | 2 | 7 | 1 | 3 | 4 | 9 | 8 |
| 6 | 2 | 7 | 1 | 9 | 8 | 5 | 4 | 3 |
| 9 | 8 | 5 | 4 | 3 | 2 | 1 | 7 | 6 |
| 3 | 4 | 1 | 6 | 7 | 5 | 8 | 2 | 9 |
| 7 | 9 | 3 | 2 | 8 | 1 | 6 | 5 | 4 |
| 4 | 1 | 8 | 5 | 6 | 9 | 2 | 3 | 7 |
| 2 | 5 | 6 | 3 | 4 | 7 | 9 | 8 | 1 |

**148**

| 1 | 9 | 6 | 2 | 4 | 7 | 3 | 8 | 5 |
| 3 | 4 | 5 | 9 | 6 | 8 | 2 | 1 | 7 |
| 2 | 8 | 7 | 3 | 1 | 5 | 9 | 4 | 6 |
| 8 | 5 | 3 | 1 | 7 | 2 | 6 | 9 | 4 |
| 6 | 7 | 1 | 8 | 9 | 4 | 5 | 3 | 2 |
| 4 | 2 | 9 | 6 | 5 | 3 | 1 | 7 | 8 |
| 5 | 3 | 4 | 7 | 2 | 1 | 8 | 6 | 9 |
| 7 | 6 | 8 | 5 | 3 | 9 | 4 | 2 | 1 |
| 9 | 1 | 2 | 4 | 8 | 6 | 7 | 5 | 3 |

**149**

| 5 | 2 | 9 | 3 | 1 | 4 | 6 | 8 | 7 |
| 7 | 3 | 6 | 9 | 2 | 8 | 1 | 4 | 5 |
| 4 | 8 | 1 | 5 | 7 | 6 | 3 | 9 | 2 |
| 8 | 1 | 2 | 4 | 5 | 9 | 7 | 6 | 3 |
| 9 | 5 | 4 | 7 | 6 | 3 | 8 | 2 | 1 |
| 3 | 6 | 7 | 1 | 8 | 2 | 9 | 5 | 4 |
| 2 | 9 | 5 | 6 | 3 | 1 | 4 | 7 | 8 |
| 1 | 4 | 8 | 2 | 9 | 7 | 5 | 3 | 6 |
| 6 | 7 | 3 | 8 | 4 | 5 | 2 | 1 | 9 |

**150**

| 4 | 8 | 5 | 7 | 1 | 6 | 9 | 3 | 2 |
| 6 | 2 | 7 | 4 | 9 | 3 | 1 | 5 | 8 |
| 3 | 9 | 1 | 8 | 2 | 5 | 6 | 4 | 7 |
| 2 | 4 | 6 | 9 | 5 | 8 | 3 | 7 | 1 |
| 9 | 1 | 3 | 2 | 6 | 7 | 5 | 8 | 4 |
| 7 | 5 | 8 | 3 | 4 | 1 | 2 | 6 | 9 |
| 5 | 6 | 4 | 1 | 8 | 2 | 7 | 9 | 3 |
| 1 | 3 | 9 | 6 | 7 | 4 | 8 | 2 | 5 |
| 8 | 7 | 2 | 5 | 3 | 9 | 4 | 1 | 6 |

**151**

| 4 | 5 | 6 | 2 | 9 | 7 | 1 | 3 | 8 |
| 7 | 9 | 3 | 4 | 8 | 1 | 6 | 5 | 2 |
| 1 | 8 | 2 | 6 | 3 | 5 | 7 | 9 | 4 |
| 8 | 4 | 1 | 5 | 7 | 6 | 9 | 2 | 3 |
| 2 | 7 | 9 | 3 | 4 | 8 | 5 | 6 | 1 |
| 6 | 3 | 5 | 1 | 2 | 9 | 8 | 4 | 7 |
| 5 | 2 | 8 | 7 | 6 | 3 | 4 | 1 | 9 |
| 9 | 6 | 4 | 8 | 1 | 2 | 3 | 7 | 5 |
| 3 | 1 | 7 | 9 | 5 | 4 | 2 | 8 | 6 |

**152**

| 6 | 5 | 4 | 2 | 9 | 3 | 1 | 8 | 7 |
| 1 | 7 | 8 | 4 | 5 | 6 | 2 | 3 | 9 |
| 3 | 2 | 9 | 7 | 1 | 8 | 5 | 6 | 4 |
| 8 | 1 | 6 | 9 | 4 | 2 | 7 | 5 | 3 |
| 2 | 4 | 5 | 3 | 7 | 1 | 6 | 9 | 8 |
| 9 | 3 | 7 | 6 | 8 | 5 | 4 | 2 | 1 |
| 4 | 9 | 3 | 5 | 2 | 7 | 8 | 1 | 6 |
| 7 | 8 | 2 | 1 | 6 | 9 | 3 | 4 | 5 |
| 5 | 6 | 1 | 8 | 3 | 4 | 9 | 7 | 2 |

**153**

| 8 | 7 | 3 | 2 | 4 | 9 | 1 | 6 | 5 |
|---|---|---|---|---|---|---|---|---|
| 2 | 9 | 5 | 6 | 8 | 1 | 7 | 3 | 4 |
| 6 | 1 | 4 | 7 | 3 | 5 | 9 | 2 | 8 |
| 3 | 5 | 1 | 4 | 7 | 8 | 2 | 9 | 6 |
| 4 | 6 | 2 | 1 | 9 | 3 | 5 | 8 | 7 |
| 7 | 8 | 9 | 5 | 2 | 6 | 4 | 1 | 3 |
| 9 | 2 | 8 | 3 | 5 | 7 | 6 | 4 | 1 |
| 1 | 3 | 7 | 9 | 6 | 4 | 8 | 5 | 2 |
| 5 | 4 | 6 | 8 | 1 | 2 | 3 | 7 | 9 |

**154**

| 3 | 4 | 7 | 2 | 1 | 9 | 5 | 8 | 6 |
|---|---|---|---|---|---|---|---|---|
| 6 | 5 | 9 | 4 | 7 | 8 | 1 | 3 | 2 |
| 8 | 2 | 1 | 5 | 6 | 3 | 4 | 7 | 9 |
| 1 | 9 | 3 | 7 | 2 | 6 | 8 | 4 | 5 |
| 7 | 6 | 5 | 1 | 8 | 4 | 2 | 9 | 3 |
| 4 | 8 | 2 | 9 | 3 | 5 | 7 | 6 | 1 |
| 2 | 7 | 4 | 6 | 9 | 1 | 3 | 5 | 8 |
| 9 | 1 | 8 | 3 | 5 | 7 | 6 | 2 | 4 |
| 5 | 3 | 6 | 8 | 4 | 2 | 9 | 1 | 7 |

**155**

| 3 | 2 | 7 | 4 | 5 | 8 | 6 | 1 | 9 |
|---|---|---|---|---|---|---|---|---|
| 4 | 8 | 6 | 3 | 9 | 1 | 5 | 7 | 2 |
| 9 | 1 | 5 | 7 | 2 | 6 | 8 | 3 | 4 |
| 7 | 5 | 1 | 9 | 6 | 3 | 2 | 4 | 8 |
| 2 | 3 | 8 | 1 | 4 | 5 | 9 | 6 | 7 |
| 6 | 4 | 9 | 8 | 7 | 2 | 1 | 5 | 3 |
| 5 | 7 | 4 | 6 | 8 | 9 | 3 | 2 | 1 |
| 1 | 9 | 2 | 5 | 3 | 7 | 4 | 8 | 6 |
| 8 | 6 | 3 | 2 | 1 | 4 | 7 | 9 | 5 |

**156**

| 1 | 5 | 2 | 9 | 8 | 7 | 4 | 3 | 6 |
|---|---|---|---|---|---|---|---|---|
| 9 | 4 | 3 | 1 | 5 | 6 | 2 | 8 | 7 |
| 8 | 6 | 7 | 4 | 3 | 2 | 9 | 5 | 1 |
| 6 | 1 | 5 | 2 | 7 | 9 | 8 | 4 | 3 |
| 7 | 3 | 9 | 5 | 4 | 8 | 6 | 1 | 2 |
| 2 | 8 | 4 | 6 | 1 | 3 | 5 | 7 | 9 |
| 5 | 2 | 8 | 3 | 6 | 1 | 7 | 9 | 4 |
| 3 | 7 | 6 | 8 | 9 | 4 | 1 | 2 | 5 |
| 4 | 9 | 1 | 7 | 2 | 5 | 3 | 6 | 8 |

**157**

| 2 | 1 | 8 | 4 | 9 | 5 | 6 | 3 | 7 |
|---|---|---|---|---|---|---|---|---|
| 6 | 3 | 9 | 8 | 1 | 7 | 2 | 5 | 4 |
| 5 | 4 | 7 | 6 | 3 | 2 | 9 | 8 | 1 |
| 4 | 6 | 3 | 1 | 7 | 8 | 5 | 9 | 2 |
| 1 | 9 | 2 | 3 | 5 | 4 | 8 | 7 | 6 |
| 7 | 8 | 5 | 9 | 2 | 6 | 4 | 1 | 3 |
| 8 | 2 | 1 | 7 | 6 | 9 | 3 | 4 | 5 |
| 3 | 5 | 4 | 2 | 8 | 1 | 7 | 6 | 9 |
| 9 | 7 | 6 | 5 | 4 | 3 | 1 | 2 | 8 |

**158**

| 5 | 3 | 4 | 1 | 7 | 9 | 8 | 2 | 6 |
|---|---|---|---|---|---|---|---|---|
| 7 | 9 | 6 | 5 | 8 | 2 | 3 | 4 | 1 |
| 2 | 1 | 8 | 6 | 4 | 3 | 9 | 5 | 7 |
| 6 | 4 | 2 | 9 | 3 | 8 | 1 | 7 | 5 |
| 3 | 7 | 1 | 4 | 5 | 6 | 2 | 9 | 8 |
| 9 | 8 | 5 | 2 | 1 | 7 | 4 | 6 | 3 |
| 8 | 6 | 3 | 7 | 2 | 4 | 5 | 1 | 9 |
| 4 | 5 | 9 | 8 | 6 | 1 | 7 | 3 | 2 |
| 1 | 2 | 7 | 3 | 9 | 5 | 6 | 8 | 4 |

**159**

| 6 | 3 | 1 | 5 | 4 | 9 | 7 | 8 | 2 |
|---|---|---|---|---|---|---|---|---|
| 5 | 9 | 2 | 1 | 7 | 8 | 3 | 4 | 6 |
| 7 | 4 | 8 | 3 | 6 | 2 | 9 | 1 | 5 |
| 2 | 1 | 4 | 9 | 8 | 5 | 6 | 7 | 3 |
| 9 | 7 | 3 | 2 | 1 | 6 | 4 | 5 | 8 |
| 8 | 5 | 6 | 7 | 3 | 4 | 2 | 9 | 1 |
| 4 | 8 | 7 | 6 | 5 | 3 | 1 | 2 | 9 |
| 3 | 2 | 5 | 4 | 9 | 1 | 8 | 6 | 7 |
| 1 | 6 | 9 | 8 | 2 | 7 | 5 | 3 | 4 |

**160**

| 7 | 8 | 1 | 9 | 2 | 3 | 6 | 5 | 4 |
|---|---|---|---|---|---|---|---|---|
| 4 | 3 | 2 | 7 | 5 | 6 | 8 | 9 | 1 |
| 9 | 6 | 5 | 4 | 1 | 8 | 7 | 3 | 2 |
| 1 | 4 | 7 | 3 | 9 | 5 | 2 | 6 | 8 |
| 8 | 2 | 9 | 1 | 6 | 7 | 3 | 4 | 5 |
| 6 | 5 | 3 | 8 | 4 | 2 | 1 | 7 | 9 |
| 5 | 1 | 8 | 6 | 3 | 9 | 4 | 2 | 7 |
| 3 | 9 | 4 | 2 | 7 | 1 | 5 | 8 | 6 |
| 2 | 7 | 6 | 5 | 8 | 4 | 9 | 1 | 3 |

**161**

| 5 | 1 | 4 | 9 | 7 | 3 | 8 | 2 | 6 |
| 2 | 3 | 6 | 5 | 1 | 8 | 4 | 7 | 9 |
| 7 | 8 | 9 | 6 | 4 | 2 | 1 | 3 | 5 |
| 9 | 2 | 8 | 7 | 3 | 5 | 6 | 4 | 1 |
| 6 | 4 | 5 | 1 | 2 | 9 | 3 | 8 | 7 |
| 3 | 7 | 1 | 4 | 8 | 6 | 5 | 9 | 2 |
| 1 | 9 | 3 | 2 | 6 | 4 | 7 | 5 | 8 |
| 4 | 6 | 2 | 8 | 5 | 7 | 9 | 1 | 3 |
| 8 | 5 | 7 | 3 | 9 | 1 | 2 | 6 | 4 |

**162**

| 6 | 2 | 3 | 1 | 9 | 7 | 5 | 8 | 4 |
| 5 | 4 | 1 | 3 | 8 | 2 | 9 | 7 | 6 |
| 8 | 7 | 9 | 4 | 6 | 5 | 1 | 2 | 3 |
| 9 | 6 | 8 | 2 | 4 | 1 | 3 | 5 | 7 |
| 1 | 3 | 2 | 7 | 5 | 8 | 4 | 6 | 9 |
| 4 | 5 | 7 | 9 | 3 | 6 | 8 | 1 | 2 |
| 2 | 9 | 6 | 8 | 1 | 4 | 7 | 3 | 5 |
| 3 | 8 | 5 | 6 | 7 | 9 | 2 | 4 | 1 |
| 7 | 1 | 4 | 5 | 2 | 3 | 6 | 9 | 8 |

**163**

| 6 | 8 | 4 | 7 | 5 | 1 | 2 | 3 | 9 |
| 3 | 9 | 5 | 6 | 2 | 8 | 1 | 7 | 4 |
| 1 | 7 | 2 | 4 | 3 | 9 | 6 | 8 | 5 |
| 8 | 3 | 7 | 1 | 6 | 5 | 4 | 9 | 2 |
| 5 | 4 | 6 | 8 | 9 | 2 | 7 | 1 | 3 |
| 2 | 1 | 9 | 3 | 7 | 4 | 8 | 5 | 6 |
| 7 | 5 | 3 | 2 | 1 | 6 | 9 | 4 | 8 |
| 4 | 6 | 1 | 9 | 8 | 3 | 5 | 2 | 7 |
| 9 | 2 | 8 | 5 | 4 | 7 | 3 | 6 | 1 |

**164**

| 3 | 6 | 7 | 2 | 1 | 8 | 9 | 5 | 4 |
| 9 | 4 | 2 | 5 | 7 | 6 | 8 | 1 | 3 |
| 5 | 1 | 8 | 3 | 9 | 4 | 2 | 7 | 6 |
| 6 | 5 | 3 | 9 | 2 | 1 | 7 | 4 | 8 |
| 8 | 2 | 1 | 4 | 3 | 7 | 5 | 6 | 9 |
| 4 | 7 | 9 | 6 | 8 | 5 | 3 | 2 | 1 |
| 7 | 8 | 6 | 1 | 5 | 9 | 4 | 3 | 2 |
| 1 | 3 | 5 | 8 | 4 | 2 | 6 | 9 | 7 |
| 2 | 9 | 4 | 7 | 6 | 3 | 1 | 8 | 5 |

**165**

| 6 | 1 | 2 | 8 | 7 | 5 | 3 | 9 | 4 |
| 9 | 4 | 3 | 2 | 1 | 6 | 5 | 8 | 7 |
| 8 | 7 | 5 | 3 | 4 | 9 | 1 | 6 | 2 |
| 5 | 6 | 9 | 1 | 8 | 4 | 2 | 7 | 3 |
| 2 | 8 | 7 | 9 | 5 | 3 | 6 | 4 | 1 |
| 1 | 3 | 4 | 7 | 6 | 2 | 8 | 5 | 9 |
| 3 | 5 | 1 | 4 | 9 | 8 | 7 | 2 | 6 |
| 4 | 2 | 8 | 6 | 3 | 7 | 9 | 1 | 5 |
| 7 | 9 | 6 | 5 | 2 | 1 | 4 | 3 | 8 |

**166**

| 8 | 5 | 4 | 1 | 3 | 6 | 2 | 9 | 7 |
| 6 | 1 | 9 | 7 | 4 | 2 | 3 | 8 | 5 |
| 3 | 7 | 2 | 5 | 9 | 8 | 1 | 4 | 6 |
| 9 | 4 | 1 | 8 | 5 | 3 | 7 | 6 | 2 |
| 2 | 6 | 3 | 9 | 7 | 1 | 4 | 5 | 8 |
| 5 | 8 | 7 | 6 | 2 | 4 | 9 | 1 | 3 |
| 4 | 9 | 6 | 2 | 8 | 7 | 5 | 3 | 1 |
| 1 | 2 | 5 | 3 | 6 | 9 | 8 | 7 | 4 |
| 7 | 3 | 8 | 4 | 1 | 5 | 6 | 2 | 9 |

**167**

| 4 | 2 | 1 | 5 | 6 | 3 | 8 | 9 | 7 |
| 6 | 3 | 7 | 9 | 8 | 2 | 4 | 1 | 5 |
| 8 | 9 | 5 | 1 | 7 | 4 | 2 | 3 | 6 |
| 5 | 7 | 3 | 6 | 1 | 8 | 9 | 2 | 4 |
| 9 | 6 | 2 | 4 | 3 | 7 | 1 | 5 | 8 |
| 1 | 4 | 8 | 2 | 9 | 5 | 6 | 7 | 3 |
| 3 | 5 | 4 | 8 | 2 | 9 | 7 | 6 | 1 |
| 2 | 8 | 6 | 7 | 5 | 1 | 3 | 4 | 9 |
| 7 | 1 | 9 | 3 | 4 | 6 | 5 | 8 | 2 |

**168**

| 8 | 2 | 9 | 7 | 4 | 5 | 1 | 6 | 3 |
| 6 | 5 | 4 | 8 | 3 | 1 | 9 | 7 | 2 |
| 7 | 3 | 1 | 6 | 9 | 2 | 5 | 8 | 4 |
| 9 | 4 | 6 | 1 | 5 | 7 | 3 | 2 | 8 |
| 3 | 7 | 8 | 9 | 2 | 4 | 6 | 1 | 5 |
| 5 | 1 | 2 | 3 | 8 | 6 | 7 | 4 | 9 |
| 2 | 6 | 3 | 4 | 7 | 9 | 8 | 5 | 1 |
| 4 | 9 | 7 | 5 | 1 | 8 | 2 | 3 | 6 |
| 1 | 8 | 5 | 2 | 6 | 3 | 4 | 9 | 7 |

**169**

| 3 | 7 | 2 | 6 | 4 | 9 | 8 | 5 | 1 |
|---|---|---|---|---|---|---|---|---|
| 1 | 4 | 5 | 2 | 7 | 8 | 6 | 3 | 9 |
| 9 | 6 | 8 | 3 | 1 | 5 | 7 | 4 | 2 |
| 2 | 1 | 7 | 5 | 6 | 4 | 9 | 8 | 3 |
| 4 | 9 | 6 | 8 | 3 | 1 | 2 | 7 | 5 |
| 5 | 8 | 3 | 9 | 2 | 7 | 4 | 1 | 6 |
| 8 | 5 | 4 | 1 | 9 | 2 | 3 | 6 | 7 |
| 7 | 3 | 9 | 4 | 5 | 6 | 1 | 2 | 8 |
| 6 | 2 | 1 | 7 | 8 | 3 | 5 | 9 | 4 |

**170**

| 5 | 4 | 2 | 8 | 7 | 1 | 6 | 9 | 3 |
|---|---|---|---|---|---|---|---|---|
| 8 | 7 | 3 | 4 | 6 | 9 | 5 | 2 | 1 |
| 1 | 6 | 9 | 2 | 5 | 3 | 4 | 7 | 8 |
| 3 | 1 | 8 | 9 | 4 | 2 | 7 | 6 | 5 |
| 2 | 5 | 6 | 3 | 1 | 7 | 8 | 4 | 9 |
| 7 | 9 | 4 | 6 | 8 | 5 | 3 | 1 | 2 |
| 6 | 3 | 7 | 1 | 2 | 8 | 9 | 5 | 4 |
| 9 | 2 | 5 | 7 | 3 | 4 | 1 | 8 | 6 |
| 4 | 8 | 1 | 5 | 9 | 6 | 2 | 3 | 7 |

**171**

| 7 | 1 | 8 | 6 | 2 | 4 | 3 | 9 | 5 |
|---|---|---|---|---|---|---|---|---|
| 2 | 3 | 9 | 1 | 7 | 5 | 6 | 8 | 4 |
| 6 | 5 | 4 | 8 | 9 | 3 | 2 | 7 | 1 |
| 5 | 7 | 3 | 4 | 8 | 9 | 1 | 6 | 2 |
| 9 | 8 | 1 | 2 | 5 | 6 | 7 | 4 | 3 |
| 4 | 6 | 2 | 3 | 1 | 7 | 8 | 5 | 9 |
| 1 | 4 | 5 | 7 | 3 | 8 | 9 | 2 | 6 |
| 8 | 2 | 6 | 9 | 4 | 1 | 5 | 3 | 7 |
| 3 | 9 | 7 | 5 | 6 | 2 | 4 | 1 | 8 |

**172**

| 8 | 2 | 3 | 6 | 4 | 1 | 7 | 9 | 5 |
|---|---|---|---|---|---|---|---|---|
| 5 | 4 | 9 | 8 | 2 | 7 | 3 | 1 | 6 |
| 7 | 6 | 1 | 9 | 5 | 3 | 2 | 4 | 8 |
| 4 | 3 | 7 | 2 | 9 | 5 | 6 | 8 | 1 |
| 6 | 9 | 2 | 3 | 1 | 8 | 4 | 5 | 7 |
| 1 | 8 | 5 | 7 | 6 | 4 | 9 | 2 | 3 |
| 2 | 5 | 4 | 1 | 7 | 6 | 8 | 3 | 9 |
| 9 | 7 | 8 | 5 | 3 | 2 | 1 | 6 | 4 |
| 3 | 1 | 6 | 4 | 8 | 9 | 5 | 7 | 2 |

**173**

| 7 | 4 | 2 | 8 | 3 | 5 | 6 | 9 | 1 |
|---|---|---|---|---|---|---|---|---|
| 1 | 9 | 3 | 7 | 6 | 4 | 2 | 5 | 8 |
| 5 | 6 | 8 | 9 | 2 | 1 | 7 | 3 | 4 |
| 2 | 5 | 9 | 4 | 1 | 3 | 8 | 6 | 7 |
| 8 | 7 | 1 | 6 | 9 | 2 | 3 | 4 | 5 |
| 4 | 3 | 6 | 5 | 8 | 7 | 9 | 1 | 2 |
| 9 | 1 | 4 | 3 | 7 | 8 | 5 | 2 | 6 |
| 3 | 8 | 5 | 2 | 4 | 6 | 1 | 7 | 9 |
| 6 | 2 | 7 | 1 | 5 | 9 | 4 | 8 | 3 |

**174**

| 4 | 1 | 2 | 3 | 6 | 5 | 9 | 8 | 7 |
|---|---|---|---|---|---|---|---|---|
| 3 | 6 | 5 | 9 | 8 | 7 | 2 | 4 | 1 |
| 8 | 9 | 7 | 1 | 4 | 2 | 6 | 3 | 5 |
| 1 | 7 | 6 | 4 | 2 | 3 | 5 | 9 | 8 |
| 5 | 3 | 9 | 8 | 7 | 1 | 4 | 6 | 2 |
| 2 | 8 | 4 | 6 | 5 | 9 | 1 | 7 | 3 |
| 9 | 2 | 3 | 7 | 1 | 6 | 8 | 5 | 4 |
| 6 | 5 | 8 | 2 | 3 | 4 | 7 | 1 | 9 |
| 7 | 4 | 1 | 5 | 9 | 8 | 3 | 2 | 6 |

**175**

| 8 | 1 | 7 | 3 | 6 | 9 | 4 | 5 | 2 |
|---|---|---|---|---|---|---|---|---|
| 4 | 9 | 3 | 5 | 2 | 7 | 1 | 6 | 8 |
| 5 | 6 | 2 | 8 | 1 | 4 | 9 | 3 | 7 |
| 7 | 8 | 6 | 2 | 5 | 1 | 3 | 4 | 9 |
| 1 | 3 | 9 | 4 | 7 | 8 | 6 | 2 | 5 |
| 2 | 5 | 4 | 6 | 9 | 3 | 7 | 8 | 1 |
| 6 | 4 | 1 | 7 | 8 | 2 | 5 | 9 | 3 |
| 9 | 2 | 5 | 1 | 3 | 6 | 8 | 7 | 4 |
| 3 | 7 | 8 | 9 | 4 | 5 | 2 | 1 | 6 |

**176**

| 1 | 2 | 4 | 8 | 3 | 9 | 7 | 6 | 5 |
|---|---|---|---|---|---|---|---|---|
| 6 | 5 | 9 | 2 | 4 | 7 | 8 | 3 | 1 |
| 7 | 8 | 3 | 6 | 1 | 5 | 2 | 9 | 4 |
| 8 | 7 | 6 | 1 | 9 | 4 | 3 | 5 | 2 |
| 9 | 1 | 5 | 3 | 2 | 6 | 4 | 8 | 7 |
| 3 | 4 | 2 | 5 | 7 | 8 | 6 | 1 | 9 |
| 4 | 9 | 1 | 7 | 6 | 3 | 5 | 2 | 8 |
| 5 | 3 | 7 | 9 | 8 | 2 | 1 | 4 | 6 |
| 2 | 6 | 8 | 4 | 5 | 1 | 9 | 7 | 3 |

**177**

**177**

| 6 | 8 | 1 | 5 | 7 | 3 | 2 | 9 | 4 |
|---|---|---|---|---|---|---|---|---|
| 5 | 3 | 2 | 8 | 9 | 4 | 7 | 6 | 1 |
| 7 | 9 | 4 | 6 | 2 | 1 | 8 | 3 | 5 |
| 8 | 4 | 9 | 3 | 6 | 5 | 1 | 7 | 2 |
| 1 | 2 | 7 | 4 | 8 | 9 | 6 | 5 | 3 |
| 3 | 6 | 5 | 7 | 1 | 2 | 4 | 8 | 9 |
| 4 | 5 | 8 | 1 | 3 | 6 | 9 | 2 | 7 |
| 9 | 1 | 6 | 2 | 5 | 7 | 3 | 4 | 8 |
| 2 | 7 | 3 | 9 | 4 | 8 | 5 | 1 | 6 |

**178**

| 3 | 6 | 2 | 7 | 4 | 5 | 8 | 9 | 1 |
|---|---|---|---|---|---|---|---|---|
| 5 | 1 | 7 | 8 | 9 | 3 | 4 | 6 | 2 |
| 4 | 8 | 9 | 6 | 1 | 2 | 7 | 3 | 5 |
| 8 | 2 | 6 | 3 | 5 | 7 | 9 | 1 | 4 |
| 1 | 9 | 3 | 2 | 6 | 4 | 5 | 8 | 7 |
| 7 | 5 | 4 | 9 | 8 | 1 | 3 | 2 | 6 |
| 6 | 3 | 5 | 1 | 7 | 8 | 2 | 4 | 9 |
| 9 | 7 | 8 | 4 | 2 | 6 | 1 | 5 | 3 |
| 2 | 4 | 1 | 5 | 3 | 9 | 6 | 7 | 8 |

**179**

| 6 | 7 | 8 | 5 | 9 | 4 | 1 | 3 | 2 |
|---|---|---|---|---|---|---|---|---|
| 3 | 2 | 5 | 8 | 6 | 1 | 4 | 9 | 7 |
| 9 | 1 | 4 | 2 | 3 | 7 | 6 | 5 | 8 |
| 2 | 6 | 7 | 9 | 1 | 3 | 8 | 4 | 5 |
| 5 | 8 | 9 | 7 | 4 | 2 | 3 | 1 | 6 |
| 1 | 4 | 3 | 6 | 5 | 8 | 2 | 7 | 9 |
| 8 | 9 | 1 | 3 | 2 | 5 | 7 | 6 | 4 |
| 7 | 3 | 6 | 4 | 8 | 9 | 5 | 2 | 1 |
| 4 | 5 | 2 | 1 | 7 | 6 | 9 | 8 | 3 |

**180**

| 5 | 8 | 4 | 6 | 7 | 3 | 2 | 9 | 1 |
|---|---|---|---|---|---|---|---|---|
| 7 | 1 | 2 | 4 | 5 | 9 | 8 | 3 | 6 |
| 6 | 3 | 9 | 1 | 8 | 2 | 4 | 7 | 5 |
| 8 | 5 | 1 | 3 | 6 | 7 | 9 | 2 | 4 |
| 2 | 6 | 7 | 9 | 4 | 1 | 5 | 8 | 3 |
| 4 | 9 | 3 | 8 | 2 | 5 | 6 | 1 | 7 |
| 1 | 4 | 6 | 7 | 9 | 8 | 3 | 5 | 2 |
| 9 | 7 | 5 | 2 | 3 | 4 | 1 | 6 | 8 |
| 3 | 2 | 8 | 5 | 1 | 6 | 7 | 4 | 9 |

**181**

| 9 | 4 | 1 | 8 | 3 | 7 | 2 | 5 | 6 |
|---|---|---|---|---|---|---|---|---|
| 5 | 3 | 7 | 6 | 2 | 4 | 1 | 8 | 9 |
| 6 | 8 | 2 | 9 | 1 | 5 | 7 | 4 | 3 |
| 8 | 7 | 6 | 2 | 5 | 1 | 3 | 9 | 4 |
| 3 | 5 | 4 | 7 | 6 | 9 | 8 | 2 | 1 |
| 1 | 2 | 9 | 3 | 4 | 8 | 5 | 6 | 7 |
| 4 | 6 | 5 | 1 | 8 | 3 | 9 | 7 | 2 |
| 7 | 1 | 8 | 4 | 9 | 2 | 6 | 3 | 5 |
| 2 | 9 | 3 | 5 | 7 | 6 | 4 | 1 | 8 |

**182**

| 8 | 2 | 5 | 1 | 7 | 3 | 6 | 9 | 4 |
|---|---|---|---|---|---|---|---|---|
| 1 | 3 | 4 | 8 | 9 | 6 | 5 | 2 | 7 |
| 9 | 7 | 6 | 2 | 5 | 4 | 8 | 1 | 3 |
| 7 | 9 | 8 | 4 | 3 | 5 | 2 | 6 | 1 |
| 3 | 6 | 2 | 7 | 1 | 9 | 4 | 8 | 5 |
| 4 | 5 | 1 | 6 | 8 | 2 | 3 | 7 | 9 |
| 5 | 8 | 3 | 9 | 6 | 7 | 1 | 4 | 2 |
| 2 | 1 | 9 | 3 | 4 | 8 | 7 | 5 | 6 |
| 6 | 4 | 7 | 5 | 2 | 1 | 9 | 3 | 8 |

**183**

| 5 | 6 | 8 | 2 | 1 | 4 | 7 | 9 | 3 |
|---|---|---|---|---|---|---|---|---|
| 1 | 2 | 7 | 8 | 3 | 9 | 4 | 6 | 5 |
| 9 | 4 | 3 | 6 | 7 | 5 | 8 | 2 | 1 |
| 2 | 7 | 6 | 4 | 8 | 1 | 5 | 3 | 9 |
| 3 | 8 | 9 | 7 | 5 | 6 | 2 | 1 | 4 |
| 4 | 5 | 1 | 9 | 2 | 3 | 6 | 7 | 8 |
| 7 | 3 | 5 | 1 | 6 | 8 | 9 | 4 | 2 |
| 6 | 1 | 4 | 5 | 9 | 2 | 3 | 8 | 7 |
| 8 | 9 | 2 | 3 | 4 | 7 | 1 | 5 | 6 |

**184**

| 9 | 5 | 7 | 8 | 2 | 6 | 4 | 1 | 3 |
|---|---|---|---|---|---|---|---|---|
| 8 | 3 | 6 | 9 | 4 | 1 | 7 | 2 | 5 |
| 2 | 1 | 4 | 5 | 3 | 7 | 8 | 9 | 6 |
| 1 | 2 | 5 | 3 | 7 | 9 | 6 | 4 | 8 |
| 3 | 4 | 9 | 6 | 8 | 5 | 1 | 7 | 2 |
| 6 | 7 | 8 | 4 | 1 | 2 | 3 | 5 | 9 |
| 5 | 9 | 3 | 1 | 6 | 4 | 2 | 8 | 7 |
| 7 | 8 | 1 | 2 | 5 | 3 | 9 | 6 | 4 |
| 4 | 6 | 2 | 7 | 9 | 8 | 5 | 3 | 1 |

**185**

| 4 | 2 | 7 | 5 | 9 | 3 | 1 | 8 | 6 |
| 8 | 1 | 9 | 4 | 7 | 6 | 3 | 2 | 5 |
| 6 | 5 | 3 | 1 | 2 | 8 | 7 | 9 | 4 |
| 1 | 4 | 2 | 3 | 8 | 5 | 6 | 7 | 9 |
| 9 | 7 | 8 | 2 | 6 | 4 | 5 | 1 | 3 |
| 5 | 3 | 6 | 9 | 1 | 7 | 8 | 4 | 2 |
| 7 | 8 | 4 | 6 | 5 | 9 | 2 | 3 | 1 |
| 2 | 9 | 5 | 7 | 3 | 1 | 4 | 6 | 8 |
| 3 | 6 | 1 | 8 | 4 | 2 | 9 | 5 | 7 |

**186**

| 6 | 3 | 7 | 1 | 9 | 8 | 2 | 4 | 5 |
| 4 | 2 | 1 | 6 | 7 | 5 | 8 | 3 | 9 |
| 8 | 9 | 5 | 3 | 4 | 2 | 6 | 1 | 7 |
| 5 | 8 | 3 | 7 | 6 | 4 | 9 | 2 | 1 |
| 7 | 4 | 2 | 5 | 1 | 9 | 3 | 8 | 6 |
| 9 | 1 | 6 | 8 | 2 | 3 | 5 | 7 | 4 |
| 3 | 5 | 4 | 9 | 8 | 1 | 7 | 6 | 2 |
| 2 | 7 | 8 | 4 | 5 | 6 | 1 | 9 | 3 |
| 1 | 6 | 9 | 2 | 3 | 7 | 4 | 5 | 8 |

**187**

| 9 | 4 | 1 | 8 | 6 | 5 | 7 | 2 | 3 |
| 8 | 6 | 5 | 3 | 7 | 2 | 9 | 4 | 1 |
| 3 | 7 | 2 | 9 | 1 | 4 | 5 | 6 | 8 |
| 5 | 8 | 3 | 2 | 9 | 6 | 4 | 1 | 7 |
| 7 | 9 | 6 | 1 | 4 | 8 | 2 | 3 | 5 |
| 1 | 2 | 4 | 7 | 5 | 3 | 8 | 9 | 6 |
| 2 | 3 | 7 | 4 | 8 | 1 | 6 | 5 | 9 |
| 4 | 5 | 9 | 6 | 3 | 7 | 1 | 8 | 2 |
| 6 | 1 | 8 | 5 | 2 | 9 | 3 | 7 | 4 |

**188**

| 8 | 3 | 4 | 7 | 5 | 1 | 6 | 2 | 9 |
| 5 | 9 | 1 | 4 | 6 | 2 | 3 | 8 | 7 |
| 2 | 7 | 6 | 9 | 8 | 3 | 4 | 1 | 5 |
| 3 | 5 | 9 | 1 | 7 | 6 | 8 | 4 | 2 |
| 6 | 2 | 8 | 3 | 4 | 5 | 7 | 9 | 1 |
| 1 | 4 | 7 | 2 | 9 | 8 | 5 | 6 | 3 |
| 9 | 1 | 5 | 6 | 3 | 4 | 2 | 7 | 8 |
| 4 | 8 | 2 | 5 | 1 | 7 | 9 | 3 | 6 |
| 7 | 6 | 3 | 8 | 2 | 9 | 1 | 5 | 4 |

**189**

| 8 | 9 | 3 | 6 | 7 | 5 | 4 | 2 | 1 |
| 7 | 6 | 1 | 4 | 8 | 2 | 9 | 5 | 3 |
| 5 | 4 | 2 | 3 | 9 | 1 | 8 | 7 | 6 |
| 6 | 1 | 4 | 8 | 5 | 3 | 2 | 9 | 7 |
| 9 | 2 | 5 | 1 | 6 | 7 | 3 | 4 | 8 |
| 3 | 7 | 8 | 9 | 2 | 4 | 1 | 6 | 5 |
| 1 | 8 | 9 | 5 | 4 | 6 | 7 | 3 | 2 |
| 4 | 5 | 7 | 2 | 3 | 8 | 6 | 1 | 9 |
| 2 | 3 | 6 | 7 | 1 | 9 | 5 | 8 | 4 |

**190**

| 7 | 1 | 4 | 5 | 8 | 9 | 6 | 2 | 3 |
| 3 | 9 | 2 | 7 | 1 | 6 | 8 | 5 | 4 |
| 8 | 5 | 6 | 4 | 2 | 3 | 7 | 1 | 9 |
| 9 | 3 | 5 | 8 | 4 | 1 | 2 | 6 | 7 |
| 1 | 4 | 7 | 3 | 6 | 2 | 5 | 9 | 8 |
| 2 | 6 | 8 | 9 | 5 | 7 | 4 | 3 | 1 |
| 5 | 8 | 9 | 6 | 3 | 4 | 1 | 7 | 2 |
| 4 | 2 | 3 | 1 | 7 | 5 | 9 | 8 | 6 |
| 6 | 7 | 1 | 2 | 9 | 8 | 3 | 4 | 5 |

**191**

| 9 | 4 | 1 | 5 | 3 | 7 | 8 | 6 | 2 |
| 2 | 6 | 3 | 4 | 9 | 8 | 5 | 7 | 1 |
| 5 | 8 | 7 | 2 | 1 | 6 | 3 | 4 | 9 |
| 4 | 1 | 8 | 6 | 7 | 3 | 9 | 2 | 5 |
| 6 | 5 | 9 | 8 | 4 | 2 | 7 | 1 | 3 |
| 7 | 3 | 2 | 1 | 5 | 9 | 4 | 8 | 6 |
| 8 | 9 | 5 | 7 | 6 | 1 | 2 | 3 | 4 |
| 1 | 2 | 4 | 3 | 8 | 5 | 6 | 9 | 7 |
| 3 | 7 | 6 | 9 | 2 | 4 | 1 | 5 | 8 |

**192**

| 8 | 3 | 4 | 6 | 2 | 9 | 1 | 7 | 5 |
| 7 | 5 | 2 | 4 | 3 | 1 | 8 | 6 | 9 |
| 9 | 1 | 6 | 7 | 8 | 5 | 2 | 3 | 4 |
| 4 | 2 | 5 | 1 | 6 | 7 | 3 | 9 | 8 |
| 3 | 6 | 9 | 8 | 4 | 2 | 7 | 5 | 1 |
| 1 | 8 | 7 | 5 | 9 | 3 | 4 | 2 | 6 |
| 2 | 9 | 8 | 3 | 1 | 6 | 5 | 4 | 7 |
| 5 | 4 | 3 | 9 | 7 | 8 | 6 | 1 | 2 |
| 6 | 7 | 1 | 2 | 5 | 4 | 9 | 8 | 3 |

| 5 | 8 | 6 | 4 | 3 | 2 | 1 | 7 | 9 |
|---|---|---|---|---|---|---|---|---|
| 2 | 4 | 1 | 9 | 6 | 7 | 5 | 3 | 8 |
| 7 | 9 | 3 | 8 | 1 | 5 | 2 | 4 | 6 |
| 6 | 2 | 9 | 7 | 8 | 3 | 4 | 5 | 1 |
| 8 | 7 | 4 | 2 | 5 | 1 | 9 | 6 | 3 |
| 1 | 3 | 5 | 6 | 9 | 4 | 8 | 2 | 7 |
| 4 | 5 | 8 | 3 | 7 | 9 | 6 | 1 | 2 |
| 9 | 1 | 7 | 5 | 2 | 6 | 3 | 8 | 4 |
| 3 | 6 | 2 | 1 | 4 | 8 | 7 | 9 | 5 |

| 9 | 4 | 5 | 8 | 6 | 3 | 1 | 7 | 2 |
|---|---|---|---|---|---|---|---|---|
| 3 | 2 | 8 | 4 | 7 | 1 | 9 | 6 | 5 |
| 6 | 1 | 7 | 2 | 9 | 5 | 4 | 3 | 8 |
| 7 | 6 | 2 | 5 | 3 | 4 | 8 | 9 | 1 |
| 5 | 3 | 4 | 1 | 8 | 9 | 6 | 2 | 7 |
| 8 | 9 | 1 | 7 | 2 | 6 | 5 | 4 | 3 |
| 2 | 5 | 9 | 3 | 4 | 8 | 7 | 1 | 6 |
| 4 | 8 | 3 | 6 | 1 | 7 | 2 | 5 | 9 |
| 1 | 7 | 6 | 9 | 5 | 2 | 3 | 8 | 4 |

| 9 | 2 | 7 | 4 | 3 | 1 | 8 | 6 | 5 |
|---|---|---|---|---|---|---|---|---|
| 1 | 4 | 5 | 7 | 6 | 8 | 2 | 9 | 3 |
| 3 | 8 | 6 | 2 | 9 | 5 | 1 | 7 | 4 |
| 5 | 9 | 8 | 3 | 2 | 6 | 7 | 4 | 1 |
| 4 | 6 | 1 | 9 | 8 | 7 | 3 | 5 | 2 |
| 7 | 3 | 2 | 1 | 5 | 4 | 9 | 8 | 6 |
| 2 | 5 | 3 | 8 | 4 | 9 | 6 | 1 | 7 |
| 6 | 7 | 9 | 5 | 1 | 3 | 4 | 2 | 8 |
| 8 | 1 | 4 | 6 | 7 | 2 | 5 | 3 | 9 |

| 9 | 3 | 6 | 2 | 5 | 8 | 7 | 1 | 4 |
|---|---|---|---|---|---|---|---|---|
| 5 | 2 | 8 | 7 | 1 | 4 | 3 | 9 | 6 |
| 7 | 4 | 1 | 3 | 9 | 6 | 5 | 2 | 8 |
| 6 | 9 | 4 | 5 | 8 | 2 | 1 | 7 | 3 |
| 1 | 8 | 7 | 6 | 3 | 9 | 2 | 4 | 5 |
| 2 | 5 | 3 | 4 | 7 | 1 | 8 | 6 | 9 |
| 3 | 7 | 9 | 1 | 4 | 5 | 6 | 8 | 2 |
| 4 | 1 | 2 | 8 | 6 | 3 | 9 | 5 | 7 |
| 8 | 6 | 5 | 9 | 2 | 7 | 4 | 3 | 1 |

| 7 | 3 | 6 | 1 | 5 | 8 | 2 | 4 | 9 |
|---|---|---|---|---|---|---|---|---|
| 2 | 5 | 9 | 4 | 3 | 7 | 8 | 1 | 6 |
| 8 | 4 | 1 | 9 | 6 | 2 | 5 | 7 | 3 |
| 4 | 1 | 5 | 8 | 7 | 3 | 9 | 6 | 2 |
| 6 | 7 | 3 | 2 | 9 | 4 | 1 | 5 | 8 |
| 9 | 8 | 2 | 6 | 1 | 5 | 7 | 3 | 4 |
| 3 | 6 | 8 | 5 | 2 | 1 | 4 | 9 | 7 |
| 5 | 2 | 7 | 3 | 4 | 9 | 6 | 8 | 1 |
| 1 | 9 | 4 | 7 | 8 | 6 | 3 | 2 | 5 |

| 5 | 4 | 8 | 9 | 3 | 2 | 7 | 6 | 1 |
|---|---|---|---|---|---|---|---|---|
| 3 | 9 | 6 | 1 | 4 | 7 | 8 | 2 | 5 |
| 7 | 1 | 2 | 6 | 8 | 5 | 4 | 3 | 9 |
| 6 | 7 | 9 | 4 | 5 | 8 | 2 | 1 | 3 |
| 2 | 3 | 1 | 7 | 6 | 9 | 5 | 8 | 4 |
| 8 | 5 | 4 | 3 | 2 | 1 | 6 | 9 | 7 |
| 9 | 2 | 5 | 8 | 7 | 3 | 1 | 4 | 6 |
| 4 | 8 | 3 | 5 | 1 | 6 | 9 | 7 | 2 |
| 1 | 6 | 7 | 2 | 9 | 4 | 3 | 5 | 8 |

| 3 | 1 | 2 | 6 | 8 | 4 | 7 | 9 | 5 |
|---|---|---|---|---|---|---|---|---|
| 4 | 6 | 7 | 2 | 5 | 9 | 1 | 8 | 3 |
| 9 | 5 | 8 | 7 | 3 | 1 | 6 | 4 | 2 |
| 1 | 7 | 3 | 4 | 6 | 2 | 9 | 5 | 8 |
| 8 | 4 | 5 | 3 | 9 | 7 | 2 | 6 | 1 |
| 6 | 2 | 9 | 5 | 1 | 8 | 3 | 7 | 4 |
| 2 | 3 | 4 | 8 | 7 | 6 | 5 | 1 | 9 |
| 7 | 8 | 1 | 9 | 2 | 5 | 4 | 3 | 6 |
| 5 | 9 | 6 | 1 | 4 | 3 | 8 | 2 | 7 |

| 5 | 7 | 9 | 8 | 2 | 3 | 4 | 6 | 1 |
|---|---|---|---|---|---|---|---|---|
| 3 | 4 | 8 | 1 | 6 | 9 | 7 | 2 | 5 |
| 2 | 1 | 6 | 4 | 7 | 5 | 9 | 8 | 3 |
| 7 | 6 | 2 | 5 | 4 | 8 | 1 | 3 | 9 |
| 1 | 3 | 5 | 6 | 9 | 7 | 8 | 4 | 2 |
| 9 | 8 | 4 | 3 | 1 | 2 | 5 | 7 | 6 |
| 6 | 5 | 3 | 7 | 8 | 1 | 2 | 9 | 4 |
| 8 | 2 | 1 | 9 | 3 | 4 | 6 | 5 | 7 |
| 4 | 9 | 7 | 2 | 5 | 6 | 3 | 1 | 8 |

**201**

| 2 | 1 | 7 | 5 | 9 | 6 | 3 | 8 | 4 |
|---|---|---|---|---|---|---|---|---|
| 5 | 8 | 4 | 7 | 1 | 3 | 6 | 2 | 9 |
| 9 | 3 | 6 | 4 | 8 | 2 | 1 | 5 | 7 |
| 4 | 9 | 1 | 3 | 5 | 8 | 2 | 7 | 6 |
| 8 | 6 | 5 | 9 | 2 | 7 | 4 | 3 | 1 |
| 7 | 2 | 3 | 1 | 6 | 4 | 8 | 9 | 5 |
| 6 | 7 | 9 | 2 | 3 | 1 | 5 | 4 | 8 |
| 3 | 5 | 8 | 6 | 4 | 9 | 7 | 1 | 2 |
| 1 | 4 | 2 | 8 | 7 | 5 | 9 | 6 | 3 |

**202**

| 2 | 5 | 3 | 8 | 7 | 1 | 6 | 4 | 9 |
|---|---|---|---|---|---|---|---|---|
| 4 | 6 | 9 | 2 | 5 | 3 | 8 | 1 | 7 |
| 8 | 1 | 7 | 4 | 9 | 6 | 3 | 5 | 2 |
| 1 | 4 | 2 | 7 | 6 | 8 | 9 | 3 | 5 |
| 9 | 8 | 6 | 5 | 3 | 2 | 1 | 7 | 4 |
| 3 | 7 | 5 | 9 | 1 | 4 | 2 | 8 | 6 |
| 5 | 9 | 8 | 3 | 2 | 7 | 4 | 6 | 1 |
| 7 | 3 | 1 | 6 | 4 | 9 | 5 | 2 | 8 |
| 6 | 2 | 4 | 1 | 8 | 5 | 7 | 9 | 3 |

**203**

| 3 | 9 | 8 | 4 | 5 | 1 | 6 | 7 | 2 |
|---|---|---|---|---|---|---|---|---|
| 7 | 6 | 2 | 8 | 9 | 3 | 4 | 5 | 1 |
| 5 | 4 | 1 | 6 | 2 | 7 | 8 | 3 | 9 |
| 6 | 8 | 7 | 3 | 1 | 5 | 9 | 2 | 4 |
| 1 | 5 | 4 | 9 | 6 | 2 | 3 | 8 | 7 |
| 9 | 2 | 3 | 7 | 8 | 4 | 1 | 6 | 5 |
| 8 | 3 | 5 | 1 | 7 | 9 | 2 | 4 | 6 |
| 4 | 7 | 9 | 2 | 3 | 6 | 5 | 1 | 8 |
| 2 | 1 | 6 | 5 | 4 | 8 | 7 | 9 | 3 |

**204**

| 5 | 1 | 6 | 9 | 7 | 4 | 8 | 2 | 3 |
|---|---|---|---|---|---|---|---|---|
| 9 | 7 | 4 | 2 | 3 | 8 | 5 | 1 | 6 |
| 2 | 8 | 3 | 5 | 1 | 6 | 4 | 9 | 7 |
| 1 | 3 | 2 | 7 | 5 | 9 | 6 | 4 | 8 |
| 4 | 5 | 8 | 3 | 6 | 2 | 1 | 7 | 9 |
| 7 | 6 | 9 | 4 | 8 | 1 | 2 | 3 | 5 |
| 8 | 9 | 7 | 1 | 2 | 5 | 3 | 6 | 4 |
| 3 | 2 | 5 | 6 | 4 | 7 | 9 | 8 | 1 |
| 6 | 4 | 1 | 8 | 9 | 3 | 7 | 5 | 2 |

**205**

| 1 | 4 | 9 | 5 | 8 | 3 | 7 | 2 | 6 |
|---|---|---|---|---|---|---|---|---|
| 5 | 6 | 8 | 7 | 2 | 9 | 1 | 4 | 3 |
| 3 | 7 | 2 | 6 | 4 | 1 | 9 | 8 | 5 |
| 4 | 2 | 6 | 1 | 9 | 5 | 3 | 7 | 8 |
| 8 | 1 | 3 | 2 | 7 | 6 | 4 | 5 | 9 |
| 9 | 5 | 7 | 8 | 3 | 4 | 2 | 6 | 1 |
| 2 | 8 | 1 | 9 | 5 | 7 | 6 | 3 | 4 |
| 6 | 3 | 5 | 4 | 1 | 2 | 8 | 9 | 7 |
| 7 | 9 | 4 | 3 | 6 | 8 | 5 | 1 | 2 |

**206**

| 3 | 7 | 2 | 4 | 9 | 6 | 1 | 5 | 8 |
|---|---|---|---|---|---|---|---|---|
| 8 | 5 | 4 | 7 | 1 | 2 | 3 | 9 | 6 |
| 9 | 1 | 6 | 3 | 5 | 8 | 4 | 2 | 7 |
| 4 | 3 | 5 | 1 | 2 | 7 | 6 | 8 | 9 |
| 2 | 9 | 1 | 8 | 6 | 3 | 5 | 7 | 4 |
| 6 | 8 | 7 | 5 | 4 | 9 | 2 | 3 | 1 |
| 1 | 2 | 8 | 9 | 3 | 4 | 7 | 6 | 5 |
| 5 | 6 | 9 | 2 | 7 | 1 | 8 | 4 | 3 |
| 7 | 4 | 3 | 6 | 8 | 5 | 9 | 1 | 2 |

**207**

| 8 | 7 | 1 | 5 | 2 | 4 | 3 | 6 | 9 |
|---|---|---|---|---|---|---|---|---|
| 3 | 6 | 4 | 1 | 8 | 9 | 2 | 5 | 7 |
| 2 | 9 | 5 | 3 | 6 | 7 | 4 | 8 | 1 |
| 6 | 2 | 8 | 4 | 7 | 5 | 1 | 9 | 3 |
| 4 | 3 | 7 | 8 | 9 | 1 | 5 | 2 | 6 |
| 5 | 1 | 9 | 6 | 3 | 2 | 8 | 7 | 4 |
| 1 | 5 | 2 | 9 | 4 | 6 | 7 | 3 | 8 |
| 7 | 8 | 6 | 2 | 1 | 3 | 9 | 4 | 5 |
| 9 | 4 | 3 | 7 | 5 | 8 | 6 | 1 | 2 |

**208**

| 1 | 8 | 2 | 7 | 9 | 5 | 3 | 6 | 4 |
|---|---|---|---|---|---|---|---|---|
| 7 | 4 | 3 | 2 | 1 | 6 | 8 | 5 | 9 |
| 6 | 5 | 9 | 4 | 3 | 8 | 7 | 1 | 2 |
| 9 | 7 | 4 | 6 | 5 | 1 | 2 | 3 | 8 |
| 3 | 1 | 8 | 9 | 4 | 2 | 5 | 7 | 6 |
| 5 | 2 | 6 | 3 | 8 | 7 | 9 | 4 | 1 |
| 8 | 3 | 5 | 1 | 6 | 9 | 4 | 2 | 7 |
| 4 | 6 | 7 | 8 | 2 | 3 | 1 | 9 | 5 |
| 2 | 9 | 1 | 5 | 7 | 4 | 6 | 8 | 3 |

**209**

| 2 | 6 | 9 | 4 | 7 | 3 | 5 | 1 | 8 |
| 4 | 8 | 7 | 2 | 5 | 1 | 9 | 3 | 6 |
| 3 | 1 | 5 | 8 | 9 | 6 | 2 | 4 | 7 |
| 9 | 7 | 8 | 3 | 6 | 5 | 1 | 2 | 4 |
| 1 | 3 | 2 | 7 | 8 | 4 | 6 | 9 | 5 |
| 6 | 5 | 4 | 1 | 2 | 9 | 8 | 7 | 3 |
| 5 | 2 | 3 | 6 | 1 | 7 | 4 | 8 | 9 |
| 8 | 4 | 6 | 9 | 3 | 2 | 7 | 5 | 1 |
| 7 | 9 | 1 | 5 | 4 | 8 | 3 | 6 | 2 |

**210**

| 9 | 5 | 4 | 8 | 6 | 1 | 7 | 2 | 3 |
| 1 | 6 | 2 | 4 | 3 | 7 | 8 | 9 | 5 |
| 3 | 7 | 8 | 5 | 9 | 2 | 1 | 6 | 4 |
| 8 | 9 | 7 | 1 | 5 | 6 | 4 | 3 | 2 |
| 6 | 1 | 3 | 7 | 2 | 4 | 5 | 8 | 9 |
| 2 | 4 | 5 | 3 | 8 | 9 | 6 | 7 | 1 |
| 7 | 2 | 6 | 9 | 4 | 5 | 3 | 1 | 8 |
| 4 | 8 | 9 | 6 | 1 | 3 | 2 | 5 | 7 |
| 5 | 3 | 1 | 2 | 7 | 8 | 9 | 4 | 6 |

**211**

| 9 | 8 | 7 | 3 | 1 | 2 | 4 | 5 | 6 |
| 3 | 2 | 6 | 5 | 9 | 4 | 1 | 8 | 7 |
| 5 | 4 | 1 | 7 | 6 | 8 | 9 | 2 | 3 |
| 7 | 1 | 3 | 8 | 5 | 9 | 6 | 4 | 2 |
| 6 | 9 | 2 | 4 | 3 | 7 | 5 | 1 | 8 |
| 4 | 5 | 8 | 6 | 2 | 1 | 7 | 3 | 9 |
| 1 | 3 | 5 | 2 | 7 | 6 | 8 | 9 | 4 |
| 2 | 7 | 4 | 9 | 8 | 5 | 3 | 6 | 1 |
| 8 | 6 | 9 | 1 | 4 | 3 | 2 | 7 | 5 |

**212**

| 3 | 8 | 1 | 9 | 5 | 7 | 2 | 4 | 6 |
| 4 | 7 | 6 | 2 | 3 | 8 | 5 | 1 | 9 |
| 9 | 2 | 5 | 4 | 6 | 1 | 7 | 3 | 8 |
| 5 | 9 | 7 | 3 | 2 | 4 | 6 | 8 | 1 |
| 2 | 4 | 3 | 8 | 1 | 6 | 9 | 5 | 7 |
| 1 | 6 | 8 | 5 | 7 | 9 | 3 | 2 | 4 |
| 6 | 1 | 2 | 7 | 4 | 3 | 8 | 9 | 5 |
| 7 | 3 | 9 | 1 | 8 | 5 | 4 | 6 | 2 |
| 8 | 5 | 4 | 6 | 9 | 2 | 1 | 7 | 3 |

**213**

| 3 | 4 | 7 | 1 | 2 | 5 | 8 | 9 | 6 |
| 8 | 2 | 6 | 9 | 7 | 3 | 5 | 1 | 4 |
| 1 | 5 | 9 | 6 | 4 | 8 | 2 | 3 | 7 |
| 7 | 6 | 5 | 4 | 8 | 9 | 1 | 2 | 3 |
| 2 | 1 | 8 | 7 | 3 | 6 | 4 | 5 | 9 |
| 4 | 9 | 3 | 5 | 1 | 2 | 7 | 6 | 8 |
| 6 | 8 | 1 | 3 | 5 | 4 | 9 | 7 | 2 |
| 9 | 7 | 2 | 8 | 6 | 1 | 3 | 4 | 5 |
| 5 | 3 | 4 | 2 | 9 | 7 | 6 | 8 | 1 |

**214**

| 5 | 3 | 4 | 9 | 1 | 2 | 6 | 8 | 7 |
| 7 | 9 | 6 | 3 | 4 | 8 | 2 | 1 | 5 |
| 8 | 2 | 1 | 6 | 7 | 5 | 3 | 9 | 4 |
| 4 | 6 | 5 | 7 | 9 | 1 | 8 | 2 | 3 |
| 1 | 8 | 2 | 5 | 6 | 3 | 4 | 7 | 9 |
| 9 | 7 | 3 | 2 | 8 | 4 | 5 | 6 | 1 |
| 3 | 1 | 7 | 8 | 5 | 6 | 9 | 4 | 2 |
| 2 | 4 | 8 | 1 | 3 | 9 | 7 | 5 | 6 |
| 6 | 5 | 9 | 4 | 2 | 7 | 1 | 3 | 8 |

**215**

| 7 | 1 | 9 | 4 | 3 | 2 | 5 | 6 | 8 |
| 6 | 2 | 5 | 1 | 8 | 7 | 4 | 9 | 3 |
| 4 | 3 | 8 | 9 | 6 | 5 | 2 | 1 | 7 |
| 3 | 5 | 4 | 7 | 9 | 6 | 8 | 2 | 1 |
| 9 | 7 | 2 | 5 | 1 | 8 | 3 | 4 | 6 |
| 1 | 8 | 6 | 2 | 4 | 3 | 7 | 5 | 9 |
| 8 | 4 | 7 | 6 | 2 | 1 | 9 | 3 | 5 |
| 5 | 9 | 1 | 3 | 7 | 4 | 6 | 8 | 2 |
| 2 | 6 | 3 | 8 | 5 | 9 | 1 | 7 | 4 |

**216**

| 1 | 3 | 4 | 6 | 7 | 9 | 5 | 2 | 8 |
| 6 | 5 | 7 | 1 | 8 | 2 | 4 | 3 | 9 |
| 2 | 8 | 9 | 4 | 3 | 5 | 6 | 1 | 7 |
| 8 | 2 | 5 | 3 | 9 | 4 | 7 | 6 | 1 |
| 9 | 7 | 3 | 2 | 1 | 6 | 8 | 5 | 4 |
| 4 | 6 | 1 | 7 | 5 | 8 | 3 | 9 | 2 |
| 7 | 4 | 2 | 5 | 6 | 1 | 9 | 8 | 3 |
| 3 | 9 | 6 | 8 | 2 | 7 | 1 | 4 | 5 |
| 5 | 1 | 8 | 9 | 4 | 3 | 2 | 7 | 6 |

**217**

| 3 | 2 | 7 | 8 | 9 | 4 | 1 | 5 | 6 |
| 9 | 5 | 4 | 7 | 6 | 1 | 3 | 8 | 2 |
| 8 | 1 | 6 | 2 | 5 | 3 | 9 | 7 | 4 |
| 2 | 3 | 1 | 6 | 7 | 8 | 5 | 4 | 9 |
| 6 | 4 | 9 | 5 | 1 | 2 | 8 | 3 | 7 |
| 7 | 8 | 5 | 3 | 4 | 9 | 2 | 6 | 1 |
| 4 | 9 | 3 | 1 | 8 | 7 | 6 | 2 | 5 |
| 1 | 6 | 8 | 4 | 2 | 5 | 7 | 9 | 3 |
| 5 | 7 | 2 | 9 | 3 | 6 | 4 | 1 | 8 |

**218**

| 4 | 1 | 7 | 8 | 2 | 3 | 5 | 9 | 6 |
| 2 | 6 | 8 | 4 | 5 | 9 | 3 | 1 | 7 |
| 9 | 5 | 3 | 7 | 6 | 1 | 4 | 8 | 2 |
| 8 | 9 | 2 | 3 | 1 | 6 | 7 | 4 | 5 |
| 3 | 7 | 5 | 9 | 8 | 4 | 2 | 6 | 1 |
| 6 | 4 | 1 | 2 | 7 | 5 | 9 | 3 | 8 |
| 5 | 8 | 4 | 6 | 9 | 7 | 1 | 2 | 3 |
| 7 | 3 | 6 | 1 | 4 | 2 | 8 | 5 | 9 |
| 1 | 2 | 9 | 5 | 3 | 8 | 6 | 7 | 4 |

**219**

| 3 | 1 | 5 | 8 | 9 | 6 | 4 | 2 | 7 |
| 9 | 6 | 7 | 2 | 5 | 4 | 8 | 1 | 3 |
| 2 | 4 | 8 | 3 | 7 | 1 | 5 | 6 | 9 |
| 1 | 8 | 4 | 9 | 2 | 7 | 6 | 3 | 5 |
| 6 | 7 | 2 | 1 | 3 | 5 | 9 | 4 | 8 |
| 5 | 3 | 9 | 4 | 6 | 8 | 1 | 7 | 2 |
| 4 | 5 | 1 | 7 | 8 | 2 | 3 | 9 | 6 |
| 8 | 2 | 3 | 6 | 1 | 9 | 7 | 5 | 4 |
| 7 | 9 | 6 | 5 | 4 | 3 | 2 | 8 | 1 |

**220**

| 8 | 3 | 4 | 7 | 6 | 9 | 2 | 5 | 1 |
| 5 | 9 | 2 | 4 | 3 | 1 | 6 | 7 | 8 |
| 6 | 7 | 1 | 5 | 2 | 8 | 3 | 9 | 4 |
| 4 | 1 | 8 | 3 | 7 | 5 | 9 | 6 | 2 |
| 2 | 5 | 7 | 9 | 1 | 6 | 4 | 8 | 3 |
| 9 | 6 | 3 | 2 | 8 | 4 | 7 | 1 | 5 |
| 7 | 2 | 5 | 8 | 9 | 3 | 1 | 4 | 6 |
| 3 | 8 | 6 | 1 | 4 | 7 | 5 | 2 | 9 |
| 1 | 4 | 9 | 6 | 5 | 2 | 8 | 3 | 7 |

**221**

| 3 | 8 | 6 | 2 | 9 | 7 | 4 | 5 | 1 |
| 9 | 1 | 4 | 5 | 8 | 3 | 7 | 2 | 6 |
| 5 | 7 | 2 | 1 | 6 | 4 | 9 | 8 | 3 |
| 1 | 5 | 3 | 7 | 4 | 6 | 2 | 9 | 8 |
| 7 | 6 | 9 | 8 | 1 | 2 | 5 | 3 | 4 |
| 4 | 2 | 8 | 9 | 3 | 5 | 6 | 1 | 7 |
| 6 | 9 | 5 | 3 | 7 | 8 | 1 | 4 | 2 |
| 8 | 4 | 1 | 6 | 2 | 9 | 3 | 7 | 5 |
| 2 | 3 | 7 | 4 | 5 | 1 | 8 | 6 | 9 |

**222**

| 3 | 6 | 7 | 4 | 5 | 8 | 1 | 2 | 9 |
| 1 | 8 | 9 | 7 | 3 | 2 | 4 | 5 | 6 |
| 4 | 2 | 5 | 9 | 6 | 1 | 8 | 7 | 3 |
| 6 | 1 | 4 | 2 | 9 | 5 | 3 | 8 | 7 |
| 9 | 5 | 3 | 1 | 8 | 7 | 2 | 6 | 4 |
| 8 | 7 | 2 | 3 | 4 | 6 | 5 | 9 | 1 |
| 7 | 4 | 6 | 5 | 2 | 3 | 9 | 1 | 8 |
| 2 | 9 | 8 | 6 | 1 | 4 | 7 | 3 | 5 |
| 5 | 3 | 1 | 8 | 7 | 9 | 6 | 4 | 2 |

**223**

| 7 | 8 | 2 | 1 | 6 | 9 | 4 | 3 | 5 |
| 5 | 3 | 4 | 2 | 8 | 7 | 6 | 1 | 9 |
| 9 | 1 | 6 | 5 | 3 | 4 | 2 | 7 | 8 |
| 3 | 9 | 8 | 7 | 5 | 2 | 1 | 4 | 6 |
| 1 | 2 | 5 | 4 | 9 | 6 | 3 | 8 | 7 |
| 6 | 4 | 7 | 8 | 1 | 3 | 9 | 5 | 2 |
| 4 | 5 | 1 | 6 | 2 | 8 | 7 | 9 | 3 |
| 2 | 7 | 9 | 3 | 4 | 5 | 8 | 6 | 1 |
| 8 | 6 | 3 | 9 | 7 | 1 | 5 | 2 | 4 |

**224**

| 5 | 4 | 2 | 1 | 3 | 6 | 8 | 7 | 9 |
| 6 | 1 | 3 | 8 | 9 | 7 | 2 | 4 | 5 |
| 8 | 9 | 7 | 2 | 5 | 4 | 6 | 3 | 1 |
| 2 | 3 | 4 | 6 | 1 | 5 | 9 | 8 | 7 |
| 9 | 6 | 1 | 3 | 7 | 8 | 4 | 5 | 2 |
| 7 | 5 | 8 | 4 | 2 | 9 | 1 | 6 | 3 |
| 3 | 2 | 6 | 5 | 4 | 1 | 7 | 9 | 8 |
| 1 | 8 | 9 | 7 | 6 | 3 | 5 | 2 | 4 |
| 4 | 7 | 5 | 9 | 8 | 2 | 3 | 1 | 6 |

## 225

| 4 | 1 | 3 | 6 | 9 | 2 | 5 | 7 | 8 |
|---|---|---|---|---|---|---|---|---|
| 8 | 2 | 5 | 3 | 1 | 7 | 9 | 4 | 6 |
| 7 | 9 | 6 | 5 | 4 | 8 | 3 | 2 | 1 |
| 9 | 5 | 7 | 4 | 6 | 1 | 2 | 8 | 3 |
| 6 | 4 | 8 | 2 | 7 | 3 | 1 | 5 | 9 |
| 1 | 3 | 2 | 9 | 8 | 5 | 7 | 6 | 4 |
| 5 | 6 | 9 | 1 | 2 | 4 | 8 | 3 | 7 |
| 3 | 7 | 4 | 8 | 5 | 9 | 6 | 1 | 2 |
| 2 | 8 | 1 | 7 | 3 | 6 | 4 | 9 | 5 |

## 226

| 3 | 7 | 4 | 1 | 6 | 5 | 2 | 9 | 8 |
|---|---|---|---|---|---|---|---|---|
| 5 | 9 | 8 | 4 | 2 | 3 | 7 | 1 | 6 |
| 6 | 2 | 1 | 9 | 7 | 8 | 4 | 5 | 3 |
| 8 | 3 | 6 | 7 | 9 | 2 | 5 | 4 | 1 |
| 9 | 5 | 2 | 8 | 1 | 4 | 6 | 3 | 7 |
| 4 | 1 | 7 | 5 | 3 | 6 | 9 | 8 | 2 |
| 7 | 8 | 9 | 6 | 5 | 1 | 3 | 2 | 4 |
| 1 | 6 | 3 | 2 | 4 | 9 | 8 | 7 | 5 |
| 2 | 4 | 5 | 3 | 8 | 7 | 1 | 6 | 9 |

## 227

| 2 | 1 | 6 | 8 | 5 | 7 | 4 | 9 | 3 |
|---|---|---|---|---|---|---|---|---|
| 7 | 5 | 8 | 3 | 9 | 4 | 1 | 6 | 2 |
| 9 | 4 | 3 | 6 | 2 | 1 | 8 | 5 | 7 |
| 5 | 6 | 4 | 9 | 8 | 2 | 3 | 7 | 1 |
| 8 | 2 | 9 | 7 | 1 | 3 | 5 | 4 | 6 |
| 3 | 7 | 1 | 5 | 4 | 6 | 2 | 8 | 9 |
| 6 | 9 | 5 | 2 | 3 | 8 | 7 | 1 | 4 |
| 1 | 8 | 2 | 4 | 7 | 9 | 6 | 3 | 5 |
| 4 | 3 | 7 | 1 | 6 | 5 | 9 | 2 | 8 |

## 228

| 3 | 6 | 7 | 8 | 5 | 1 | 2 | 4 | 9 |
|---|---|---|---|---|---|---|---|---|
| 8 | 1 | 4 | 6 | 9 | 2 | 3 | 7 | 5 |
| 5 | 9 | 2 | 4 | 7 | 3 | 8 | 1 | 6 |
| 1 | 7 | 5 | 3 | 6 | 9 | 4 | 2 | 8 |
| 4 | 8 | 6 | 5 | 2 | 7 | 1 | 9 | 3 |
| 9 | 2 | 3 | 1 | 4 | 8 | 6 | 5 | 7 |
| 2 | 3 | 8 | 7 | 1 | 5 | 9 | 6 | 4 |
| 6 | 5 | 1 | 9 | 8 | 4 | 7 | 3 | 2 |
| 7 | 4 | 9 | 2 | 3 | 6 | 5 | 8 | 1 |

## 229

| 2 | 3 | 5 | 7 | 6 | 8 | 9 | 1 | 4 |
|---|---|---|---|---|---|---|---|---|
| 4 | 6 | 7 | 2 | 1 | 9 | 5 | 3 | 8 |
| 9 | 1 | 8 | 3 | 5 | 4 | 6 | 2 | 7 |
| 3 | 4 | 6 | 5 | 2 | 7 | 1 | 8 | 9 |
| 5 | 9 | 2 | 1 | 8 | 3 | 4 | 7 | 6 |
| 8 | 7 | 1 | 4 | 9 | 6 | 3 | 5 | 2 |
| 7 | 5 | 3 | 9 | 4 | 2 | 8 | 6 | 1 |
| 1 | 8 | 9 | 6 | 7 | 5 | 2 | 4 | 3 |
| 6 | 2 | 4 | 8 | 3 | 1 | 7 | 9 | 5 |

## 230

| 2 | 9 | 8 | 4 | 6 | 1 | 5 | 3 | 7 |
|---|---|---|---|---|---|---|---|---|
| 7 | 6 | 5 | 3 | 8 | 9 | 2 | 1 | 4 |
| 3 | 4 | 1 | 7 | 2 | 5 | 6 | 8 | 9 |
| 8 | 3 | 7 | 9 | 1 | 6 | 4 | 2 | 5 |
| 5 | 2 | 4 | 8 | 7 | 3 | 1 | 9 | 6 |
| 6 | 1 | 9 | 2 | 5 | 4 | 3 | 7 | 8 |
| 1 | 7 | 6 | 5 | 3 | 8 | 9 | 4 | 2 |
| 9 | 5 | 2 | 1 | 4 | 7 | 8 | 6 | 3 |
| 4 | 8 | 3 | 6 | 9 | 2 | 7 | 5 | 1 |

## 231

| 7 | 4 | 3 | 2 | 6 | 1 | 9 | 8 | 5 |
|---|---|---|---|---|---|---|---|---|
| 2 | 8 | 5 | 3 | 9 | 4 | 6 | 7 | 1 |
| 6 | 1 | 9 | 7 | 8 | 5 | 3 | 2 | 4 |
| 3 | 5 | 7 | 6 | 2 | 9 | 4 | 1 | 8 |
| 9 | 2 | 1 | 5 | 4 | 8 | 7 | 3 | 6 |
| 8 | 6 | 4 | 1 | 7 | 3 | 5 | 9 | 2 |
| 5 | 3 | 2 | 9 | 1 | 6 | 8 | 4 | 7 |
| 1 | 9 | 8 | 4 | 5 | 7 | 2 | 6 | 3 |
| 4 | 7 | 6 | 8 | 3 | 2 | 1 | 5 | 9 |

## 232

| 2 | 9 | 3 | 5 | 4 | 6 | 1 | 8 | 7 |
|---|---|---|---|---|---|---|---|---|
| 6 | 5 | 1 | 8 | 7 | 2 | 4 | 3 | 9 |
| 4 | 7 | 8 | 3 | 9 | 1 | 6 | 5 | 2 |
| 1 | 3 | 4 | 6 | 8 | 7 | 2 | 9 | 5 |
| 9 | 2 | 5 | 1 | 3 | 4 | 8 | 7 | 6 |
| 7 | 8 | 6 | 2 | 5 | 9 | 3 | 1 | 4 |
| 3 | 1 | 9 | 4 | 6 | 5 | 7 | 2 | 8 |
| 5 | 6 | 2 | 7 | 1 | 8 | 9 | 4 | 3 |
| 8 | 4 | 7 | 9 | 2 | 3 | 5 | 6 | 1 |

**233**

| 7 | 4 | 8 | 1 | 9 | 5 | 6 | 3 | 2 |
| 2 | 6 | 3 | 4 | 8 | 7 | 9 | 1 | 5 |
| 9 | 1 | 5 | 2 | 3 | 6 | 4 | 8 | 7 |
| 6 | 3 | 4 | 7 | 5 | 8 | 1 | 2 | 9 |
| 8 | 2 | 1 | 3 | 4 | 9 | 7 | 5 | 6 |
| 5 | 9 | 7 | 6 | 1 | 2 | 3 | 4 | 8 |
| 1 | 5 | 6 | 9 | 2 | 3 | 8 | 7 | 4 |
| 4 | 7 | 2 | 8 | 6 | 1 | 5 | 9 | 3 |
| 3 | 8 | 9 | 5 | 7 | 4 | 2 | 6 | 1 |

**234**

| 7 | 8 | 6 | 4 | 2 | 3 | 5 | 9 | 1 |
| 5 | 3 | 4 | 9 | 1 | 6 | 8 | 7 | 2 |
| 2 | 9 | 1 | 8 | 7 | 5 | 6 | 4 | 3 |
| 3 | 2 | 8 | 6 | 5 | 9 | 4 | 1 | 7 |
| 9 | 1 | 5 | 3 | 4 | 7 | 2 | 6 | 8 |
| 6 | 4 | 7 | 1 | 8 | 2 | 9 | 3 | 5 |
| 4 | 7 | 2 | 5 | 6 | 1 | 3 | 8 | 9 |
| 1 | 6 | 9 | 2 | 3 | 8 | 7 | 5 | 4 |
| 8 | 5 | 3 | 7 | 9 | 4 | 1 | 2 | 6 |

**235**

| 2 | 5 | 4 | 7 | 3 | 8 | 1 | 6 | 9 |
| 3 | 8 | 1 | 4 | 6 | 9 | 5 | 2 | 7 |
| 9 | 7 | 6 | 2 | 5 | 1 | 3 | 4 | 8 |
| 1 | 9 | 3 | 5 | 7 | 4 | 6 | 8 | 2 |
| 4 | 2 | 8 | 1 | 9 | 6 | 7 | 5 | 3 |
| 7 | 6 | 5 | 3 | 8 | 2 | 9 | 1 | 4 |
| 6 | 3 | 9 | 8 | 2 | 5 | 4 | 7 | 1 |
| 8 | 1 | 7 | 6 | 4 | 3 | 2 | 9 | 5 |
| 5 | 4 | 2 | 9 | 1 | 7 | 8 | 3 | 6 |

**236**

| 8 | 2 | 4 | 7 | 6 | 9 | 3 | 5 | 1 |
| 9 | 5 | 7 | 4 | 1 | 3 | 2 | 8 | 6 |
| 6 | 3 | 1 | 2 | 8 | 5 | 9 | 7 | 4 |
| 4 | 9 | 2 | 1 | 7 | 6 | 8 | 3 | 5 |
| 5 | 8 | 3 | 9 | 4 | 2 | 1 | 6 | 7 |
| 1 | 7 | 6 | 5 | 3 | 8 | 4 | 2 | 9 |
| 2 | 4 | 8 | 6 | 5 | 1 | 7 | 9 | 3 |
| 7 | 6 | 9 | 3 | 2 | 4 | 5 | 1 | 8 |
| 3 | 1 | 5 | 8 | 9 | 7 | 6 | 4 | 2 |

**237**

| 5 | 6 | 4 | 7 | 1 | 8 | 3 | 2 | 9 |
| 8 | 1 | 2 | 3 | 6 | 9 | 4 | 7 | 5 |
| 3 | 9 | 7 | 5 | 4 | 2 | 1 | 6 | 8 |
| 2 | 5 | 1 | 4 | 9 | 7 | 8 | 3 | 6 |
| 9 | 8 | 6 | 1 | 3 | 5 | 7 | 4 | 2 |
| 7 | 4 | 3 | 8 | 2 | 6 | 9 | 5 | 1 |
| 6 | 3 | 9 | 2 | 8 | 4 | 5 | 1 | 7 |
| 4 | 2 | 5 | 9 | 7 | 1 | 6 | 8 | 3 |
| 1 | 7 | 8 | 6 | 5 | 3 | 2 | 9 | 4 |

**238**

| 1 | 9 | 5 | 2 | 4 | 8 | 7 | 3 | 6 |
| 7 | 8 | 6 | 1 | 9 | 3 | 4 | 2 | 5 |
| 3 | 2 | 4 | 7 | 5 | 6 | 9 | 8 | 1 |
| 8 | 4 | 2 | 5 | 3 | 1 | 6 | 9 | 7 |
| 9 | 1 | 3 | 4 | 6 | 7 | 2 | 5 | 8 |
| 5 | 6 | 7 | 9 | 8 | 2 | 3 | 1 | 4 |
| 6 | 3 | 1 | 8 | 7 | 9 | 5 | 4 | 2 |
| 4 | 7 | 8 | 3 | 2 | 5 | 1 | 6 | 9 |
| 2 | 5 | 9 | 6 | 1 | 4 | 8 | 7 | 3 |

**239**

| 1 | 5 | 7 | 9 | 2 | 6 | 8 | 4 | 3 |
| 6 | 9 | 8 | 7 | 3 | 4 | 5 | 1 | 2 |
| 4 | 3 | 2 | 1 | 5 | 8 | 6 | 7 | 9 |
| 9 | 4 | 1 | 5 | 8 | 2 | 3 | 6 | 7 |
| 8 | 7 | 6 | 3 | 1 | 9 | 2 | 5 | 4 |
| 3 | 2 | 5 | 4 | 6 | 7 | 1 | 9 | 8 |
| 2 | 6 | 4 | 8 | 7 | 1 | 9 | 3 | 5 |
| 7 | 8 | 3 | 6 | 9 | 5 | 4 | 2 | 1 |
| 5 | 1 | 9 | 2 | 4 | 3 | 7 | 8 | 6 |

**240**

| 7 | 9 | 1 | 6 | 3 | 2 | 8 | 4 | 5 |
| 3 | 5 | 2 | 1 | 8 | 4 | 6 | 9 | 7 |
| 8 | 4 | 6 | 7 | 5 | 9 | 3 | 1 | 2 |
| 9 | 1 | 4 | 8 | 6 | 7 | 5 | 2 | 3 |
| 2 | 7 | 8 | 3 | 4 | 5 | 9 | 6 | 1 |
| 6 | 3 | 5 | 2 | 9 | 1 | 7 | 8 | 4 |
| 5 | 8 | 9 | 4 | 2 | 3 | 1 | 7 | 6 |
| 4 | 6 | 7 | 5 | 1 | 8 | 2 | 3 | 9 |
| 1 | 2 | 3 | 9 | 7 | 6 | 4 | 5 | 8 |

## 241

| 3 | 1 | 8 | 9 | 6 | 4 | 7 | 2 | 5 |
| 5 | 6 | 7 | 3 | 8 | 2 | 1 | 4 | 9 |
| 4 | 2 | 9 | 5 | 7 | 1 | 3 | 8 | 6 |
| 6 | 3 | 5 | 1 | 9 | 8 | 2 | 7 | 4 |
| 1 | 7 | 2 | 4 | 3 | 6 | 5 | 9 | 8 |
| 9 | 8 | 4 | 2 | 5 | 7 | 6 | 3 | 1 |
| 7 | 4 | 1 | 6 | 2 | 9 | 8 | 5 | 3 |
| 8 | 9 | 3 | 7 | 1 | 5 | 4 | 6 | 2 |
| 2 | 5 | 6 | 8 | 4 | 3 | 9 | 1 | 7 |

## 242

| 2 | 4 | 8 | 3 | 1 | 9 | 7 | 6 | 5 |
| 9 | 1 | 6 | 2 | 7 | 5 | 8 | 3 | 4 |
| 3 | 7 | 5 | 8 | 6 | 4 | 1 | 2 | 9 |
| 7 | 3 | 1 | 9 | 8 | 2 | 5 | 4 | 6 |
| 6 | 9 | 2 | 4 | 5 | 7 | 3 | 8 | 1 |
| 5 | 8 | 4 | 6 | 3 | 1 | 9 | 7 | 2 |
| 4 | 5 | 7 | 1 | 2 | 3 | 6 | 9 | 8 |
| 1 | 6 | 9 | 7 | 4 | 8 | 2 | 5 | 3 |
| 8 | 2 | 3 | 5 | 9 | 6 | 4 | 1 | 7 |

## 243

| 7 | 5 | 1 | 8 | 3 | 9 | 6 | 4 | 2 |
| 6 | 8 | 9 | 5 | 2 | 4 | 1 | 7 | 3 |
| 2 | 4 | 3 | 7 | 1 | 6 | 5 | 8 | 9 |
| 4 | 9 | 8 | 2 | 6 | 5 | 7 | 3 | 1 |
| 5 | 6 | 7 | 3 | 8 | 1 | 9 | 2 | 4 |
| 3 | 1 | 2 | 4 | 9 | 7 | 8 | 5 | 6 |
| 9 | 7 | 5 | 6 | 4 | 2 | 3 | 1 | 8 |
| 1 | 3 | 4 | 9 | 7 | 8 | 2 | 6 | 5 |
| 8 | 2 | 6 | 1 | 5 | 3 | 4 | 9 | 7 |

## 244

| 7 | 2 | 1 | 5 | 9 | 8 | 3 | 4 | 6 |
| 3 | 8 | 9 | 6 | 1 | 4 | 7 | 2 | 5 |
| 4 | 6 | 5 | 2 | 7 | 3 | 9 | 1 | 8 |
| 2 | 7 | 3 | 1 | 6 | 9 | 8 | 5 | 4 |
| 5 | 9 | 6 | 4 | 8 | 2 | 1 | 3 | 7 |
| 1 | 4 | 8 | 7 | 3 | 5 | 6 | 9 | 2 |
| 6 | 1 | 2 | 9 | 4 | 7 | 5 | 8 | 3 |
| 9 | 3 | 4 | 8 | 5 | 6 | 2 | 7 | 1 |
| 8 | 5 | 7 | 3 | 2 | 1 | 4 | 6 | 9 |

## 245

| 5 | 8 | 6 | 4 | 1 | 2 | 9 | 3 | 7 |
| 4 | 7 | 1 | 8 | 3 | 9 | 6 | 5 | 2 |
| 3 | 2 | 9 | 7 | 5 | 6 | 8 | 4 | 1 |
| 7 | 6 | 8 | 9 | 4 | 3 | 2 | 1 | 5 |
| 2 | 4 | 3 | 1 | 6 | 5 | 7 | 8 | 9 |
| 9 | 1 | 5 | 2 | 7 | 8 | 3 | 6 | 4 |
| 1 | 3 | 4 | 6 | 2 | 7 | 5 | 9 | 8 |
| 8 | 5 | 2 | 3 | 9 | 1 | 4 | 7 | 6 |
| 6 | 9 | 7 | 5 | 8 | 4 | 1 | 2 | 3 |

## 246

| 3 | 9 | 4 | 5 | 1 | 7 | 2 | 8 | 6 |
| 2 | 6 | 8 | 4 | 9 | 3 | 1 | 7 | 5 |
| 1 | 5 | 7 | 8 | 6 | 2 | 3 | 9 | 4 |
| 8 | 2 | 3 | 7 | 4 | 5 | 9 | 6 | 1 |
| 4 | 1 | 5 | 9 | 3 | 6 | 7 | 2 | 8 |
| 6 | 7 | 9 | 2 | 8 | 1 | 4 | 5 | 3 |
| 7 | 4 | 2 | 1 | 5 | 8 | 6 | 3 | 9 |
| 5 | 3 | 1 | 6 | 7 | 9 | 8 | 4 | 2 |
| 9 | 8 | 6 | 3 | 2 | 4 | 5 | 1 | 7 |

## 247

| 9 | 3 | 5 | 7 | 1 | 8 | 2 | 4 | 6 |
| 1 | 8 | 6 | 9 | 4 | 2 | 3 | 5 | 7 |
| 2 | 4 | 7 | 5 | 6 | 3 | 9 | 8 | 1 |
| 4 | 9 | 3 | 8 | 7 | 6 | 5 | 1 | 2 |
| 7 | 5 | 2 | 1 | 3 | 9 | 8 | 6 | 4 |
| 6 | 1 | 8 | 4 | 2 | 5 | 7 | 9 | 3 |
| 5 | 2 | 1 | 3 | 8 | 4 | 6 | 7 | 9 |
| 3 | 7 | 9 | 6 | 5 | 1 | 4 | 2 | 8 |
| 8 | 6 | 4 | 2 | 9 | 7 | 1 | 3 | 5 |

## 248

| 6 | 4 | 5 | 9 | 1 | 3 | 7 | 8 | 2 |
| 9 | 7 | 1 | 5 | 8 | 2 | 4 | 3 | 6 |
| 8 | 2 | 3 | 7 | 4 | 6 | 1 | 9 | 5 |
| 1 | 8 | 2 | 6 | 7 | 5 | 9 | 4 | 3 |
| 7 | 5 | 9 | 4 | 3 | 8 | 6 | 2 | 1 |
| 3 | 6 | 4 | 1 | 2 | 9 | 8 | 5 | 7 |
| 5 | 1 | 7 | 3 | 9 | 4 | 2 | 6 | 8 |
| 4 | 3 | 8 | 2 | 6 | 7 | 5 | 1 | 9 |
| 2 | 9 | 6 | 8 | 5 | 1 | 3 | 7 | 4 |

**249**

| 2 | 8 | 5 | 1 | 3 | 4 | 7 | 9 | 6 |
| 4 | 1 | 9 | 8 | 7 | 6 | 2 | 5 | 3 |
| 3 | 6 | 7 | 2 | 9 | 5 | 1 | 8 | 4 |
| 1 | 3 | 2 | 4 | 8 | 9 | 6 | 7 | 5 |
| 7 | 5 | 4 | 3 | 6 | 1 | 8 | 2 | 9 |
| 8 | 9 | 6 | 5 | 2 | 7 | 4 | 3 | 1 |
| 9 | 7 | 3 | 6 | 4 | 2 | 5 | 1 | 8 |
| 6 | 2 | 1 | 9 | 5 | 8 | 3 | 4 | 7 |
| 5 | 4 | 8 | 7 | 1 | 3 | 9 | 6 | 2 |

**250**

| 6 | 8 | 4 | 1 | 3 | 9 | 2 | 7 | 5 |
| 9 | 5 | 2 | 4 | 7 | 6 | 3 | 1 | 8 |
| 3 | 7 | 1 | 2 | 5 | 8 | 9 | 4 | 6 |
| 5 | 3 | 9 | 6 | 2 | 1 | 4 | 8 | 7 |
| 8 | 4 | 6 | 7 | 9 | 3 | 1 | 5 | 2 |
| 2 | 1 | 7 | 8 | 4 | 5 | 6 | 3 | 9 |
| 7 | 6 | 3 | 5 | 1 | 2 | 8 | 9 | 4 |
| 4 | 9 | 8 | 3 | 6 | 7 | 5 | 2 | 1 |
| 1 | 2 | 5 | 9 | 8 | 4 | 7 | 6 | 3 |

**251**

| 7 | 1 | 8 | 5 | 4 | 3 | 6 | 2 | 9 |
| 9 | 5 | 4 | 6 | 7 | 2 | 3 | 1 | 8 |
| 2 | 6 | 3 | 8 | 9 | 1 | 7 | 4 | 5 |
| 6 | 3 | 2 | 4 | 5 | 7 | 9 | 8 | 1 |
| 1 | 4 | 9 | 2 | 6 | 8 | 5 | 3 | 7 |
| 8 | 7 | 5 | 3 | 1 | 9 | 2 | 6 | 4 |
| 5 | 2 | 7 | 1 | 8 | 6 | 4 | 9 | 3 |
| 3 | 9 | 1 | 7 | 2 | 4 | 8 | 5 | 6 |
| 4 | 8 | 6 | 9 | 3 | 5 | 1 | 7 | 2 |

**252**

| 7 | 1 | 4 | 8 | 6 | 9 | 5 | 3 | 2 |
| 2 | 6 | 9 | 3 | 7 | 5 | 1 | 4 | 8 |
| 3 | 5 | 8 | 4 | 1 | 2 | 9 | 6 | 7 |
| 1 | 3 | 2 | 5 | 9 | 4 | 7 | 8 | 6 |
| 6 | 4 | 5 | 2 | 8 | 7 | 3 | 1 | 9 |
| 9 | 8 | 7 | 6 | 3 | 1 | 4 | 2 | 5 |
| 8 | 7 | 3 | 9 | 4 | 6 | 2 | 5 | 1 |
| 5 | 9 | 6 | 1 | 2 | 3 | 8 | 7 | 4 |
| 4 | 2 | 1 | 7 | 5 | 8 | 6 | 9 | 3 |

**253**

| 3 | 9 | 6 | 1 | 4 | 8 | 7 | 2 | 5 |
| 4 | 2 | 8 | 3 | 7 | 5 | 1 | 6 | 9 |
| 5 | 1 | 7 | 2 | 6 | 9 | 4 | 8 | 3 |
| 2 | 8 | 3 | 7 | 1 | 4 | 9 | 5 | 6 |
| 1 | 7 | 9 | 8 | 5 | 6 | 2 | 3 | 4 |
| 6 | 4 | 5 | 9 | 2 | 3 | 8 | 1 | 7 |
| 7 | 6 | 2 | 5 | 9 | 1 | 3 | 4 | 8 |
| 9 | 3 | 4 | 6 | 8 | 2 | 5 | 7 | 1 |
| 8 | 5 | 1 | 4 | 3 | 7 | 6 | 9 | 2 |

**254**

| 9 | 5 | 7 | 1 | 8 | 2 | 6 | 3 | 4 |
| 8 | 6 | 3 | 7 | 5 | 4 | 2 | 9 | 1 |
| 4 | 1 | 2 | 3 | 9 | 6 | 5 | 7 | 8 |
| 7 | 2 | 6 | 9 | 4 | 8 | 3 | 1 | 5 |
| 5 | 3 | 8 | 6 | 2 | 1 | 9 | 4 | 7 |
| 1 | 9 | 4 | 5 | 7 | 3 | 8 | 6 | 2 |
| 3 | 4 | 5 | 2 | 1 | 9 | 7 | 8 | 6 |
| 6 | 7 | 1 | 8 | 3 | 5 | 4 | 2 | 9 |
| 2 | 8 | 9 | 4 | 6 | 7 | 1 | 5 | 3 |

**255**

| 6 | 5 | 7 | 3 | 9 | 1 | 4 | 8 | 2 |
| 3 | 9 | 2 | 5 | 8 | 4 | 7 | 6 | 1 |
| 1 | 4 | 8 | 6 | 2 | 7 | 9 | 5 | 3 |
| 2 | 3 | 4 | 9 | 7 | 8 | 5 | 1 | 6 |
| 8 | 7 | 9 | 1 | 5 | 6 | 3 | 2 | 4 |
| 5 | 6 | 1 | 2 | 4 | 3 | 8 | 9 | 7 |
| 4 | 1 | 6 | 8 | 3 | 9 | 2 | 7 | 5 |
| 9 | 2 | 3 | 7 | 6 | 5 | 1 | 4 | 8 |
| 7 | 8 | 5 | 4 | 1 | 2 | 6 | 3 | 9 |

**256**

| 3 | 8 | 1 | 7 | 6 | 9 | 4 | 5 | 2 |
| 6 | 9 | 7 | 4 | 2 | 5 | 8 | 3 | 1 |
| 4 | 5 | 2 | 1 | 8 | 3 | 7 | 9 | 6 |
| 8 | 7 | 5 | 3 | 4 | 1 | 6 | 2 | 9 |
| 2 | 1 | 6 | 9 | 7 | 8 | 5 | 4 | 3 |
| 9 | 3 | 4 | 2 | 5 | 6 | 1 | 7 | 8 |
| 7 | 2 | 3 | 8 | 1 | 4 | 9 | 6 | 5 |
| 1 | 6 | 9 | 5 | 3 | 7 | 2 | 8 | 4 |
| 5 | 4 | 8 | 6 | 9 | 2 | 3 | 1 | 7 |

**257**

| 5 | 1 | 4 | 9 | 3 | 2 | 6 | 7 | 8 |
|---|---|---|---|---|---|---|---|---|
| 9 | 2 | 3 | 7 | 8 | 6 | 1 | 5 | 4 |
| 8 | 7 | 6 | 5 | 4 | 1 | 9 | 3 | 2 |
| 7 | 5 | 9 | 2 | 6 | 3 | 8 | 4 | 1 |
| 6 | 3 | 8 | 4 | 1 | 7 | 2 | 9 | 5 |
| 1 | 4 | 2 | 8 | 5 | 9 | 7 | 6 | 3 |
| 4 | 9 | 1 | 6 | 2 | 5 | 3 | 8 | 7 |
| 3 | 6 | 5 | 1 | 7 | 8 | 4 | 2 | 9 |
| 2 | 8 | 7 | 3 | 9 | 4 | 5 | 1 | 6 |

**258**

| 3 | 5 | 9 | 8 | 1 | 7 | 4 | 2 | 6 |
|---|---|---|---|---|---|---|---|---|
| 6 | 2 | 8 | 5 | 3 | 4 | 9 | 1 | 7 |
| 1 | 4 | 7 | 6 | 2 | 9 | 8 | 3 | 5 |
| 8 | 1 | 4 | 2 | 6 | 3 | 7 | 5 | 9 |
| 9 | 6 | 2 | 4 | 7 | 5 | 1 | 8 | 3 |
| 5 | 7 | 3 | 1 | 9 | 8 | 6 | 4 | 2 |
| 7 | 9 | 5 | 3 | 8 | 1 | 2 | 6 | 4 |
| 4 | 8 | 6 | 7 | 5 | 2 | 3 | 9 | 1 |
| 2 | 3 | 1 | 9 | 4 | 6 | 5 | 7 | 8 |

**259**

| 5 | 6 | 1 | 4 | 7 | 3 | 8 | 2 | 9 |
|---|---|---|---|---|---|---|---|---|
| 4 | 8 | 9 | 6 | 2 | 5 | 3 | 7 | 1 |
| 7 | 3 | 2 | 1 | 9 | 8 | 5 | 6 | 4 |
| 3 | 1 | 7 | 8 | 4 | 2 | 9 | 5 | 6 |
| 6 | 4 | 8 | 9 | 5 | 7 | 1 | 3 | 2 |
| 9 | 2 | 5 | 3 | 1 | 6 | 7 | 4 | 8 |
| 2 | 9 | 4 | 5 | 3 | 1 | 6 | 8 | 7 |
| 8 | 7 | 3 | 2 | 6 | 9 | 4 | 1 | 5 |
| 1 | 5 | 6 | 7 | 8 | 4 | 2 | 9 | 3 |

**260**

| 7 | 4 | 8 | 3 | 6 | 1 | 5 | 9 | 2 |
|---|---|---|---|---|---|---|---|---|
| 1 | 2 | 9 | 4 | 8 | 5 | 3 | 7 | 6 |
| 3 | 6 | 5 | 7 | 9 | 2 | 8 | 4 | 1 |
| 9 | 1 | 4 | 6 | 7 | 8 | 2 | 5 | 3 |
| 8 | 3 | 2 | 1 | 5 | 9 | 7 | 6 | 4 |
| 6 | 5 | 7 | 2 | 4 | 3 | 9 | 1 | 8 |
| 5 | 9 | 6 | 8 | 3 | 4 | 1 | 2 | 7 |
| 2 | 7 | 3 | 5 | 1 | 6 | 4 | 8 | 9 |
| 4 | 8 | 1 | 9 | 2 | 7 | 6 | 3 | 5 |

**261**

| 7 | 1 | 3 | 5 | 2 | 9 | 6 | 8 | 4 |
|---|---|---|---|---|---|---|---|---|
| 6 | 8 | 4 | 1 | 7 | 3 | 5 | 9 | 2 |
| 2 | 9 | 5 | 6 | 8 | 4 | 1 | 3 | 7 |
| 1 | 5 | 6 | 9 | 4 | 8 | 2 | 7 | 3 |
| 3 | 4 | 2 | 7 | 6 | 5 | 8 | 1 | 9 |
| 9 | 7 | 8 | 2 | 3 | 1 | 4 | 6 | 5 |
| 4 | 2 | 9 | 8 | 1 | 7 | 3 | 5 | 6 |
| 8 | 3 | 7 | 4 | 5 | 6 | 9 | 2 | 1 |
| 5 | 6 | 1 | 3 | 9 | 2 | 7 | 4 | 8 |

**262**

| 9 | 1 | 5 | 2 | 7 | 4 | 8 | 3 | 6 |
|---|---|---|---|---|---|---|---|---|
| 4 | 8 | 3 | 6 | 5 | 9 | 1 | 2 | 7 |
| 6 | 2 | 7 | 3 | 1 | 8 | 9 | 4 | 5 |
| 2 | 9 | 6 | 7 | 8 | 5 | 3 | 1 | 4 |
| 5 | 4 | 1 | 9 | 2 | 3 | 7 | 6 | 8 |
| 7 | 3 | 8 | 4 | 6 | 1 | 5 | 9 | 2 |
| 3 | 5 | 2 | 1 | 4 | 7 | 6 | 8 | 9 |
| 1 | 7 | 4 | 8 | 9 | 6 | 2 | 5 | 3 |
| 8 | 6 | 9 | 5 | 3 | 2 | 4 | 7 | 1 |

**263**

| 1 | 2 | 3 | 8 | 6 | 9 | 4 | 5 | 7 |
|---|---|---|---|---|---|---|---|---|
| 9 | 4 | 7 | 2 | 3 | 5 | 6 | 8 | 1 |
| 8 | 5 | 6 | 7 | 1 | 4 | 2 | 3 | 9 |
| 4 | 9 | 1 | 6 | 8 | 2 | 5 | 7 | 3 |
| 6 | 3 | 2 | 9 | 5 | 7 | 1 | 4 | 8 |
| 7 | 8 | 5 | 1 | 4 | 3 | 9 | 2 | 6 |
| 5 | 1 | 4 | 3 | 7 | 6 | 8 | 9 | 2 |
| 2 | 7 | 8 | 4 | 9 | 1 | 3 | 6 | 5 |
| 3 | 6 | 9 | 5 | 2 | 8 | 7 | 1 | 4 |

**264**

| 8 | 3 | 6 | 1 | 5 | 2 | 4 | 9 | 7 |
|---|---|---|---|---|---|---|---|---|
| 9 | 5 | 2 | 3 | 7 | 4 | 1 | 6 | 8 |
| 7 | 1 | 4 | 6 | 8 | 9 | 3 | 2 | 5 |
| 2 | 8 | 9 | 4 | 6 | 1 | 5 | 7 | 3 |
| 5 | 4 | 7 | 2 | 3 | 8 | 6 | 1 | 9 |
| 1 | 6 | 3 | 7 | 9 | 5 | 2 | 8 | 4 |
| 4 | 7 | 5 | 8 | 1 | 6 | 9 | 3 | 2 |
| 3 | 2 | 1 | 9 | 4 | 7 | 8 | 5 | 6 |
| 6 | 9 | 8 | 5 | 2 | 3 | 7 | 4 | 1 |

**265**

| 7 | 1 | 3 | 8 | 4 | 6 | 2 | 5 | 9 |
| 2 | 6 | 4 | 1 | 5 | 9 | 3 | 7 | 8 |
| 8 | 9 | 5 | 3 | 2 | 7 | 6 | 4 | 1 |
| 9 | 2 | 8 | 6 | 1 | 5 | 7 | 3 | 4 |
| 5 | 3 | 1 | 2 | 7 | 4 | 9 | 8 | 6 |
| 4 | 7 | 6 | 9 | 3 | 8 | 1 | 2 | 5 |
| 3 | 8 | 2 | 5 | 9 | 1 | 4 | 6 | 7 |
| 1 | 5 | 7 | 4 | 6 | 3 | 8 | 9 | 2 |
| 6 | 4 | 9 | 7 | 8 | 2 | 5 | 1 | 3 |

**266**

| 2 | 5 | 3 | 9 | 6 | 1 | 8 | 7 | 4 |
| 8 | 4 | 7 | 3 | 5 | 2 | 6 | 9 | 1 |
| 1 | 9 | 6 | 8 | 7 | 4 | 2 | 3 | 5 |
| 7 | 2 | 4 | 5 | 8 | 9 | 1 | 6 | 3 |
| 9 | 8 | 5 | 6 | 1 | 3 | 7 | 4 | 2 |
| 6 | 3 | 1 | 2 | 4 | 7 | 5 | 8 | 9 |
| 3 | 1 | 9 | 7 | 2 | 6 | 4 | 5 | 8 |
| 4 | 6 | 8 | 1 | 3 | 5 | 9 | 2 | 7 |
| 5 | 7 | 2 | 4 | 9 | 8 | 3 | 1 | 6 |

**267**

| 2 | 1 | 9 | 5 | 8 | 3 | 7 | 4 | 6 |
| 5 | 8 | 4 | 9 | 7 | 6 | 1 | 2 | 3 |
| 6 | 7 | 3 | 2 | 4 | 1 | 8 | 9 | 5 |
| 4 | 6 | 8 | 3 | 9 | 7 | 2 | 5 | 1 |
| 7 | 5 | 1 | 4 | 2 | 8 | 6 | 3 | 9 |
| 9 | 3 | 2 | 1 | 6 | 5 | 4 | 8 | 7 |
| 1 | 2 | 6 | 8 | 3 | 9 | 5 | 7 | 4 |
| 8 | 9 | 5 | 7 | 1 | 4 | 3 | 6 | 2 |
| 3 | 4 | 7 | 6 | 5 | 2 | 9 | 1 | 8 |

**268**

| 2 | 4 | 5 | 6 | 9 | 1 | 3 | 8 | 7 |
| 9 | 7 | 3 | 2 | 8 | 4 | 1 | 5 | 6 |
| 6 | 8 | 1 | 5 | 3 | 7 | 4 | 9 | 2 |
| 1 | 3 | 9 | 4 | 7 | 5 | 2 | 6 | 8 |
| 8 | 6 | 7 | 9 | 1 | 2 | 5 | 3 | 4 |
| 5 | 2 | 4 | 8 | 6 | 3 | 9 | 7 | 1 |
| 3 | 5 | 2 | 7 | 4 | 8 | 6 | 1 | 9 |
| 4 | 9 | 8 | 1 | 5 | 6 | 7 | 2 | 3 |
| 7 | 1 | 6 | 3 | 2 | 9 | 8 | 4 | 5 |

**269**

| 8 | 7 | 1 | 9 | 3 | 6 | 5 | 2 | 4 |
| 9 | 2 | 3 | 4 | 5 | 7 | 8 | 6 | 1 |
| 6 | 5 | 4 | 2 | 8 | 1 | 9 | 7 | 3 |
| 4 | 3 | 5 | 7 | 2 | 9 | 1 | 8 | 6 |
| 2 | 6 | 7 | 8 | 1 | 3 | 4 | 9 | 5 |
| 1 | 9 | 8 | 6 | 4 | 5 | 2 | 3 | 7 |
| 5 | 4 | 2 | 3 | 6 | 8 | 7 | 1 | 9 |
| 3 | 1 | 9 | 5 | 7 | 2 | 6 | 4 | 8 |
| 7 | 8 | 6 | 1 | 9 | 4 | 3 | 5 | 2 |

**270**

| 4 | 3 | 8 | 2 | 1 | 5 | 6 | 9 | 7 |
| 6 | 2 | 5 | 8 | 7 | 9 | 4 | 3 | 1 |
| 7 | 1 | 9 | 3 | 6 | 4 | 2 | 8 | 5 |
| 2 | 8 | 1 | 5 | 9 | 7 | 3 | 4 | 6 |
| 5 | 9 | 6 | 1 | 4 | 3 | 8 | 7 | 2 |
| 3 | 7 | 4 | 6 | 2 | 8 | 5 | 1 | 9 |
| 8 | 5 | 7 | 9 | 3 | 2 | 1 | 6 | 4 |
| 9 | 6 | 2 | 4 | 8 | 1 | 7 | 5 | 3 |
| 1 | 4 | 3 | 7 | 5 | 6 | 9 | 2 | 8 |

**271**

| 5 | 8 | 9 | 2 | 7 | 4 | 1 | 3 | 6 |
| 4 | 1 | 2 | 5 | 6 | 3 | 7 | 9 | 8 |
| 3 | 7 | 6 | 1 | 9 | 8 | 5 | 4 | 2 |
| 8 | 4 | 3 | 9 | 1 | 7 | 6 | 2 | 5 |
| 6 | 9 | 5 | 3 | 8 | 2 | 4 | 7 | 1 |
| 1 | 2 | 7 | 6 | 4 | 5 | 3 | 8 | 9 |
| 7 | 5 | 4 | 8 | 2 | 1 | 9 | 6 | 3 |
| 9 | 3 | 8 | 4 | 5 | 6 | 2 | 1 | 7 |
| 2 | 6 | 1 | 7 | 3 | 9 | 8 | 5 | 4 |

**272**

| 2 | 9 | 1 | 5 | 3 | 6 | 4 | 8 | 7 |
| 4 | 5 | 7 | 9 | 2 | 8 | 6 | 3 | 1 |
| 6 | 3 | 8 | 7 | 1 | 4 | 5 | 2 | 9 |
| 3 | 1 | 9 | 4 | 5 | 2 | 7 | 6 | 8 |
| 7 | 4 | 5 | 6 | 8 | 1 | 2 | 9 | 3 |
| 8 | 6 | 2 | 3 | 7 | 9 | 1 | 4 | 5 |
| 1 | 7 | 6 | 8 | 4 | 3 | 9 | 5 | 2 |
| 9 | 2 | 3 | 1 | 6 | 5 | 8 | 7 | 4 |
| 5 | 8 | 4 | 2 | 9 | 7 | 3 | 1 | 6 |

**273**

| 3 | 6 | 8 | 7 | 4 | 9 | 2 | 1 | 5 |
|---|---|---|---|---|---|---|---|---|
| 2 | 5 | 7 | 3 | 6 | 1 | 4 | 8 | 9 |
| 9 | 1 | 4 | 5 | 2 | 8 | 6 | 7 | 3 |
| 7 | 8 | 3 | 4 | 9 | 5 | 1 | 2 | 6 |
| 5 | 9 | 1 | 6 | 7 | 2 | 3 | 4 | 8 |
| 6 | 4 | 2 | 1 | 8 | 3 | 5 | 9 | 7 |
| 1 | 2 | 5 | 9 | 3 | 7 | 8 | 6 | 4 |
| 4 | 3 | 9 | 8 | 1 | 6 | 7 | 5 | 2 |
| 8 | 7 | 6 | 2 | 5 | 4 | 9 | 3 | 1 |

**274**

| 3 | 7 | 5 | 1 | 2 | 8 | 4 | 6 | 9 |
|---|---|---|---|---|---|---|---|---|
| 9 | 4 | 6 | 3 | 5 | 7 | 1 | 8 | 2 |
| 1 | 8 | 2 | 9 | 6 | 4 | 7 | 5 | 3 |
| 6 | 2 | 4 | 7 | 9 | 5 | 3 | 1 | 8 |
| 5 | 1 | 8 | 6 | 3 | 2 | 9 | 4 | 7 |
| 7 | 9 | 3 | 4 | 8 | 1 | 5 | 2 | 6 |
| 4 | 3 | 9 | 2 | 1 | 6 | 8 | 7 | 5 |
| 2 | 5 | 1 | 8 | 7 | 9 | 6 | 3 | 4 |
| 8 | 6 | 7 | 5 | 4 | 3 | 2 | 9 | 1 |

**275**

| 3 | 7 | 5 | 6 | 4 | 8 | 1 | 9 | 2 |
|---|---|---|---|---|---|---|---|---|
| 2 | 8 | 9 | 3 | 5 | 1 | 4 | 6 | 7 |
| 4 | 1 | 6 | 9 | 7 | 2 | 8 | 3 | 5 |
| 9 | 6 | 7 | 4 | 8 | 3 | 5 | 2 | 1 |
| 8 | 4 | 2 | 5 | 1 | 9 | 3 | 7 | 6 |
| 1 | 5 | 3 | 7 | 2 | 6 | 9 | 8 | 4 |
| 6 | 2 | 4 | 8 | 9 | 5 | 7 | 1 | 3 |
| 7 | 3 | 8 | 1 | 6 | 4 | 2 | 5 | 9 |
| 5 | 9 | 1 | 2 | 3 | 7 | 6 | 4 | 8 |

**276**

| 9 | 3 | 2 | 5 | 8 | 1 | 7 | 6 | 4 |
|---|---|---|---|---|---|---|---|---|
| 8 | 1 | 7 | 3 | 6 | 4 | 5 | 9 | 2 |
| 5 | 6 | 4 | 7 | 2 | 9 | 3 | 8 | 1 |
| 6 | 5 | 3 | 2 | 1 | 7 | 9 | 4 | 8 |
| 1 | 4 | 9 | 6 | 5 | 8 | 2 | 7 | 3 |
| 2 | 7 | 8 | 4 | 9 | 3 | 1 | 5 | 6 |
| 4 | 8 | 5 | 1 | 7 | 2 | 6 | 3 | 9 |
| 3 | 2 | 6 | 9 | 4 | 5 | 8 | 1 | 7 |
| 7 | 9 | 1 | 8 | 3 | 6 | 4 | 2 | 5 |

**277**

| 9 | 6 | 1 | 5 | 2 | 8 | 4 | 7 | 3 |
|---|---|---|---|---|---|---|---|---|
| 2 | 7 | 3 | 1 | 6 | 4 | 5 | 8 | 9 |
| 4 | 5 | 8 | 9 | 3 | 7 | 1 | 6 | 2 |
| 6 | 8 | 2 | 4 | 9 | 5 | 3 | 1 | 7 |
| 1 | 4 | 9 | 3 | 7 | 6 | 8 | 2 | 5 |
| 7 | 3 | 5 | 8 | 1 | 2 | 6 | 9 | 4 |
| 5 | 9 | 6 | 2 | 4 | 1 | 7 | 3 | 8 |
| 3 | 1 | 4 | 7 | 8 | 9 | 2 | 5 | 6 |
| 8 | 2 | 7 | 6 | 5 | 3 | 9 | 4 | 1 |

**278**

| 2 | 9 | 8 | 6 | 4 | 1 | 7 | 3 | 5 |
|---|---|---|---|---|---|---|---|---|
| 5 | 4 | 1 | 3 | 8 | 7 | 9 | 6 | 2 |
| 3 | 6 | 7 | 5 | 9 | 2 | 8 | 4 | 1 |
| 4 | 8 | 2 | 7 | 6 | 3 | 5 | 1 | 9 |
| 9 | 3 | 6 | 1 | 5 | 8 | 2 | 7 | 4 |
| 1 | 7 | 5 | 4 | 2 | 9 | 6 | 8 | 3 |
| 8 | 1 | 3 | 9 | 7 | 5 | 4 | 2 | 6 |
| 7 | 5 | 4 | 2 | 1 | 6 | 3 | 9 | 8 |
| 6 | 2 | 9 | 8 | 3 | 4 | 1 | 5 | 7 |

**279**

| 9 | 8 | 1 | 5 | 3 | 7 | 2 | 4 | 6 |
|---|---|---|---|---|---|---|---|---|
| 5 | 2 | 6 | 8 | 4 | 1 | 9 | 3 | 7 |
| 7 | 3 | 4 | 9 | 2 | 6 | 8 | 1 | 5 |
| 6 | 7 | 3 | 2 | 5 | 9 | 4 | 8 | 1 |
| 8 | 4 | 5 | 6 | 1 | 3 | 7 | 9 | 2 |
| 2 | 1 | 9 | 4 | 7 | 8 | 5 | 6 | 3 |
| 1 | 9 | 8 | 7 | 6 | 2 | 3 | 5 | 4 |
| 3 | 5 | 7 | 1 | 8 | 4 | 6 | 2 | 9 |
| 4 | 6 | 2 | 3 | 9 | 5 | 1 | 7 | 8 |

**280**

| 2 | 9 | 8 | 5 | 7 | 6 | 3 | 1 | 4 |
|---|---|---|---|---|---|---|---|---|
| 3 | 1 | 5 | 8 | 4 | 2 | 7 | 9 | 6 |
| 7 | 6 | 4 | 9 | 1 | 3 | 8 | 5 | 2 |
| 1 | 5 | 3 | 6 | 2 | 7 | 4 | 8 | 9 |
| 8 | 2 | 9 | 1 | 5 | 4 | 6 | 3 | 7 |
| 6 | 4 | 7 | 3 | 9 | 8 | 1 | 2 | 5 |
| 9 | 7 | 6 | 2 | 8 | 1 | 5 | 4 | 3 |
| 5 | 3 | 1 | 4 | 6 | 9 | 2 | 7 | 8 |
| 4 | 8 | 2 | 7 | 3 | 5 | 9 | 6 | 1 |

**281**

| 1 | 7 | 3 | 6 | 4 | 8 | 9 | 2 | 5 |
|---|---|---|---|---|---|---|---|---|
| 5 | 6 | 8 | 1 | 9 | 2 | 7 | 3 | 4 |
| 4 | 9 | 2 | 7 | 5 | 3 | 6 | 1 | 8 |
| 2 | 8 | 1 | 4 | 7 | 9 | 3 | 5 | 6 |
| 3 | 5 | 9 | 8 | 6 | 1 | 4 | 7 | 2 |
| 7 | 4 | 6 | 3 | 2 | 5 | 8 | 9 | 1 |
| 8 | 2 | 4 | 9 | 1 | 7 | 5 | 6 | 3 |
| 6 | 1 | 7 | 5 | 3 | 4 | 2 | 8 | 9 |
| 9 | 3 | 5 | 2 | 8 | 6 | 1 | 4 | 7 |

**282**

| 6 | 5 | 7 | 2 | 4 | 8 | 1 | 9 | 3 |
|---|---|---|---|---|---|---|---|---|
| 4 | 1 | 3 | 6 | 7 | 9 | 2 | 5 | 8 |
| 9 | 8 | 2 | 3 | 1 | 5 | 4 | 7 | 6 |
| 3 | 4 | 6 | 7 | 9 | 2 | 8 | 1 | 5 |
| 8 | 7 | 1 | 5 | 3 | 4 | 9 | 6 | 2 |
| 5 | 2 | 9 | 1 | 8 | 6 | 7 | 3 | 4 |
| 2 | 6 | 4 | 9 | 5 | 1 | 3 | 8 | 7 |
| 7 | 9 | 5 | 8 | 2 | 3 | 6 | 4 | 1 |
| 1 | 3 | 8 | 4 | 6 | 7 | 5 | 2 | 9 |

**283**

| 3 | 1 | 9 | 8 | 2 | 6 | 4 | 7 | 5 |
|---|---|---|---|---|---|---|---|---|
| 5 | 7 | 8 | 4 | 9 | 1 | 6 | 2 | 3 |
| 4 | 2 | 6 | 5 | 7 | 3 | 8 | 9 | 1 |
| 7 | 6 | 4 | 3 | 8 | 5 | 9 | 1 | 2 |
| 2 | 8 | 3 | 7 | 1 | 9 | 5 | 6 | 4 |
| 9 | 5 | 1 | 6 | 4 | 2 | 3 | 8 | 7 |
| 6 | 9 | 2 | 1 | 5 | 4 | 7 | 3 | 8 |
| 1 | 4 | 7 | 9 | 3 | 8 | 2 | 5 | 6 |
| 8 | 3 | 5 | 2 | 6 | 7 | 1 | 4 | 9 |

**284**

| 2 | 3 | 5 | 9 | 6 | 1 | 8 | 7 | 4 |
|---|---|---|---|---|---|---|---|---|
| 6 | 8 | 9 | 4 | 2 | 7 | 5 | 3 | 1 |
| 4 | 1 | 7 | 5 | 3 | 8 | 2 | 9 | 6 |
| 3 | 9 | 2 | 7 | 1 | 5 | 6 | 4 | 8 |
| 7 | 4 | 1 | 6 | 8 | 2 | 3 | 5 | 9 |
| 8 | 5 | 6 | 3 | 9 | 4 | 1 | 2 | 7 |
| 9 | 6 | 8 | 2 | 7 | 3 | 4 | 1 | 5 |
| 5 | 7 | 3 | 1 | 4 | 6 | 9 | 8 | 2 |
| 1 | 2 | 4 | 8 | 5 | 9 | 7 | 6 | 3 |

**285**

| 9 | 2 | 4 | 1 | 6 | 5 | 3 | 8 | 7 |
|---|---|---|---|---|---|---|---|---|
| 7 | 5 | 8 | 3 | 2 | 9 | 6 | 4 | 1 |
| 1 | 3 | 6 | 7 | 4 | 8 | 9 | 2 | 5 |
| 6 | 1 | 7 | 8 | 3 | 4 | 2 | 5 | 9 |
| 8 | 4 | 5 | 2 | 9 | 7 | 1 | 6 | 3 |
| 3 | 9 | 2 | 5 | 1 | 6 | 4 | 7 | 8 |
| 5 | 6 | 3 | 9 | 7 | 2 | 8 | 1 | 4 |
| 2 | 8 | 9 | 4 | 5 | 1 | 7 | 3 | 6 |
| 4 | 7 | 1 | 6 | 8 | 3 | 5 | 9 | 2 |

**286**

| 8 | 9 | 2 | 3 | 7 | 1 | 4 | 6 | 5 |
|---|---|---|---|---|---|---|---|---|
| 1 | 6 | 3 | 4 | 8 | 5 | 2 | 7 | 9 |
| 5 | 4 | 7 | 9 | 6 | 2 | 3 | 1 | 8 |
| 7 | 2 | 8 | 6 | 5 | 4 | 1 | 9 | 3 |
| 4 | 5 | 9 | 2 | 1 | 3 | 6 | 8 | 7 |
| 6 | 3 | 1 | 7 | 9 | 8 | 5 | 2 | 4 |
| 9 | 8 | 4 | 5 | 2 | 6 | 7 | 3 | 1 |
| 2 | 7 | 5 | 1 | 3 | 9 | 8 | 4 | 6 |
| 3 | 1 | 6 | 8 | 4 | 7 | 9 | 5 | 2 |

**287**

| 4 | 1 | 8 | 9 | 2 | 3 | 5 | 6 | 7 |
|---|---|---|---|---|---|---|---|---|
| 5 | 7 | 2 | 8 | 4 | 6 | 1 | 9 | 3 |
| 6 | 9 | 3 | 5 | 7 | 1 | 2 | 8 | 4 |
| 9 | 5 | 7 | 4 | 6 | 8 | 3 | 2 | 1 |
| 2 | 6 | 4 | 1 | 3 | 9 | 8 | 7 | 5 |
| 8 | 3 | 1 | 7 | 5 | 2 | 9 | 4 | 6 |
| 7 | 4 | 9 | 2 | 1 | 5 | 6 | 3 | 8 |
| 1 | 8 | 6 | 3 | 9 | 7 | 4 | 5 | 2 |
| 3 | 2 | 5 | 6 | 8 | 4 | 7 | 1 | 9 |

**288**

| 7 | 9 | 8 | 6 | 1 | 5 | 3 | 2 | 4 |
|---|---|---|---|---|---|---|---|---|
| 1 | 5 | 3 | 4 | 7 | 2 | 8 | 9 | 6 |
| 2 | 6 | 4 | 3 | 8 | 9 | 1 | 5 | 7 |
| 4 | 8 | 1 | 2 | 6 | 7 | 9 | 3 | 5 |
| 6 | 2 | 5 | 1 | 9 | 3 | 7 | 4 | 8 |
| 9 | 3 | 7 | 5 | 4 | 8 | 6 | 1 | 2 |
| 3 | 1 | 6 | 8 | 5 | 4 | 2 | 7 | 9 |
| 5 | 7 | 2 | 9 | 3 | 6 | 4 | 8 | 1 |
| 8 | 4 | 9 | 7 | 2 | 1 | 5 | 6 | 3 |

## 289

| 6 | 7 | 8 | 5 | 1 | 4 | 2 | 3 | 9 |
|---|---|---|---|---|---|---|---|---|
| 3 | 9 | 2 | 6 | 7 | 8 | 5 | 4 | 1 |
| 4 | 5 | 1 | 2 | 9 | 3 | 7 | 8 | 6 |
| 5 | 1 | 9 | 7 | 3 | 6 | 8 | 2 | 4 |
| 8 | 6 | 3 | 1 | 4 | 2 | 9 | 7 | 5 |
| 7 | 2 | 4 | 8 | 5 | 9 | 1 | 6 | 3 |
| 2 | 3 | 5 | 9 | 6 | 7 | 4 | 1 | 8 |
| 1 | 8 | 6 | 4 | 2 | 5 | 3 | 9 | 7 |
| 9 | 4 | 7 | 3 | 8 | 1 | 6 | 5 | 2 |

## 290

| 2 | 6 | 8 | 3 | 7 | 4 | 5 | 1 | 9 |
|---|---|---|---|---|---|---|---|---|
| 4 | 5 | 9 | 6 | 8 | 1 | 7 | 2 | 3 |
| 7 | 1 | 3 | 5 | 9 | 2 | 6 | 4 | 8 |
| 9 | 2 | 7 | 4 | 5 | 6 | 3 | 8 | 1 |
| 3 | 4 | 1 | 8 | 2 | 7 | 9 | 6 | 5 |
| 6 | 8 | 5 | 1 | 3 | 9 | 4 | 7 | 2 |
| 8 | 3 | 2 | 7 | 4 | 5 | 1 | 9 | 6 |
| 1 | 9 | 4 | 2 | 6 | 3 | 8 | 5 | 7 |
| 5 | 7 | 6 | 9 | 1 | 8 | 2 | 3 | 4 |

## 291

| 4 | 2 | 6 | 5 | 3 | 1 | 7 | 8 | 9 |
|---|---|---|---|---|---|---|---|---|
| 3 | 9 | 5 | 6 | 7 | 8 | 2 | 4 | 1 |
| 8 | 7 | 1 | 2 | 9 | 4 | 6 | 3 | 5 |
| 2 | 1 | 4 | 8 | 5 | 6 | 3 | 9 | 7 |
| 5 | 8 | 9 | 7 | 2 | 3 | 4 | 1 | 6 |
| 6 | 3 | 7 | 4 | 1 | 9 | 8 | 5 | 2 |
| 1 | 6 | 3 | 9 | 8 | 2 | 5 | 7 | 4 |
| 9 | 5 | 2 | 3 | 4 | 7 | 1 | 6 | 8 |
| 7 | 4 | 8 | 1 | 6 | 5 | 9 | 2 | 3 |

## 292

| 5 | 7 | 8 | 3 | 4 | 2 | 6 | 1 | 9 |
|---|---|---|---|---|---|---|---|---|
| 1 | 9 | 2 | 5 | 7 | 6 | 4 | 8 | 3 |
| 4 | 3 | 6 | 8 | 9 | 1 | 7 | 5 | 2 |
| 7 | 8 | 4 | 1 | 5 | 9 | 3 | 2 | 6 |
| 6 | 1 | 3 | 2 | 8 | 4 | 5 | 9 | 7 |
| 9 | 2 | 5 | 6 | 3 | 7 | 1 | 4 | 8 |
| 3 | 5 | 1 | 9 | 6 | 8 | 2 | 7 | 4 |
| 8 | 6 | 7 | 4 | 2 | 5 | 9 | 3 | 1 |
| 2 | 4 | 9 | 7 | 1 | 3 | 8 | 6 | 5 |

## 293

| 8 | 7 | 9 | 6 | 5 | 2 | 1 | 4 | 3 |
|---|---|---|---|---|---|---|---|---|
| 5 | 6 | 3 | 9 | 1 | 4 | 2 | 8 | 7 |
| 2 | 4 | 1 | 8 | 3 | 7 | 5 | 6 | 9 |
| 7 | 5 | 6 | 4 | 9 | 8 | 3 | 2 | 1 |
| 1 | 3 | 2 | 7 | 6 | 5 | 4 | 9 | 8 |
| 4 | 9 | 8 | 3 | 2 | 1 | 7 | 5 | 6 |
| 9 | 8 | 4 | 5 | 7 | 3 | 6 | 1 | 2 |
| 3 | 2 | 5 | 1 | 8 | 6 | 9 | 7 | 4 |
| 6 | 1 | 7 | 2 | 4 | 9 | 8 | 3 | 5 |

## 294

| 9 | 1 | 4 | 7 | 6 | 8 | 5 | 3 | 2 |
|---|---|---|---|---|---|---|---|---|
| 2 | 8 | 3 | 5 | 4 | 1 | 7 | 9 | 6 |
| 6 | 7 | 5 | 3 | 9 | 2 | 4 | 8 | 1 |
| 3 | 2 | 6 | 4 | 5 | 7 | 8 | 1 | 9 |
| 8 | 9 | 7 | 6 | 1 | 3 | 2 | 4 | 5 |
| 4 | 5 | 1 | 8 | 2 | 9 | 6 | 7 | 3 |
| 1 | 6 | 8 | 9 | 7 | 5 | 3 | 2 | 4 |
| 7 | 4 | 2 | 1 | 3 | 6 | 9 | 5 | 8 |
| 5 | 3 | 9 | 2 | 8 | 4 | 1 | 6 | 7 |

## 295

| 5 | 1 | 9 | 8 | 7 | 2 | 4 | 6 | 3 |
|---|---|---|---|---|---|---|---|---|
| 8 | 7 | 2 | 6 | 4 | 3 | 5 | 1 | 9 |
| 3 | 4 | 6 | 1 | 5 | 9 | 8 | 2 | 7 |
| 2 | 6 | 8 | 4 | 1 | 7 | 3 | 9 | 5 |
| 7 | 3 | 4 | 9 | 2 | 5 | 1 | 8 | 6 |
| 1 | 9 | 5 | 3 | 6 | 8 | 7 | 4 | 2 |
| 4 | 8 | 7 | 5 | 9 | 6 | 2 | 3 | 1 |
| 9 | 5 | 1 | 2 | 3 | 4 | 6 | 7 | 8 |
| 6 | 2 | 3 | 7 | 8 | 1 | 9 | 5 | 4 |

## 296

| 1 | 7 | 2 | 3 | 6 | 8 | 4 | 9 | 5 |
|---|---|---|---|---|---|---|---|---|
| 3 | 8 | 4 | 1 | 5 | 9 | 6 | 2 | 7 |
| 6 | 9 | 5 | 7 | 2 | 4 | 8 | 1 | 3 |
| 8 | 4 | 1 | 2 | 3 | 7 | 9 | 5 | 6 |
| 7 | 2 | 6 | 8 | 9 | 5 | 3 | 4 | 1 |
| 9 | 5 | 3 | 4 | 1 | 6 | 7 | 8 | 2 |
| 5 | 3 | 7 | 9 | 8 | 1 | 2 | 6 | 4 |
| 2 | 1 | 8 | 6 | 4 | 3 | 5 | 7 | 9 |
| 4 | 6 | 9 | 5 | 7 | 2 | 1 | 3 | 8 |

**297**

| | | | | | | | | |
|---|---|---|---|---|---|---|---|---|
| 2 | 1 | 9 | 3 | 5 | 4 | 8 | 6 | 7 |
| 7 | 6 | 4 | 9 | 2 | 8 | 1 | 3 | 5 |
| 8 | 5 | 3 | 1 | 7 | 6 | 2 | 4 | 9 |
| 4 | 8 | 1 | 7 | 6 | 5 | 9 | 2 | 3 |
| 5 | 3 | 2 | 8 | 4 | 9 | 6 | 7 | 1 |
| 6 | 9 | 7 | 2 | 3 | 1 | 5 | 8 | 4 |
| 9 | 4 | 5 | 6 | 8 | 7 | 3 | 1 | 2 |
| 1 | 2 | 6 | 4 | 9 | 3 | 7 | 5 | 8 |
| 3 | 7 | 8 | 5 | 1 | 2 | 4 | 9 | 6 |

**298**

| | | | | | | | | |
|---|---|---|---|---|---|---|---|---|
| 5 | 9 | 7 | 4 | 1 | 3 | 6 | 8 | 2 |
| 4 | 8 | 6 | 7 | 9 | 2 | 5 | 3 | 1 |
| 1 | 2 | 3 | 8 | 5 | 6 | 9 | 4 | 7 |
| 9 | 3 | 5 | 2 | 4 | 1 | 7 | 6 | 8 |
| 8 | 7 | 2 | 3 | 6 | 5 | 1 | 9 | 4 |
| 6 | 1 | 4 | 9 | 7 | 8 | 3 | 2 | 5 |
| 2 | 6 | 9 | 1 | 8 | 7 | 4 | 5 | 3 |
| 7 | 5 | 8 | 6 | 3 | 4 | 2 | 1 | 9 |
| 3 | 4 | 1 | 5 | 2 | 9 | 8 | 7 | 6 |

**299**

| | | | | | | | | |
|---|---|---|---|---|---|---|---|---|
| 6 | 8 | 3 | 4 | 1 | 2 | 7 | 5 | 9 |
| 9 | 7 | 5 | 8 | 3 | 6 | 1 | 4 | 2 |
| 4 | 1 | 2 | 5 | 7 | 9 | 8 | 6 | 3 |
| 1 | 5 | 9 | 6 | 2 | 4 | 3 | 8 | 7 |
| 8 | 4 | 6 | 3 | 9 | 7 | 5 | 2 | 1 |
| 3 | 2 | 7 | 1 | 5 | 8 | 4 | 9 | 6 |
| 7 | 6 | 8 | 9 | 4 | 1 | 2 | 3 | 5 |
| 2 | 3 | 4 | 7 | 6 | 5 | 9 | 1 | 8 |
| 5 | 9 | 1 | 2 | 8 | 3 | 6 | 7 | 4 |

**300**

| | | | | | | | | |
|---|---|---|---|---|---|---|---|---|
| 3 | 6 | 4 | 2 | 5 | 9 | 7 | 8 | 1 |
| 5 | 7 | 1 | 4 | 3 | 8 | 2 | 6 | 9 |
| 8 | 2 | 9 | 6 | 1 | 7 | 5 | 4 | 3 |
| 9 | 3 | 8 | 5 | 2 | 4 | 1 | 7 | 6 |
| 7 | 1 | 5 | 3 | 8 | 6 | 4 | 9 | 2 |
| 2 | 4 | 6 | 7 | 9 | 1 | 8 | 3 | 5 |
| 1 | 5 | 7 | 9 | 4 | 3 | 6 | 2 | 8 |
| 6 | 9 | 2 | 8 | 7 | 5 | 3 | 1 | 4 |
| 4 | 8 | 3 | 1 | 6 | 2 | 9 | 5 | 7 |